FIREPOWER

FIREPOWER

THE MOST SPECTACULAR FRAUD
IN AUSTRALIAN HISTORY

GERARD RYLE

ALLEN&UNWIN

First published in 2009

Allen & Unwin
83 Alexander Street
Crows Nest NSW 2065
Australia
Phone: (61 2) 8425 0100
Fax: (61 2) 9906 2218
Email: info@allenandunwin.com
Web: www.allenandunwin.com

Cataloguing-in-Publication details are available from
the National Library of Australia
www.librariesaustralia.nla.gov.au

ISBN 978 1 74175 355 4

Set in 13/15.9 pt Granjon by Midland Typesetters, Australia

10 9 8 7 6 5 4 3 2 1

CONTENTS

ACKNOWLEDGEMENTS

This book would not have been possible without the time, help and advice of many special people. In no particular order, I want to thank Marie Fox and Seamus Bradley for their endless patience in reading early drafts of the manuscript; Adrian Mogos and Paul Cristian Radu for their research in Romania and for generously acting as my guides when I visited that country; Glenda Kwek for her help in Singapore; Chris Carey for his help in the United States; Rod Allen, Mark Polden, Richard Coleman and Jacquelin Magnay for their boundless support and encouragement; the *Sydney Morning Herald* and its management and editors for allowing me to stick with a difficult story in difficult times; Allen & Unwin Chairman, Patrick Gallagher; Nicola O'Shea and Alexandra Nahlous, my skillful editors at Allen & Unwin; Kate Hyde, my publicist at Allen & Unwin; Richard Walsh, for commissioning the book and for his vision and continuous assistance; and David Round, to whom I owe particular gratitude. I'm indebted to my wife Kimberley Porteous for her tolerance, guidance and affection; and to my family, friends and other workmates.

PROLOGUE: THE JOKE

Tim Johnston needed a distraction.

Sport was a distraction. In Australia, it was a national obsession. More than anything else, Australians admired someone who could leap higher or run faster or strike a ball cleaner off a wooden bat. Where else would athletes regularly nudge aside doctors, scientists and humanitarians to the nation's highest honours?

Johnston's friend Peter O'Meara had a sporting team. O'Meara was chief executive officer of the Western Force, a franchise that played in the best rugby union league in the world, a competition that pitted the finest players from Australia, New Zealand and South Africa against each other. But O'Meara's team was the worst team in that league. Johnston wanted a proper distraction, a big one.

It was 2006 and by then Johnston had moved from poverty to plenty with barely a hitch in his stride. Already people were tipping him for greatness. Just as Thomas Edison had revolutionised the world with the invention of the light bulb, many believed Johnston was about to radically affect the biggest emergency facing mankind—the global energy crisis. Some of Australia's brightest business leaders figured him to be the new Bill Gates, the billionaire founder of the world's biggest company, Microsoft. Johnston was surely about to enjoy the same commercial success. Like Edison, his product also fitted neatly into the palm of one hand. It was a little brown pill about the size of a five-cent piece.

Johnston was 50 years old and given to hyperbole. He had been asked by Prime Minister John Howard to advise the country on the pressing issue of climate change. The British prime minister, Tony Blair, was a silent investor in his various schemes. Both houses of the Russian parliament had ordered that his technology be adopted in every farm and factory and furnace across the vast former Soviet empire. The contracts were worth millions. Perhaps billions.

It was sometimes difficult to know where the untruths began and ended with Johnston. His world was filled with unexpected surprise. John Howard did invite him to dinner. They dined at the Lodge, the prime minister's official residence in Canberra. They dined with Julie Bishop, the minister for science, and they discoursed on the issue of Johnston's great invention. The prime minister invited him back to dine again. And Johnston, who liked to study the Bible, gave thanks to his God for the meals. His favourite topic of conversation—outside his yearning to save the planet—was his professed desire for honesty and integrity. The contradiction was not always immediately apparent.

Johnston began his marketing career as a shampoo salesman. His clean-cut image served him well when he moved on to other things. Like selling bacteria that ate cow dung, or cures for medical ailments, or paint that was so light that aircraft manufacturers were animated about its fuel-saving possibilities. And it was here, in the area of fuel saving, that he finally hit it big. Not with the paint, but with the little brown pill.

It was easy to see the attraction. By the time Johnston arrived on the scene in Australia, the public had breached another record in its collective indulgence in oil consumption. The appetite was such that, according to Department of Infrastructure, Transport, Regional Development and Local Government statistics, there was nearly one truck or car for every man, woman and child, devouring more than 36.3 billion litres of petrol and diesel each year. Johnston's little brown pill promised to cut this $29 billion annual bill by 20 per cent in one easy stroke. Moreover, he claimed that the pill would virtually eliminate all of the poisonous gases emitted by each vehicle.

The excitement over his invention allowed Johnston to collect money from all corners of the globe. He had formed a company called Firepower and to potential investors the message was clear: get on board or lose out on the chance of a lifetime. The pill, he said, was going to make everyone extremely wealthy. And by the time he finished, they had handed over more than $100 million.

Johnston surrounded himself with substantial people. His business partners included Gordon Hill, a former West Australian police minister. There was Warren Anderson, one of the country's best-known property developers, and Grigory Luchansky, a Russian oligarch who regularly featured in newspaper stories around the world. Both the Governor-General Major-General Michael Jeffery and the Queensland premier Peter Beattie turned up for Firepower-sponsored events. Bill Moss, the former Macquarie Bank director, was scheduled to be the chairman of Firepower and Firepower's chief executive officer was John Finnin, one of Australia's most senior public servants. Johnston told everyone they were going to be rich when he listed his company on the London Stock Exchange.

Even in these heady days, Firepower appeared too good to be true. So good in fact that rumours sprang up that it was really a money-laundering front for the Russian mafia, or a product of the KGB or the CIA. The reasons were never quite clear, but nobody seemed to care as long as the money flowed. And flow it did. But few took the time to find out what Firepower was really about, or to take the time to look into Johnston's colourful personal history.

Johnston spent much of 2006 on board first-class flights and on private jets. He spent long hours explaining the deals he was signing up. World leaders—prime ministers and presidents—were begging for his help. They wanted to improve their refineries, their factories and their methods of food production. His technology, he elucidated, also had many military applications. That made it a danger to powerful interests—not least the big oil companies. And until that year came to an end, everything was holding up.

But we have all felt panic, the sudden rush of doubt; and Johnston came to feel it well before then. The various strands of his story had grown contradictory. The portrait he built up remained unconvincing. Despite the millions of words that were poured into explaining the gulf between science and science fiction the two remain unreconciled. In short, Johnston needed a distraction. He needed something to draw attention away from the fundamental question that people had yet to ask, the proof he had yet to offer, the stock market listing he had yet to deliver. He found it in sport.

Johnston conceived his plan for the big distraction over Sunday afternoon drinks at his friend Peter O'Meara's comfortable pad in the Perth beachside suburb of Cottesloe, not far from the $16 million mansion Johnston himself had recently moved into. He began by luring the best rugby players in the land away from other franchises to the Western Force. They included Matt Giteau and Drew Mitchell, the stars of the Australian national team. Firepower turned the Western Force from the worst Australian team to one of the best teams in the tri-nations competition, and Johnston was soon the most powerful person in West Australian rugby.

But Johnston had mammoth ambitions. As his boasts grew, so did the distraction. He began to build the biggest sporting sponsorship portfolio Australia had ever seen. The Firepower name was soon brashly displayed across the country, in boxing rings, on horse tracks, on racing cars, on motorbikes, even on surfboards. He began sponsoring the Sydney Kings, Australia's best-known basketball team, and ended up buying the franchise.

Johnston's brash style often clashed with those who were more culturally conservative, but many were drawn to his fervour and his money. He was good at identifying weaknesses in others. He was good at understanding rules and laws and the ways they could be broken. He was good at making sure people who might have spoken up couldn't, because they were compromised. Those who probably should have known better often left their good sense behind when they signed on for the camaraderie, the dollars, and the excitement. And like treasured guests at a children's party, people didn't doubt the integrity of the magician.

At the height of his popularity, in September 2006, a 4200-tonne navy-guided missile frigate was handed over at taxpayers' expense for a gala sponsorship function soon after Defence Force chiefs became Firepower investors. The HMAS *Sydney* was moored at the navy's base at Garden Island, with views over the Opera House, when it was used for the official launch of the Sydney Kings basketball season. By then, the head of the Australian Defence Force, Air Chief Marshal Angus Houston, the deputy chief of navy, Rear Admiral Davyd Thomas, a former senior naval officer, Commodore Kevin Taylor, and the former air force chief, Air Marshal Errol McCormack, were all on board the dream as investors, though none were involved in the decision to hand over the boat.

Johnston's attentions weren't confined to Australia. His sporting heroes were scattered across the world, from New Zealand to Tonga to Russia. He had his people draw up plans to sponsor Chelsea soccer club in the English Premier League and Formula One motor racing. By then, he was also funding a rugby team in Wales.

For a time, all things seemed possible. Johnston began socialising with Russell Crowe, the Oscar-winning Hollywood actor, and Peter Holmes à Court, one of Australia's best-known businessmen. The two men owned the iconic South Sydney Rabbitohs rugby league team in Sydney. Firepower had just become one of the team's major sponsors. This team too was struggling on the field of play. But Johnston's millions would surely help turn that around.

Johnston's investors came from all walks of life. They were doctors, accountants, public servants, media figures and mum and dad speculators. They came from the airy elite of international diplomacy, like the Australian High Commissioner to Pakistan, Zorica McCarthy. They even came from the centre of Johnston's own big distraction—the world of sport itself.

A group of Australian Rules football players had decided that Firepower was the next big thing. Leading the investment scramble was Mark Ricciuto, the captain of the Adelaide Crows, and Wayne Carey, the former all-Australian captain. Carey told current and former players it was a great way to not just triple their money, but increase it tenfold. Most of the Adelaide Crows team became investors, including the coaching staff. And Johnston drew up plans to share profits from the sale of his pills with the Crows Foundation, the club's charitable arm.

One of the former players who invested had a radio show in Adelaide, on the Triple-M network. So the friends began to play a game. The players and former players began to compete with each other over how many times they could use the word 'firepower' during on-air interviews. It got so that the city's major newspaper wrote about it in the social pages. The private comedy became public. And all and sundry was laughing at Johnston's distraction.

But the real joke was on them.

1 PERPETUAL MOTION

Australian investors have long had a weakness for fuel-saving devices.

Ever since Ralph Sarich appeared on the ABC television show *The Inventors* in 1972 and revealed a new type of engine, fortunes have been won and lost on assurances to revolutionise the car industry. Sarich's compact design promised more power, fewer emissions and significant fuel economy. The fact that his Orbital engine remained untested failed to dampen the resultant frenzy. Australia's largest company, BHP, formed a joint venture to develop the technology. Shares that once traded for 20 cents went to $24 each. Investors and analysts brimmed with confidence about the potential for lucrative multimillion-dollar contracts from big car manufacturers.

Governments got involved. During the 1987 federal election campaign, the then prime minister, Bob Hawke, announced that $500 000 of taxpayers' money would be used to assess the viability of an Orbital engine manufacturing plant. He was responding to fears that Australia would lose the project to foreign interests. But the inflated confidence overlooked a number of fundamental problems. Key components of the Sarich engine couldn't be cooled. Others couldn't be readily lubricated. The engine was susceptible to overheating and was eventually deemed too impractical.

By 2004, the Orbital Engine Company had accumulated losses of $480 million, and had defeated BHP, which unloaded its stock in 1998 and 1999 at prices below $1 per share. Sarich had been fortunate enough to get out sooner. He sold his shares for $3 each and did what every sensible millionaire does—he bought property in Perth's central business district.

But the perceived success of Orbital spawned a number of imitators. In 1988, another radical engine design began making headlines. Split-Cycle Technology also promised more power, fewer emissions and better fuel economy. Rick Mayne, the New Zealand inventor, had appeared in Australia two years earlier. He had previously made his living selling caravans and trailers built from second-hand parts, arguing that because the material he used was second-hand, no sales tax was payable.

Mayne sold shares to the general public in his new Split-Cycle venture without going through the usual step of listing on a stock exchange. Instead, trading in the shares occurred at the Split-Cycle headquarters on the Gold Coast and during sweaty revival-hall-style gatherings in packed hotel rooms. One story told by promoters was of the Split-Cycle dealer who made $139 000 running up and down between different floors of the Split-Cycle offices between buyers and sellers. Doctors, nightclub owners and accountants abandoned their careers to join the action, often contacting each other through newspaper advertisements, where the trading was perpetuated. An estimated 111 million shares changed hands.

Stimulating the interest were Mayne's confident assertions. In 1992, he said his engine would be powering its first car within eighteen months. Soon after, he announced the multimillion-dollar sale of development rights to a Slovakian company. He also unveiled plans for an ambitious multi-billion-dollar joint research venture with four major American universities.

The publicity-conscious Mayne enlisted the celebrity train robber Ronald Biggs as a representative, and hired three-time Formula One world champion Sir Jack Brabham to chair the company. At its peak, Split-Cycle was valued at more than $200 million. Mayne, as the biggest shareholder, was worth $50 million. In 1993, he was named as one of Australia's richest people, the owner of a string of exotic cars, including a $670 000 Lamborghini. That same year he was arrested when he returned to his native New Zealand for evading a $1 million tax bill on the caravans and trailers. The tax dispute was settled, but Mayne eventually shuffled off into the sunset, leaving behind thousands of empty-handed shareholders and a posse of frustrated corporate regulators.

Market governance failed to save investors in Red River Limited, once one of the most traded stocks on the Australian Stock Exchange. The company's share price went from 9 cents in December 1993 to $1.85 in early May 1994 after it released test results on a device that claimed to radically reduce petrol consumption using a common garden hose.

Red River had started life as a mining company, and its journey to automotive technology had involved prior stints importing waterbeds, trading confectionery and managing time-share properties. But it hit the big time when tests on its contraption the Econo Power apparently showed a 75 per cent fuel saving on a 1986 Holden Commodore driven over a distance of 1400 kilometres, without any loss of performance or other adverse occurrences. The Econo Power involved installing a separate water tank in the boot of the car, converting the water into vapour, then combining it with petrol before injecting the mixture into the engine. The company was expected to complete further independent trials with a major automotive company or university within four months. But only days after going public with the test result, the car burst into flames.

Celebrities have often been caught up in the folly. The late Kevin Charles 'Pro' Hart came up with his own fuel-saving concept in the mid-1980s, but his initial prototype for the Zero Emission Fuel Saver was too large to be practical. The world-renowned Australian bush painter spent more than a decade refining the device before sharing his secret in 1997 with the fast-talking and charismatic Jeffrey Alan Muller.

Muller was a one-time Sydney real-estate salesman who was then in his late forties. Like many in the fuel-saving business, he laid claim to an extraordinary personal history. He was a former champion speedway driver, a one-time successful property developer, and a friend of celebrities such as Ted Turner, Olivia Newton-John and John Denver. He also boasted ownership of a now defunct rugby league team called the Gold Coast Chargers. What he failed to mention was that the sporting franchise was taken away from him after only a couple of months. He hadn't come good with the promised finance, had brought in a faith healer and, according to a judge, had ineptly interfered in the club's affairs 'creating such instability that its chief executive officer and some other important personnel associated with it resigned'.

Hart and Muller met by chance on the Gold Coast and according to a *Sydney Morning Herald* article dated April 2001, Muller claimed to have secured a 'marketing and manufacturing agreement' that would give the entrepreneur exclusive worldwide distribution rights to the device, in exchange for 20 per cent of the anticipated profits. Hart denied ever having signed this agreement, never received a cent from Muller, and was outraged by what happened next. Muller bought a United States shelf company, changed its name to Save The World Air Inc, made himself president and sold the company his rights to the device.

Save The World Air Inc was premised entirely on a piece of shiny metal the size of a packet of cigarettes with holes drilled through it—a compact and updated version of Hart's original prototype—that sold for US$195. The company claimed it could decrease fuel consumption by 42 per cent and virtually eliminate poisonous exhaust gases.

This wasn't the first time that Muller had attempted to profit from green technology. Some years earlier, the *Sydney Morning Herald* reported that he'd claimed to have developed an engine 'which runs on nothing but compressed air'. He then got involved in promoting something he called a 'super kiri tree', which he claimed was the world's fastest-growing hardwood. This turned out to be a small plantation of paulownia trees, a popular tax-minimisation scheme of the mid-1990s.

Even amid the high-tech hyperventilation of the late 1990s, the promotion of Save The World Air Inc was extraordinary. Muller was relentless. He pumped out scores of media releases via the internet. He demonstrated the device on Fox TV and was written up in the *New York Times*. He recruited a stable of sporting and show business celebrities to endorse the product, including Sir Jack Brabham, the Split-Cycle chairman, and champion golfer Wayne Grady. According to the *Sydney Morning Herald*, Steven Seagal, the Hollywood movie star, videotaped a testimonial for the gadget, and John Brown, the former Australian sports minister, wrote: 'I have never been more impressed over my long life in business and politics with any other venture'. All later repudiated those endorsements. But whipped along by internet chatter—some of it planted by Muller's friends—shares in Save The World Air Inc went from being worth a few cents each when it listed in 1999 to a peak of US$28 each in July 2000. This valued the company at an extraordinary $420 million. And Muller, who owned about one-quarter of the stock, joined the ranks of Australia's wealthiest men, worth more than $100 million on paper.

'I've been told we've got the potential to be as big as Microsoft,' he crowed to a Bloomberg business wire reporter after he claimed to have just sold his first distribution franchise for 'a guaranteed $4 million' to a Jamaican auto-parts dealer. According to the *Herald*, he said he planned to sell a hundred more for $20 million a piece—a cool $2 billion.

But the deals promised by Muller came to nothing. Unlike Microsoft, the company never manufactured anything. The only Zero Emission Fuel Savers in existence were about a dozen closely guarded prototypes used for demonstrations. Adrian Menzell of Ashmore Wreckers, a Gold Coast car-parts yard, had knocked them up using simple, cheap magnets. 'Once somebody sees one and holds one in their hand they can go out and make one in their garage,' Muller's former associate Joe Daniels told the *Sydney Morning Herald* in April 2001. 'He's got no product—he's out there peddling air.'

Muller had another problem, one that would bring his wild ride to a grinding halt. His claims for the device had never been independently tested or scientifically verified. Muller had only ever performed undemanding demonstrations using rudimentary pollution-testing apparatus. Despite this, the company's press releases heralded the 'successful test' of the device by two service technicians at a local New York auto dealership; another assessment conducted by 'Sun Electric and Snap On Tools' at a due diligence conference for stockbrokers in Boca Raton, Florida; and two others carried out at a petrol station in Brentwood, California and a car dealership in Los Angeles. Also featured prominently on the Save The World Air

Inc website was an apparent endorsement from an academic at Queensland's Griffith University. The website claimed that Dr Allan Edwards certified that he had seen the machine work under 'credible circumstances' and believed it to be 'highly effective'. But when contacted by the *Sydney Morning Herald* in April 2001, Edwards said he had no expertise in vehicle emissions. He was, in fact, a teacher of sports management and marketing. Muller was a friend who had invited him to a demonstration of the device and he had written the letter not realising how it would be used. 'I feel really ashamed and angry,' he said. 'I was a frightful goose.'

Muller's golden run came to an end in July 2000 when the consumer website Stock Patrol published a two-part investigation headlined 'Stock or Schlock?', which focused on the fact that the hot 'tech' company appeared to have no assets and no prospects. The next day, as the share price fluctuated wildly, the US Securities and Exchange Commission moved in. Citing a misleading media release implying the Ford Motor Company was interested in the device, the corporate watchdog suspended trading in the stock on 20 July 2000, saying in a press release it was 'because of questions raised about the accuracy and adequacy of publicly disseminated information concerning the results of tests of Zero Emission Fuel Saver'.

The commission sued Muller for fraud. It claimed in the US District Court he made a personal profit of US$9 million and had 'carried out a fraudulent promotional campaign using press releases, internet postings, an elaborate website, and televised media events to disseminate false and materially misleading information about STWA's product and commercial prospects'. Purported licensing agreements, it said, and other business developments 'simply did not exist'.

On 15 November 2005, a US District Court in New York ordered Muller to hand over US$7.5 million and another

US$100 000 in civil penalties. He was barred from being an officer of a company for twenty years.

But that wasn't the end of Save The World Air Inc. Muller was replaced as the company's chief executive officer by the late Edward Masry, better known as the Californian attorney who hired the struggling single mother Erin Brockovich as a legal assistant and, with her, achieved a landmark environmental legal victory, as portrayed in the Hollywood movie that won Julia Roberts an Oscar.

Another fuel-saving celebrity was the late Peter Brock, an Australian rally driver known to an adoring public as Peter Perfect. Before his untimely death in a car accident in September 2006, Brock had achieved a long list of memorable moments. His first win at Bathurst, Australia's premier road-racing event, was in 1972, driving single-handed for 500 miles in a customised Holden Torana. He underlined his superiority at the event in 1979, winning by six laps and setting a record on his last lap. In 1980, he became the first driver to win Bathurst, Sandown and the Australian Touring Car title in the same year. Many Brock stories passed into folklore. How he developed his legendary skills by thrashing an old Austin around his father's farm on the northern fringes of Melbourne. How fans asked for his autograph on their body, then tattooed over their hero's scrawl.

Less remembered is Brock's stubborn belief—inspired by his spiritual teacher, Eric Dowker—in a mysterious device said to improve the performance and fuel economy of his cars. It was called the Energy Polariser and was nothing more than an assortment of common magnets and crystals wrapped in tinfoil. But Brock claimed it was a highly advanced energy machine that altered molecular structures, bringing order to an otherwise random pattern and rendering it more efficient.

Brock claimed the device had been tested and approved by General Motors, and that the giant global corporation was so impressed it was considering attaching them to all their vehicles. The bond between Brock and Holden—the local arm of General Motors—ran deep, dating back to 1980 when Brock's special vehicle company began building thousands of modified high-performance Holden Commodore cars that were offered for sale through the Holden dealership network. In return, the dealers contributed to the running of Brock's Commodore race team. It was a successful relationship that lasted seven years. Brock's well-funded Commodores were regular winners on the track, and the limited-build Brock Commodore road cars were strong sellers in the showrooms. They had image, prestige and a fat margin on the sticker price. In the dark days of the early 1980s when Holden lost the market leadership it had held for more than thirty years in Australia to its main rival Ford, and Commodore sales slumped from a high of 64 000 to barely 35 000 units a year, Brock was the one bright spot on a bleak corporate horizon.

But his insistence that the Energy Polariser be fitted to the engine bay of all cars bearing his name ultimately cost him his relationship with his main sponsor. Holden knew its parent company hadn't carried out any scientific trials in the United States, as Brock had implied. Instead, Holden itself had subjected the Energy Polariser to a series of tests over four days in late 1986, at its proving ground at Lang Lang, about 150 kilometres from Melbourne. The device was found to make no difference, either to performance or to fuel economy, and Holden was anxious to distance itself from the nonsensical claims.

Yet right to the very end, Brock's faith in the Energy Polariser was unswayed. 'How do we prove it works?' he said to the Melbourne's *Herald Sun* newspaper shortly before his death. 'They haven't invented the machine yet to prove it works.'

Such absolute personal conviction—in the absence of any scientific proof—goes some way towards explaining how these supposed fuel-saving devices appear again and again in Australia's recent history.

Australia doesn't have a dedicated laboratory for testing the various fuel-saving devices that emerge on the market. What it does have is Project 55 at the Railway Cooperative Research Centre, headed by Dr Damon Honnery and funded by Australia's biggest private railways in an attempt to cut their half-a-billion-dollar-a-year fuel bills. The testing is done on a stripped-down truck engine that sits in a room at the back of the engineering wing of the sprawling Clayton campus of Monash University in Melbourne.

When it first opened in 2003, the centre didn't advertise what it was doing. The scientists simply went out and purchased a selection of the many fuel-saving devices available, ranging from additives to a set of flow ionisers (magnets) similar to Brock's Energy Polariser. With so much at stake, Project 55 will listen to anything, even the promise of a 1 per cent saving. Some of the devices offered savings of up to 45 per cent.

'For the railways, this was very challenging because it is a very beguiling offer,' Honnery explained in a 2008 interview. 'Any major transport fuel user wants the magic bullet for their fuel consumption. And they are continually being offered them.'

Honnery took the claims and tested them. None of the devices worked. He wasn't surprised. He says that getting a fuel saving of 20 per cent or more in a modern engine—as many of the products tested advertised—is almost thermodynamically impossible.

In the early days of the motor car so many fuel-saving devices flooded the market that the United States government set up a separate department to register them all. In 1971, it went a step further and tasked the Environmental Protection Agency (EPA) with assessing whether any of them worked.

The methods employed by the EPA at its testing centre in Ann Arbor, a university town about 60 kilometres from Detroit, in the heart of the American motor industry, are tried and proven. Other testing centres around the world copy the methods, and they show that it is possible to measure precisely whether something works or not.

The machine used is a dynamometer, an apparatus that simulates road conditions. Typically, two vehicles are placed on it and driven three times to establish a base line for a test. The product being tested is then installed—either added to the fuel or attached to the car, as instructed by the manufacturer—and the same three test drives are conducted again.

Any changes in fuel economy and emissions are measured. The results are then made public, and can be downloaded free from the internet by anyone who cares to take the time. Significantly, of the 93 additives and devices that have been tested at the laboratory since 1971, none has received the agency's seal of approval.

Dr Michael J. Brear, head of the Advanced Centre for Automotive Research and Testing at Melbourne University, tells a similar tale. He uses the Ford proving ground near Geelong to test fuel-saving products and says he gets 'a call every two weeks' from someone with a new device or additive. 'We tell them straightaway that we are not particularly hopeful,' he says. 'That we can't see how it could work from the basic science.'

So far, Brear hasn't been proved wrong. Nothing has worked. He points out the obvious. The annual research budget at a company like Daimler-Benz is hundreds of millions of dollars, he says; that one company alone probably spends more on research and development than all of the industries and universities in Australia combined. 'If they could get a 5 per cent reduction in fuel consumption in one of their engines they would be over the moon. That would be a huge improvement.'

So if someone did come up with a genuine fuel-saving device, the rewards of going straight to one of the big car companies would be far greater than attempting to sell it directly to consumers.

But common sense doesn't always apply.

A remarkable new product captured the New Zealand motoring market in late 1991. It was a small blue waxy cylinder about half the size of the average thumb. Plop one in a petrol tank and vehicle owners could expect a 17 per cent improvement in fuel consumption, an increase in power of up to 12 per cent, and a reduction in harmful exhaust emissions.

These claims appeared in advertising leaflets with the slogan: 'Is your car on the pill?' They stated the pill would also clean carburettors, plugs and injectors, and greatly improve the reliability of any vehicle.

The timing was fortuitous. Petrol prices were increasing, and a broad and growing concern over the destruction of the environment was about to become mainstream. That year, more than one hundred heads of state gathered in Rio de Janeiro, Brazil, for an Earth Summit where they signed the first international Convention on Climate Change, marking the beginning of a seismic shift in political thought that would eventually become the global environmental movement juggernaut.

Within months of the first appearance of the little blue pills, a network of about 3000 small distributors was selling them across New Zealand. The distributors had been recruited at quasi-evangelical gatherings in hotel rooms from Auckland to Christchurch, with promises of freedom from debt, high annual incomes and more time to spend with their families. The company marketing the pills, Power Plan International, was able to exploit a legal loophole that allowed it to make such extravagant assertions. Though it was an offence under the

New Zealand *Fair Trading Act* to make false advertising claims, the law provided an escape if the person advertising a product had reasonable grounds for believing what they were saying was true. Power Plan International could point to sheaves of positive testimonials from users of the little blue pill.

For instance, an opal miner in Australia found that his generator ran for three hours and fifty minutes on a drum of fuel that had the pill added, compared to only two hours and thirty-five minutes without the pill. The owner of a temperamental chainsaw found his machine now started sweetly. The owner of a Chrysler Regal motor vehicle got a 19.5 per cent fuel saving. In New Zealand, satisfied users of the pill included an Eltham motorist (20 per cent improvement in economy), a Queens-town marketing man (34 per cent) and an Auckland surveyor (20 per cent).

No one could check if these people were genuine customers or just friends and family, because none were named.

An Auckland automotive technician called Dale Nixon carried out unspecified tests using the pill in a Toyota Corolla. His testimony included an extraordinary exercise of intuition: 'Although not able to carry out fuel-consumption tests, all my other testing and knowledge leads me to conclude that there is no basis to object to the fuel-saving claims made on the literature I have read regarding the Petrol Pill.'

Power Plan International was structured across multiple levels, with each new set of recruits encouraged to create a new level below them. The higher the distributor could go, the greater the reward. This type of trade—known as multi-level marketing—can trace its roots to pyramid selling.

Charles Ponzi, an Italian immigrant to the United States, brought the concept to public attention when he organised the Securities Exchange Company in Boston in 1919. He issued promissory notes payable in ninety days with 50 per cent interest and triggered a storm of investment frenzy that duped just about everyone. He purported to make his money by trading international reply postal coupons, but he simply used the money of new investors to pay old investors huge profits.

In 1967, Glenn W. Turner began an incredible distribution network in Orlando, Florida. His line purported to be cosmetics, featuring mink oil as a special ingredient. But little selling of the cosmetics actually took place because the real money was to be made in the sale of new distributorships. Participants were encouraged to attend elaborately staged gatherings where clean-cut young men subjected them to the rigours of high-pressure salesmanship. These 'Adventure Meetings' or 'Golden Opportunity Meetings' were directed towards the joys of making easy money. In just five years, Turner parlayed US$10 000 into a conglomerate that generated a cash flow of US$200 million and duped as many as 100 000 people.

More recently, multi-level marketing gained legitimacy thanks to Amway. Two childhood friends founded Amway Corporation in Michigan in 1959, deriving the name from a contraction of the words 'American Way'. The company, which expanded to Australia in 1971, employs a novel means of product distribution using what are termed independent business owners—individuals who earn rewards by selling the products to customers who are often family and friends. In 1979, the company was accused by United States government authorities of being an illegal pyramid scheme. But in a landmark case, the Federal Trade Commission determined that although Amway engaged in deceptive practices, as long as profits were made through the sale of a product the company could continue to operate within the law.

The ruling opened the way to the effective legalisation of a multi-billion-dollar industry. In the United States alone it is estimated that at any one time 10 million people belong to one kind of multi-level marketing scheme or another. Given that the great majority of distributors drop out of the system within a year, only to be replaced by a new set of hopefuls, it is all the more pervasive.

Comparisons are often made between multi-level marketing and religion. Each has its own form of catechism, to be studied, recited and taught by followers. It is also compared to the medieval science of alchemy, the tortured search for a mystical substance called the philosopher's stone that could transform lead into gold. Observers point out that the wealth and influence that accrued to the alchemists didn't come from achieving their enticing goal; rather their power came from developing a philosophy that attracted the support of those who believed transmutation could be accomplished. In the Middle Ages, alchemy's promise of worldly riches drew some of history's best minds, from theologian Thomas Aquinas to scientist Roger Bacon. It also appealed to a selection of history's most famous liars and cheats.

Tens of thousands of the small blue petrol pills were sold in New Zealand before the product came to the attention of the country's influential Automobile Association. The motoring organisation suspected a scam, and decided to find out who was at the top of Power Plan International's triangular-like structure.

It found Tim Johnston.

2 CHOOSING SIDES

Timothy Francis Johnston was born in Brisbane on 30 September 1956. Back then, Brisbane wasn't the tropical easygoing wonderland of today. It was a place where religious belief still influenced social status and where a fear of Catholicism hung over the city like a tropical storm. The Labor Party, the absolute political power that had dominated Queensland for decades, had been divided by religion. Those changes in what had seemed so unchangeable allowed the Country Party under Sir Francis Nicklin to be elected, and in turn paved the way for the institutionally corrupt and conservative nineteen-year reign of Sir Joh Bjelke-Petersen.

Johnston was a Catholic. He lived with his parents and two sisters in a regular suburban home, and attended St Laurence's College, a large all-boys school located in the south of the city, run by the strict Irish Christian Brothers religious organisation.

The sport of choice at St Laurence's was rugby union. Johnston found himself scrumming with Peter O'Meara, a young man who years later would escape a stultifying career in middle management at the Commonwealth Bank to become the inaugural chief executive of the Western Force Super 14 team—the rugby union franchise that Johnston would also become involved with. Both youths played for Souths, although Johnston spent more time on the reserve bench than on the field. Shane Richardson played for Souths too, but would later switch rugby codes and administer rugby league teams. By coincidence, one of his future jobs would be chief executive of the iconic South Sydney Rabbitohs, another team Johnston would be linked with.

When Johnston left school, he joined the Brisbane offices of the petrol-retailing company Ampol as a management trainee. Later, this stage of his career would appear on his CV as 'an extensive background in the oil industry'. From there, encouraged by a hairdressing friend, he joined the beauty company L'Oreal and began marketing shampoo. By now, he'd developed a confident manner; the lanky schoolboy had grown into a tall, handsome salesman. Customers weakened at his patter. Johnston had found his calling.

The new job required him to move to Sydney, a city that in the 1980s presented many opportunities. The glistening expanse of harbour was just waking up to a new dawn, with the nation getting ready to celebrate its bicentenary, and a flotilla of images about to be beamed across the world. It was an era before the domination of corporate lawyers and the big merchant banks. When both the politicians and the crooks had a clearer understanding of the rules. And where enduring decisions were often sealed at clandestine meetings, using brown-paper bags full of cash.

Much of the colourful history of this period would later emerge in a series of stark public inquiries that offered a rare communal glimpse of Sydney's murky underbelly, depicting brutal images far removed from the jaunty representations beamed overseas. One such inquiry was the 1991 Gyles Royal Commission into illegal activities in the Sydney building trade and it is here, buried away in faded transcripts and containing an incorrect spelling of his name, that a fascinating insight into Johnston's early life in Sydney emerges. The transcripts record that in December 1984 Jim Masterton, a wealthy Sydney property developer and the owner of Masterton Homes, bought a company called Knebel Kitchens from its previous owner Richard Knebel. By agreement, Knebel had retained a small shareholding in the business and stayed on as managing director. Masterton insisted on only one change after the sale. He wanted to install a new general manager to serve under Knebel, a young man who was about to marry his daughter, Sue. This man would be entrusted with the day-to-day running of the business. His name was Tim Johnston.

Before going to work for his future father-in-law, Johnston had progressed from L'Oreal to a junior management position at Kwikasair, a division of the giant TNT transport group. This position would also undergo some creative transformation in Johnston's CV, elevating him to 'group general manager' of the entire TNT Australian operation.

Johnston's ego clashed with the concept of being an understudy, and from the moment he walked into Knebel Kitchens he undermined Knebel, convincing Masterton that the business was rife with petty thievery and union issues and hinting heavily that Knebel himself was behind the trouble. His strategy was successful, to the extent that the Royal Commission recounts that by the middle of 1985 Knebel had become 'nothing more than a figurehead' in the business that he had started.

Then events took a sinister turn. The Royal Commission heard that Johnston informed Masterton that Knebel had taken out a contract on his life. Masterton was to be executed by Lennie

McPherson, the notorious Kings Cross underworld figure responsible for bashings, shootings, theft and extortion going back to the 1950s. Alarmed, Masterton turned to Tim Bristow for help, a former policeman turned private eye with a reputation as a violent and brutal standover man. Before his death in 2003, he was one of the country's most notorious convicted criminals. The royal commission heard that Masterton and Bristow had been introduced indirectly through the racing circles that Masterton's daughter—Johnston's fiancée—moved in and that Johnston was a 'good friend' of Bristow's son, Stephen Bristow.

'Tim Johnston was in a car, allegedly, with Richard Knebel when the first threat was made,' Tim Bristow told the inquiry. 'It was in the nature that Len McPherson was going to do something to Jim Masterton. I said "that couldn't be true". That's why I organised the meeting.'

Bristow met with Masterton and, though he continued to cast doubt on the story Johnston had spun about the contract killing, he said he would help to deal with Knebel. But Masterton told the royal commission that he declined Bristow's offer of assistance.

Nevertheless, on 2 August 1985 Bristow visited the premises of Knebel Kitchens in the company of McPherson and two other associates and informed Knebel he was to pack his things. A truck would be provided to drive his belongings home. Faced with the obvious threat, Knebel didn't resist, but he asked to be allowed to drive home in his company car, a white Mercedes. Bristow called a cab for Knebel and arranged with Masterton to exchange Knebel's white Mercedes for his own, 'a similar model but in poorer condition'.

Masterton told the royal commission he felt acutely embarrassed over the incident. He insisted he had not arranged the visit. It was then alleged that it had been initiated by Johnston, who had paid Bristow $9000 for his services on the understanding that half would go to McPherson. During the inquiry, Bristow gave evidence that Johnston had been called away to the phone at the crucial moment when the thugs walked into Knebel's office. 'I think he was disappointed he wouldn't see the look on Knebel's face,' Bristow said.

An unpleasant picture emerged at the inquiry about what life was later like at Knebel Kitchens under Johnston's management. With Knebel gone, the company regularly employed associates of McPherson and Bristow, including Bristow's son, Stephen, and the notorious convicted killer Jack 'Mad Dog' Cooper. Cooper, whom Bristow had met in jail, wore a metal glove and, if antagonised, used it to tear off a person's skin. He also dealt in guns, bringing AK-47 assault rifles from New Guinea into Sydney.

Tim Johnston wasn't present to defend himself at the Royal Commission, and no adverse findings were ever made against him. By then he had disappeared to New Zealand, having fallen out with the Masterton family when his relationship with Sue Masterton ended, before the marriage.

Johnston wasn't single for long. He told friends he met his future wife through Warren Anderson, a former wheat farmer and bulldozer driver from Perth who had also moved to Sydney to seek his fortune. Anderson built shopping centres—dozens of them—for the country's biggest supermarket chain, Coles New World. He owned Boomerang, Sydney's most famous art deco mansion at Elizabeth Bay, as well as a massive cattle station in the Northern Territory and a sprawling farm in Sydney's Blue Mountains with its own zoo, race track and stables. By coincidence Anderson's name also came up in the Building Industry Royal Commission. Six weeks after Johnston and Sandra Meeks met, she was pregnant with their first child, Madeleine. Two years later, they had a second child, Emily. Anderson's version is that although he did know Meeks—she shared an apartment with Anderson's then secretary—he did not meet Johnston until years later.

Meeks was an attractive brunette, born in Fiji and raised in New Zealand, who, according to friends, had worked as a private detective in Sydney in an era when there were few female private detectives anywhere. After the suicide of her first husband, she joined the Jehovah's Witness church, with its promise of heavenly paradise; and then linked up with Johnston, whose promise of earthly rewards were a little more immediate.

Johnston quickly abandoned the remnants of his Catholicism and adopted the religious beliefs of his new wife. He told friends he was swayed by the Jehovah's Witnesses' teaching in relation to blood (members are usually obliged to refuse blood transfusions) because, he claimed, he had contracted a mysterious illness through a blood transfusion, causing a liver condition that would plague him throughout his adult life, sometimes rendering him unfit for days at a time.

Membership of the Jehovah's Witness church's relatively closed community afforded Johnston a certain protection. It was a kinship he could hide behind, as well as exploit as a resource for his many get-rich-quick schemes. However, his adherence to the church's other teachings, such as honesty and integrity, would later be questioned.

When Johnston first arrived in Auckland, he became one of those well-dressed men in suits who go from residence to residence carrying a Bible and spruiking the Jehovah's Witness cause. When he tired of having doors slammed in his face, he went into selling real estate. Then he met an American woman called Sandra Dedina who opened up for him the wondrous world of multi-level marketing.

Associates recall Dedina, then in her early sixties, as the kind of person who had ten businesses going at once, and ten more waiting in the wings. She was based in Cathedral City, California, and ran a company called CYI Techni-Lube—the letters stood for Create Youth International—through which she peddled miracle face sprays, anti-cancer pills and bacteria that ate cow dung and chip fat. Johnston sold all of these before settling on the little blue fuel pills.

Johnston didn't know it at the time, but he was part of a larger pyramid himself. Power Plan International was getting its fuel pills from Dedina, who in turn was sourcing them from a Californian company called PSP Gas Saver Inc, based at Radio Avenue, San Diego. The letters stood for Petroleum Specialty Products. The inventor of the merchandise—the Super Power Stik and the Power Pill—was another American phoney called Ray C. McVeigh. To add one more layer to the equation, McVeigh's products were manufactured by yet another Californian firm called US Lubricants.

McVeigh wasn't afraid to make remarkable claims for his products. They were said to be good for everything from fuel economy to rust prevention. There was no scientific proof, just the usual reams of personal testimonials from customers. For instance, the company's promotional literature included an endorsement from a US Coast Guard commander called Harold G. Reed claiming better fuel economy and a 'significant decrease in maintenance time and expense' from using the products. There was also a letter from a W.E. Becker, described as the general service manager of Electro-Motive, a division of the giant General Motors Corporation, stating that using the products would not affect vehicle warranties. McVeigh claimed his products had been tested at San Diego State University but there were no details about the types of trials that were carried out.

McVeigh was squeezing Dedina hard on price, and she in turn was squeezing Power Plan International. Power Plan International was squeezing the mum and dad distributors.

By the time the pills reached retail level—the 3000 or so people recruited by Johnston in New Zealand—they were being sold for $5 each. It made no sense on a number of levels. Even if people were able to achieve the promised savings attributed to the pill, the maximum savings amounted to about $5—the same price as one of the pills.

The Automobile Association began to ask questions. It wanted to know why there was no trace of any such marvellous fuel-saving compounds in the world's scientific literature. It also wanted to know why there were no scientific studies to back up the claims made for the pill.

'When you think about it, Petrol Pills, if they worked, would be one of the world's greatest inventions. This is a product that ought to interest not just motorists, but governments,' said a feature entitled 'The Miracle Product That Isn't' that appeared in the September 1992 edition of the Association's magazine.

'If the product does "massively reduce" exhaust emissions, it ought to have been a talking point at the Earth Summit in Rio . . . Why is there no pressure on governments to have the product compulsorily included in all brands of petrol? And wouldn't that make far greater profits for the owners of the formula than the present method of distribution?'

They rapped on Johnston's door looking for the answers.

Power Plan International was based at 79 Carbine Road in the light industrial suburb of Mount Wellington in Auckland. It had other offices at 34 Anderson Road in the western Sydney suburb of Kings Langley, and salespeople in Fiji, Indonesia, China, Hong Kong and Malaysia. Johnston had designs on Britain and Germany too. The planned expansion was not only geographical but also in the range of fuel-saving products. Dedina had promised liquid versions of the pill, an oil conditioner, a transmission conditioner, an anti-freeze for fuel and a conditioner for furnace fuel.

By the time the Automobile Association came knocking, Johnston had teamed up with a fellow member of the local Jehovah's Witness community named Ross Johnston (no relative). He was a brown-haired, heavy-set man, then in his early fifties, whose crumpled suits, saggy eyelids and fondness for a social beer contrasted with his younger business partner's dapper appearance. He was a salesman at his mother's brush factory, which had regional offices in Malaysia and sold brooms across Asia and Australia. The two Johnstons would remain business partners.

It was the debonair younger Johnston who was interviewed by the Automobile Association at Power Plan International's cramped Auckland offices. When asked how the pill worked, his answer is recorded in the Association's magazine: 'I don't know how the product works. And I don't think they [CYI Techni-Lube] know themselves. It was invented by a fluke.'

That wasn't good enough for the Automobile Association, which was concerned that most of the testimonials provided by Johnston—which had clearly been passed down the pyramid by McVeigh, the inventor of the pill—were ancient. One letter from the owner of a trucking company was written in 1974. The testimonial from the US Coast Guard commander relating to the pill's alleged ability to clean out fuel fungus was dated 1978. 'We found it odd that such dated testimonials continued to be used, rather than new ones,' the Association later wrote in the September 1992 article.

The Automobile Association was also shown a test by a 'state university' purporting to demonstrate improvements in fuel economy. But this was simply 'two sheets of typed paper with no letterhead, no address, no signature and no clear indication of findings'. A second trial by a Californian research centre claimed a 17 per cent fuel saving. It too was no more than two typewritten sheets that bore 'no letterhead, no address, no date, no signature'.

Johnston was clearly under pressure. So he lied. He claimed two New Zealand government authorities were testing the product, but was vague about the details. Then his interrogators finally struck something solid. At the end of the interview Johnston made a reference to tests being carried out in Australia by the Royal Automobile Club of Victoria and the National Roads and Motorists Association of New South Wales that would ensure the product's endorsement. Both were sister organisations of the Automobile Association. Johnston had made a mistake. The Australian organisations denied knowledge of the pill. They also denied knowledge of any test results. It was at this point that the Automobile Association took matters into its own hands and decided to test the pill.

The vehicle used was a 1992 Toyota Corolla 1600 GL with 9000 kilometres on the clock. It was brought to the Automobile Association's Auckland testing centre, the same place where the Association determined fuel usage in cars for the New Zealand government. The car was placed on an inertia dynamometer.

'Tim Johnston had been at pains to stress that no test of his product is valid until the vehicle has done five per cent of its total mileage with the pill in its tank. For a car that has done 50 000 km that would mean running it for 2500 km before the test proper could begin,' the Association later wrote in its magazine. 'That proviso does not appear in the company's advertising, which therefore becomes very misleading. The clear indication in the advertising is that the Pill works straight away, and there is no suggestion you will not get the full benefits until you have driven the vehicle for five per cent of its total mileage.

'Nevertheless we complied with the requirement. We first tested its petrol consumption in the test centre without the Pill. Then with the Pill in tank we ran it for more than five per cent of its mileage on the road. Finally, we returned to the test centre and tested it again using the Pill in prescribed quantities.'

The news for Johnston was not good. The test indicated use of the pill worsened fuel consumption in around-town driving by 3.67 per cent. During simulated highway driving at 100 kilometres per hour, fuel consumption improved by 1.54 per cent. The average result was a worsening in fuel consumption of 0.73 per cent.

'Our engineers concluded the Pills have a nil effect on fuel consumption,' the Automobile Association wrote. 'We also did tests of exhaust emissions and our engineers concluded these were within the manufacturer's specifications both with the Pill and without.'

The Association prepared an article on the test results and sent a draft to Johnston for comment. He replied through his lawyers and sought to stop publication by seeking an injunction in the High Court of New Zealand. Then he made another mistake. In preparation for the case, he entered a sworn affidavit to the court in which he claimed Kel Glare, the then chief of the Victoria Police, had 'tested the product with outstanding results'.

'We have just recently received an order for 20 litres in liquid form which I understand is to be placed in the Police Force fuel storage tanks,' Johnston's statement read. 'We have been surveyed by the New Zealand Commerce Commission. Its representative Tom Wilson told us that we appear to have a very good product and a very fair multi-level marketing plan.'

The Automobile Association contacted the Victoria Police. It was informed that Mr Glare had no knowledge of the claims made in respect of the product. The Commerce Commission also said its representative had made it plain to Johnston that it did not give any endorsements and that such statements were not to be made. Johnston's lawyers advised him to ditch his attempt for an injunction.

But the Automobile Association didn't abandon its chase. By then it had carried out a second test of the pills, in response to Johnston's insistence that the first test was invalid because it was carried out on a 'new' car.

'We disagreed that a car with 9000 km on the clock is new, and in any case the company's advertising nowhere says the product will not work on new cars. Nonetheless in our second test we took care to choose an older car, a 1988 Nissan Bluebird two-litre automatic sedan which had done 48 843 km,' the magazine article continued. 'Again we complied with the tedious requirement to run the vehicle for five per cent of its total mileage with the Pills in the tank before beginning the test.'

The test on the Nissan produced similar results to the Toyota. There was no improvement in fuel consumption, no improvement in power output and no significant change in emissions. The publication of the article went ahead. 'It is far too easy for promoters of such products to make extravagant claims,' it read, 'and very difficult, time-consuming and expensive to challenge such claims.'

Johnston appears to have been undeterred by the Automobile Association's findings. At this moment of absolute public humiliation and defeat, he began to conceive the steps that would eventually lead to his greatest triumph.

3 ABRACADABRA

Johnston landed in California on Christmas Day 1994. He had learned that the original source of the pills was the US Lubricants plant at 10735 Kadota Avenue, Pomona. He wanted to cut Dedina out of the pyramid and buy direct.

The trip proved more spectacularly successful than even he could have imagined. As the days unfolded, Johnston discovered that McVeigh, the inventor of the blue pills, had died more than twelve months earlier. As nobody had come to claim the formula, the plant owner, Fred Chorney—an ex-Korean War veteran of Ukrainian heritage in his early sixties—had simply continued to churn the pills out for a variety of middlemen around the world.

Johnston found a kindred spirit in the cantankerous factory owner. He was impressed by Chorney's apparent willingness to bend the rules and even more pleased when he discovered that the fuel-saving liquids offered by Dedina were based on Chorney's own formulas. The liquids were marketed under the brand name Techni-Lube, hence the origin of the second part of Dedina's company name, CYI Techni-Lube.

Chorney—a once-talented chemist—liked to start his drinking by midday. Johnston, in turn, liked to ask questions. And it was from Chorney that Johnston learned much of the faux-science that later littered his product brochures. The old chemist explained, for instance, how unburned hydrocarbons from the engine combustion process undergo complex cracking and polymerisation to produce gums, lacquers and varnishes that sometimes find their way into fuel lines, carburettors and injectors. This, he said, translated into poor engine performance, poor fuel economy and the shortened service life of engine components.

Chorney showed Johnston an old copy of a newsletter from the construction and mining equipment manufacturer Caterpillar, dated 1979, that stated sulphur action was also one of the main causes of engine-wear. He claimed that naturally occurring sulphur in fuel would often combine with water to form sulphuric acid, which was one of the causes of acid rain in third world countries.

Faux-science or not, Johnston took it all in. More importantly, Chorney gave him access to a series of test reports he claimed verified the assertions he made for his products and for the pill. They included the originals of the testimonial letters and trials that had been examined and queried by the Automobile Association of New Zealand. They dated back two decades, to the 1970s. It was at this point that Johnston created a kind of Pandora's box, into which he stowed copies of the reports that would form the basis of the massive swindle he was going to carry out. Every time he opened it he would unleash misery.

Back home, Power Plan International escaped prosecution by New Zealand authorities after Johnston stoutly insisted that the reputed properties for the blue waxy pill were real. He begged for time to get new tests done. The matter dragged on for so long that the Commerce Commission eventually deemed that achieving a conviction was simply too difficult. Power Plan International was struck off the New Zealand companies' register in March 1994 and, as far as the local authorities were concerned, that was the end of the whole distasteful episode.

But Johnston had other ideas. He determined that the next time the government came knocking he would be ready. Somewhere along the way he had made the delightful discovery that throwing a little money at an air-conditioned, empty-shell office in a faraway island went a long way to ensuring a manner of protected living.

During the early 1990s, some remote tax sanctuaries advertised on the internet offering the opportunity to start a corporation there for as little as a few thousand dollars. Make up a name, fill out a few forms—it was as simple as that. For the governments of the South Pacific the equation was clear-cut. The web-based entities provided them with a much-needed source of revenue via registration and management fees. But whereas standard corporations are required to stick to rules and keep an audit trail of money and people coming in and going out—such as an annual company report or an annual account statement to authorities—the kind of tax haven Johnston favoured didn't burden its firms with such fussiness. Nor were firms required to tell foreign government authorities who its principals were. If investigators questioned them, they would find it impossible to get answers.

Tax havens that will hide your tracks and your money have always existed. But until the advent of the internet, they were more of a rich man's benefit, associated with old-world grandeur and located in places like Switzerland. The internet lowered the cost, making it easier for middle-income con men like Johnston to take advantage of the practice.

Among the companies Johnston became associated with about this time was a weighty-sounding Vanuatu firm called Prole Bank Limited, as well as a company registered in the Isle of Man called Marello Corporation. Another Vanuatu company, US Lubricants International, deliberately suggested a link with Chorney's firm, the California-based US Lubricants, even though the two did not appear to be otherwise related.

Johnston established Australian and New Zealand sections of the labyrinth by registering a whole new set of companies in both countries, all of which somehow featured the letters TLC—a play on Techni-Lube Corporation, the name on many of the questionable trials and reports he had copied from Chorney. These new companies also shared unusual share structures that sometimes involved the entities in the tax havens.

Adding further to the complexity was another series of satellite companies Johnston encouraged all of his new business associates to register. Many were Jehovah's Witnesses who had signed up to be part of Johnston's pyramid and were selling Chorney's pills and liquids out of their homes and garages. These new businesses also had similar-sounding names, again usually based on the letters TLC.

The intricacy was almost impossible to penetrate.

Johnston wasn't alone in discovering the joys of the online era. The advent of South Pacific internet banking became a major issue for law enforcement about this time, coinciding as it did with the break-up of the Soviet Union and the formation of a number of powerful new Russian crime syndicates. Authorities identified many of the leaders of these syndicates as former spies from the old Communist secret service, the KGB. The deputy chairman of the Russian Central Bank, Victor Melnikov, went public in October 1999 with estimates that $US70 billion in dirty money was laundered through accounts in Nauru alone during the early and middle 1990s. The leading international agency on money laundering, the Financial Action Task Force, also highlighted its concern by saying in its 1998/99 annual report that 'a heavy concentration of financial activity related to Russian organised crime has been observed, specifically in Western Samoa, Nauru, Vanuatu and the Cook Islands'.

The United States government specifically identified Vanuatu—one of the havens favoured by Johnston—as a 'jurisdiction of prime concern' in relation to money laundering and drug trafficking. The February 1999 US State Department report said the country had failed to criminalise laundering activity and also had no requirement for banks to report suspicious transactions to regulators or law enforcement agencies.

Back in New Zealand, much of the public attention over this issue was focused on a mysterious entity called Prok Bank and a related entity called Prok Enterprises. Prok Bank was registered in Vanuatu on 28 March 1992, and set up an office in Auckland in August that same year with share capital of just $NZ10 000. But the firm wasn't a bank in the ordinary sense of the word: it didn't borrow or take deposits from customers at retail counters, and its doors weren't open to the public. The only statement of its intent was to 'finance trade between the Soviet Union and New Zealand' even though at that stage the Soviet Union had well and truly crumbled.

Prok Enterprises was the parent entity in New Zealand. The biggest shareholder in both companies was a former leader of the Communist Party in the crime-ridden eastern Russian city of Nakhodka, where Prok was headquartered. Prok triggered front-page headlines and a national political crisis in New Zealand in August 1995, with news that a serving minister in the then national government of Jim Bolger had joined its board. Conservative MP Ross Meurant was no stranger to controversy. A former deputy head of the infamous police Red Squad (riot squad) during the 1981 Springbok tour, Meurant had hung onto his junior ministry despite several previous crises, including his involvement in a scheme to sell New Zealand army surplus weapons to a British government agent. His directorship of Prok Bank had reputedly come about after he helped the bank broker a commercial fishing deal. As well as the discomfiture of a minister being involved in an organisation that had shades of grey, the directorship was perceived to be in conflict with Meurant's job as undersecretary of agriculture and forestry. He was asked to relinquish the directorship; when he refused, he was sacked from the government.

Prok Bank made headlines again the following year when it was revealed that the New Zealand Serious Fraud Office was investigating its parent company, Prok Enterprises, over suspicions of money laundering. Prok Enterprises was eventually cleared, but Prok Bank was the subject of yet another investigation by regulatory authorities in 2000, which this time spread to Australia. The third inquiry, by the Reserve Bank of New Zealand, centred on whether Prok broke banking rules by acting as a normal domestic bank when it had no authority to do so. In Australia, Westpac Bank complained that Prok's web pages had inappropriately advertised a relationship between it and Prok. There was no link, and the web pages were later withdrawn.

Prok did, however, have a link to Tim Johnston. He had convinced Prok Enterprises—the organisation investigated and cleared of money-laundering charges—of the merits of his Techni-Lube products, and for about three years during the mid-1990s Prok Enterprises helped fund a series of dubious trials in Russia, the Ukraine and Vietnam aimed at proving the products' worth.

The renamed Techni-Lube-Prok liquid product was tested on dump trucks in Kiev, on a ship carrying timber from Russia to Japan, and on some vehicles belonging to the Vietnamese army. Though the tests weren't able to prove anything, the relationship provided Johnston with an insight into the ways of doing business in Russia. It also gave him an introduction to an elderly, white-haired gentleman who would appear in numerous brochures over the years proclaiming the remarkable properties of Johnston's products. Professor Gennadiy Rozenblit from the Kharkov State Academy of Railway Transport of the Ukraine was quoted as having tested the Techni-Lube-Prok product in 1996 and obtained fuel savings of 9 per cent and an emissions reduction of up to 50 per cent. Johnston later claimed to staff he had paid for the endorsement.

Johnston also had operations in Europe about this time. He sold the European distribution rights for the little blue fuel pill to a group of businessmen in the Isle of Man, one of whom in turn signed up a distributor in Northern Ireland called Steven Templeton. Templeton was the son of a well-known Irish motorcycle racer, which was no coincidence. The Europe distributors felt the market for the pill was through motorcycle shops and they began to sponsor sporting events as a way of bringing the product to public attention—events such as the annual Isle of Man TT motorcycle race.

Many of the claims made for the pill were drawn directly from the material supplied by Chorney and added to by Johnston from his experiences in Russia, such as the paid-for endorsement from Professor Rozenblit. The work of the New Zealand Automobile Association was conveniently forgotten. But the Irish were sceptical, so Templeton figured it would be a good idea to give the pill some local credibility. As proper scientific trials were expensive, he turned to a friend, Dr Roy Douglas, who was a senior lecturer in the School of Mechanical and Process Engineering at the respected Queen's University of Belfast.

He convinced Douglas to carry out a series of tests on the pill using the motorbike engine test facilities at Queen's University and then to speak about the results of these tests on videotape. The intended kindness continues to haunt Douglas today. He had no concept of how his words would be used and twisted by Johnston and others over the years, purporting to support a stream of unrelated liquid and pill products. 'These [the tests] showed no improvement in fuel consumption, no change in power output and no significant change in emissions,' Dr Douglas said in an interview in 2007. But when cut and spliced in the right way, the videotape could be manipulated to tell a different story. The tests indicated no fuel savings, but they did indicate that the fuel burned better during the test on the two-stroke engine. This in itself was not statistically significant—it only indicated that further tests needed to be done to determine the cause and if the increased burn rate could be repeated. But Johnston seized upon it as proof that his American-sourced products created a more complete burn.

To call Johnston a compulsive storyteller would be to underrate him. It wouldn't do justice to the sheer exuberant scale of his fancy. To some people, he told an impressive but fictitious tale about being run out of Australia in fear of his life by the union movement because of his extraordinary success in eliminating union rorting and in turning around the profits of TNT. To others, he implied a period of employment in the United States, where he claimed to have headed up the marketing division of a company called US Lubricants International (actually his own Vanuatu-registered firm) and, according to his CV, spent eight years as 'chairman of the board' of TLC Limited, though no such company existed in the United States.

His travels also took him to England, a country that had bestowed upon him the astonishing honour of inviting him to become a member of 'the prestigious Chartered Institute of Transport of London'. Such an organisation did once exist, but its modern equivalent has no record of Johnston being a member.

Johnston claimed to have three separate university honours degrees—in transport management, business management and marketing—though he never mentioned the universities by name. 'Mr. Johnston is an internationally recognized businessman with many years experience in the Oil and Transport industries,' the CV continued. 'Having lived and worked in various parts of the world, Mr. Johnston has a natural feel for international trade and negotiations. Many multimedia articles have been written as well as radio and Television interviews about the international success of businesses headed by Mr. Johnston.'

In many ways Johnston was like the Humpty Dumpty character in Lewis Carroll's famous book about Alice going through the looking glass in that when he used a word it meant just what he chose it to mean, neither more nor less.

His sales pitches were based on a sequence of scientific gibberish that he had garnered from Chorney's stories and from McVeigh's old product literature, and which he would often deliver using his favourite tool—a whiteboard. He would begin by writing a sequence of chemical formulas on the board and talking about the subtle but important difference the addition of one atom could make to each. His standard line was that by adding one more atom of oxygen to water you get hydrogen peroxide. 'Drink that and it will be your last,' he would say. 'See the difference one atom makes?'

The presentation was illogical and difficult to understand, with a beginning and an end but no real middle. But by the time Johnston had finished drawing what he called a tadpole diagram, with a fuel tank at one end and a list of chemical equations at the other, he usually had the full attention of the room. Few of those he addressed had even the most basic understanding of chemistry.

His party piece was to direct a gimmicky act that involved two small test tubes and an assistant dressed in a white lab coat, posing as a chemist. Each of the glass tubes was filled with a small amount of diesel. His product was then added to one of them, coating it in an oily residue. A quote from the vehicle manufacturer Caterpillar flashed up on screen, claiming that sulphur action was the cause of most engine-wear (the quote came via Chorney, and was taken from *Caterpillar Engine News*, 7 March 1979, a newsletter produced by the Caterpillar Tractor Company that talked about high sulphur fuel in some unnamed countries). At this point Johnston would put five drops of sulphuric acid into the test tube 'replicating the conditions within the combustion chamber before your eyes'. He claimed the acid represented 5000 kilometres of normal driving in an engine. The final touch involved applying a laboratory burner to the bottom of each test tube. The test tube containing Johnston's product remained clear. The other tube blackened and burned.

'This test was guaranteed to blow everyone away,' one of Johnston's former employees says. 'But I am not sure what it was meant to prove.'

Each presentation concluded with a graphic contending to show the burn rate using Johnston's products, as measured by Dr Douglas from Queen's University, Belfast. 'This faster burn condition,' Johnston would explain, 'is normally conducive to better power and lower emissions.'

But behind the tricks, Johnston's business was a ramshackle, amateurish mess. Company literature from the time—encompassing numerous grammatical and spelling errors—shows an ambition that was at odds with reality. The brochures featured a superimposed photograph of the US Lubricants plant in Pomona, California, described as one of several factories the company owned around the world.

'Established in 1990, TLC is a company committed to supplying the latest proven technology. To supply world markets TLC as a virtual manufacturer has strategically positioned itself by aquiring [*sic*] products from refineries and blending facilities that can produce the required quality products that meet the customers challenges and demands,' reads the TLC (NZ) Ltd Licencee's Information Manual dated August 1998.

The brochure sketches a vigorous research and development arm that 'leads the world in the development of solid and liquid super concentrates'. These fuel conditioners, it claimed, 'have achieved international credibility for superior performance by improving fuel efficiency, greater equipment performance and reducing harmful exhaust emissions'. The brochure also claimed that Johnston's products were on sale 'from Siberia through Europe to Africa and Asia to the smallest Islands in the South Pacific'.

Johnston's philosophy seemed to be: if you are going to tell a lie, tell a big one.

4 BIG CONCEPTS

On one of his trips to California, Johnston met Jim Grebe. Grebe had worked in sales and marketing at the giant United States oil company Chevron, and at the smaller fuel additive companies STP Corporation and the Wynn Oil Company, before deciding to go into business for himself. In 1992, he began to produce his own fuel-saving and fuel-injector-cleaning products under the brand Chemplex Automotive Group Inc.

Chemplex was a tiny operation, so small that it didn't even have its own factory, and it sold only three products. Each—like the McVeigh merchandise—was manufactured and packaged at Chorney's US Lubricants plant. Two were liquids that cleaned fuel-injectors and carburettors. A third product—called Chemplex FE-3—was a little brown fuel pill that was said to perform similar miracles to the blue, waxy pill Johnston had been peddling in New Zealand.

The letters FE in the name referred to the chemical composition of the product—an iron-based chemical called ferrocene. There was nothing particularly new or secret about ferrocene. A Harvard chemist had discovered it in 1953 and it had caused a lot of initial excitement in the scientific community for its remarkable properties. It showed great potential as an anti-knock agent or octane enhancer in fuel. At one point, it was considered as a realistic alternative for lead in petrol. Boffins involved in the United States rocket program experimented with its use in solid rocket fuel. Ferrocene also had a marked effect on diesel. By adding even a small portion, the amount of soot produced from an engine was drastically reduced.

But several problems soon emerged. Ferrocene-laced fuel often left deposits on spark plugs, catalysts and other exhaust system parts. These fine abrasive deposits of iron oxide (also known as jeweller's rouge) caused catastrophic and premature failure of the spark plugs. Engineers also found that iron oxide acted as a physical barrier between the catalyst/oxygen sensor and the exhaust gases in an engine, leading to erosion and plugging of the catalyst. Emission control systems were not always able to function as designed, causing actual emissions of toxic gases to increase.

Even the soot-reducing properties that were observed in diesel engines weren't quite the bonus they at first seemed. The visible amount of soot decreased, but tests showed that the number of overall toxic emissions actually increased. The particles were just smaller.

But what most concerned engineers was that the presence of iron oxide in the vehicle lubrication system often led to premature wear of critical engine components, such as the pistons and the rings. In short, the addition of ferrocene to fuel could slowly destroy an engine.

The problems with ferrocene caused it to be banned from the fuel specifications of most western countries, including by the Environmental Protection Agency in the United States. However, it is a peculiar quirk of the United States and other western regulatory systems that aftermarket fuel additives do not have to follow the same rules as pre-mixed fuel. Therefore ferrocene—though it is generally excluded from bowser fuel—has never been banned as a fuel additive.

Johnston was unlikely to have known any of this when he first set his eyes on the little brown pill. As far as he was concerned, it simply had qualities that better suited his purposes than the old blue paraffin-based formula that had been devised by McVeigh. The most obvious advantage was that the brown pills didn't melt at Australian, New Zealand and Asian summer temperatures—a constant problem since the early days of Power Plan International and the waxy blue paraffin pills. Whether it worked may have been altogether irrelevant.

Johnston, with all the luck of a Napoleonic general, had arrived on the scene during a delicate period in the business relationship that had developed between Chorney, the owner of US Lubricants, and Grebe, the maker of the ferrocene pill. Chorney had recently purchased a state-of-the-art chemical-blending facility from the giant Quaker Chemical Company. But the opportunity of a lifetime—the sale included a chemical-blending contract with Quaker worth US$500 000 a year—coincided with a desire by Chorney to spend more time on the golf course. An arrangement was struck whereby Grebe would purchase US Lubricants, but the sale would be executed over a period of several years. In the meantime, Grebe would run the day-to-day operations of US Lubricants, as well as his own little company, Chemplex, and Chorney would take a back seat. Eventually, Grebe would assume full control of everything.

But the relationship between Chorney and Grebe had soured. Chorney spent less time on the golf course than anticipated and Grebe resented his interference. The animosity between the two men built up, and the final straw came when Johnston approached Grebe and told him that Chorney was secretly selling the ferrocene-based pill out the back door—to him and to others. Whether the allegation was true or not is hard to determine. But Grebe immediately moved his Chemplex operation away from the US Lubricants plant. And he showed his gratitude to Johnston by signing him up as his exclusive agent in Australia, New Zealand and Asia. Johnston had just been handed the pill that would be central to his later adventures.

Jim Grebe and his wife, Carol, were never entirely comfortable with the relationship, however. They became increasingly perplexed and concerned by some of Johnston's requests. One was his suggestion that Chemplex open a bank account in Vanuatu. 'I don't recall the exact details of the conversation, but he was basically talking about avoiding taxes,' Carol Grebe, president of the company says. 'He was very condescending when I declined and [he] proceeded to explain that everyone does it—implying that that is how business is done.'

When the Grebes paid a visit to New Zealand, they were stunned to find that Johnston had scrawled the name 'TL Chemplex' in big painted letters over the door of his offices. They had never given permission for their company name to be used. The Grebes also discovered they had been downgraded in one of Johnston's product brochures from the owners of Chemplex to merely the Californian distributor of Johnston's products.

Then there were the strange visits. One day Johnston turned up at the Grebes' Orange County homestead in California with a group of Russian businessmen who were described as potential customers. 'They met at the plant and then we had a Texas-style barbecue for them outside by the pool,' Carol Grebe recalls. 'Tim told us one of them was KGB.'

Among the group was the elderly, white-haired Professor Rozenblit from the Kharkov State Academy of Railway Transport of the Ukraine, wearing an open-necked shirt and over-sized glasses. A photograph showing him beside Jim and Carol Grebe's swimming pool was used in Johnston's later brochures. The Russian introduced as 'Victor' (the KGB agent) was thought to be Victor Shumilo, the president of Prok Bank.

The biggest mystery was how Johnston made his money. He was barely selling enough Chemplex products to cover his enormous expenses, which involved flying around the world, usually in business or first-class cabins. And he was constantly short of cash.

'We would be out, and suddenly he didn't have his credit card on him,' says Carol Grebe. 'Or he would have one of his employees pick up the tab for him. Then we would find out later that he had run up thousands and thousands of dollars in expenses that they never got back.'

Johnston, it seemed, was more interested in selling a big concept than in selling an actual product.

The Grebes soon learned that doing business with Johnston meant doing business with Graeme Clegg. Clegg, like Johnston, had the clean-cut appearance of an American television evangelist, and though by then in his fifties could easily have passed for a man many years younger. He was a fellow member of the Jehovah's Witness church, a fervent networker and regular speaker on the New Zealand motivational circuit, and the owner of New Image International, then one of the most successful multi-level marketing companies in Australia, New Zealand and South East Asia.

In low-cost rooms across the region, Clegg delivered free introductory lectures that always ended with the same high-pressure sales pitch he had refined for years. When everyone was seated, his warm-up man would bound onto the stage and repeatedly ask in an increasingly high-pitched voice, 'Are we enthusiastic?' Then the white-toothed, white-suited Clegg would appear, playing the crowd like a beaming paternal pastor. Sometimes, he dressed in a Superman costume and threw wads of small bills into the crowd to the sounds of chanting and near hysteria.

Clegg's involvement with multi-level marketing dated back to the early 1980s, when he picked up some of the remnant products—shampoos and the like—of a company called Total Image. Total Image had fallen foul of authorities in Australia after it was accused of being an illegal pyramid-selling scheme. Photographs of the company's supporters chaining themselves to Parliament House in Sydney to protest over the action by the then New South Wales state government had become one of the defining images of the era.

Total Image had been caught up in the widespread public concern about the cult-like behaviour of multinational pyramid-selling firms like Golden Products and Holiday Magic, which developed out of the Human Potential Movement that bloomed in the 1960s and 1970s. It was a time of pseudo-psychology and encounter groups, and the concern was that the companies were using deceptive and indirect techniques of persuasion and control.

The American principal behind Holiday Magic, which sold products ranging from motor-oil additives to banana-flavoured body lotions, also offered a bizarre program called Leadership Dynamics, which consisted of a four-day course that put participants through a physically and mentally abusive regimen designed to promote a more creative and constructive life. Some participants were ordered into closed coffins; others were suspended from large wooden crosses; and some were told to strip naked while fellow participants insulted and taunted them. In one session, a man was forced to perform fellatio on an artificial penis watched by a group of women.

Graeme Clegg's business ventures seemed based on a deep

fear of his own mortality after his brother died of melanoma and his parents both died of colon cancer, and an overwhelming desire, like Johnston, to make sure that this life was as rewarding as the next one promised by his religious beliefs. Soon after he formed New Image International, he added to the shampoos, skin creams and foot scrubs his own range of controversial health food products. Clegg claimed he had an epiphany during an awful winter storm on his family's Wairarapa sheep farm. He noticed how lambs that almost froze to death could be revived 'miraculously' with a dose of colostrum, the pre-milk fluid produced by mammalian mothers during the first few days after a baby is born. Clegg began taking the fluid daily, and claimed it made him immune to everything from the common flu to jetlag. He bought excess colostrum from local dairy farmers and turned it into a range of products that made big claims but had little scientific backing.

Clegg later set up his own research centre to try to support his assertions that his products could promote a 15 per cent increase in muscle mass and a 14 per cent increase in strength. But rather than sell his miracle products in the normal way through health food stores or chemists (where, presumably, they would come under more regulatory scrutiny), Clegg continued to use multi-level marketing. He built a vast network of independent direct-selling contractors throughout New Zealand, Australia, Indonesia, Malaysia, the Philippines, Singapore and Taiwan. At one point he claimed to employ thirty people at his factory but another 100 000 as salespeople, all of whom worked for themselves marketing his products to their friends, families and associates. His reasoning was that by cutting out the middleman all of his independent contractors could share in the wealth. In reality, it was just another multi-level marketing company that used a similar program of rewards and techniques to those used by other direct-selling organisations around the world.

For instance, Clegg's best salesmen got paid when they turned up to his meetings. At a prearranged cue, armed security guards would wheel out suitcases of money, all carefully folded and arranged like the fantail of a peacock. The suitcases would be lined up and flaunted for maximum effect.

Johnston and Clegg had hooked up in 1994, cross-pollinating their respective enterprises. Now Johnston convinced the Grebes of the merits of shipping the raw ingredients of their ferrocene pill to Clegg's factory, where the products would be finished and packaged. It was a decision the Grebes would come to regret.

The pills were relatively easy to make. Apart from the finely powdered ferrocene, the main item needed was a commercial press—the same tool used to make common pharmaceuticals. The finished products were then sold under various brand names. Johnston called his the PowerMax Pill and the FuelMax Pill. Clegg's identical product was called the Power Pill FE-3. Perhaps to create a point of difference, each man told contradictory stories about the origins of the pill. In one tale, it had been developed in Russia at the end of the Second World War. In another, it had been refined and patented in the United States, and tested as a rocket propellant by the space agency NASA. Today, Clegg even maintains a third story: that it was he who invented the pill, after years of scientific research that involved studying an obscure rocket program initiated by the Swiss. Like any recollection of an accident or major event, he says, you always get ten different versions of what really happened.

The Grebes, whose recollection of events seems the most believable, soon discovered that Johnston was making all kinds of assertions for their product that he couldn't prove scientifically. Tests related to other merchandise—McVeigh's blue pill and US Lubricants' liquid products—were now being taken out of Johnston's Pandora's box and used to support the brown ferrocene pill. 'At first we thought Tim didn't know what he was doing, that he didn't have a technical understanding of the products,' says Carol Grebe. 'But it soon became apparent that he took great liberties in using data where it seemed most beneficial from a marketing standpoint, even when it didn't relate to the product.'

Clegg, too, appeared willing to bend the truth. Even today on one of his many websites, Dr Douglas, the engineer from Queen's University in Belfast, features in a long promotional video allegedly talking about the amazing qualities of the Power Pill FE-3, which Clegg still sells all over the world. It is a manipulated copy of the video shot by Templeton in 1996 in which Douglas talked about the blue waxy pill.

Clegg's business has now gone mainstream. His company is listed on the New Zealand Stock Exchange—one of the many penny stocks that potter along near the bottom of the market. His headquarters at 19 Mahunga Drive has a slightly world-weary feel, despite the gigantic poster on the wall of a group of young people jumping with health. The drab floors, worn sofa chairs and blue rodent bait in the corner contrast with the sign over reception: 'This Is A No Neg Zone, Sales In Progress'. But the radiant optimism is still evident in the pictures that line the walls. They are photographs taken across Asia of the best New Image International salesmen and women. They sit on mock thrones draped in blue and gold cloaks and wearing fake glittering crowns, clutching suitcases full of brightly coloured fantails of money.

Johnston didn't just fool Chemplex. He misrepresented himself everywhere he went. Sometimes he was the head of a nonexistent independent California-based fuel conditioner manufacturer called TLC USA. At other times he was the head of US Lubricants International, the company registered in Vanuatu but also presented as being from the United States. Occasionally, he was simply in charge of a business called TLC International, which didn't appear to officially exist anywhere.

The lies were usually consistent though. He said his products were being sold in ninety-one countries and that he was exploring the possibility of setting up a manufacturing facility in whatever country he was visiting at the time.

During a series of sales circuses in Malaysia, Singapore and Thailand in 1998, Johnston was often greeted by senior government ministers and state officials, all keen to promote his range of products in the hope of attracting new jobs and industry. He even got his version of the ferrocene pill endorsed by the Automobile Association of Malaysia, which claimed to have tested the product and found that it worked. That report, too, added to his Pandora's box.

Reports in Malaysian and Chinese language newspapers—often accompanied by photographs of Johnston shaking the hands of prominent locals—recounted how motorists could get 'a higher motoring pleasure' through improved engine performance by using his products.

'TLC USA, an independent California-based fuel conditioner manufacturer, is considering setting up a manufacturing base in Malaysia, which will be used to export its products to the region,' reads a *Business Times* report from Malaysia, dated 13 February 1998. 'No details are available yet, but company officials said a feasibility study is already being carried out. Its managing director Tim Johnston said negotiations are also being carried out with local lubricant companies to manufacture the product.'

At revival-style meetings held in local hotels and sometimes attended by up to 1500 people, Johnston spruiked the qualities of his goods.

'The company promoting this American product here has testimonials and test reports from the US to the sub-zero regions of the Central Asian Republics, Africa and Asia to back up its claim,' reads another newspaper report from Malaysia, dated 1 March 1998. 'It has also been tested by General Motors, Singapore Standards Institute, Belfast University and many other international testing bodies.'

In Kuala Lumpur, Johnston's products were launched at the Hilton Hotel by the deputy minister for science, technology and the environment, Dato Abu Bakar bin Daud. There were 150 VIP guests present.

'Based on the same elements as commercially available fuel, PowerMax's secret in helping the internal combustion engines to improve their operation is to separate the sulphur and water contents in the fuel before they reach the combustion chambers,' said the *Malaysia Sun* newspaper, dated 8 May 1998. 'With PowerMax fuel conditioner added to every fresh tankful of fuel, the conditioned fuel will burn more completely which means less pollutants discharged.'

The beneficial claims were also sometimes extended to include large industry.

'At difficult times like now, imagine the money a factory would save with at least 10 per cent improvement in fuel consumed not to mention less downtime and higher power,' the *Malaysia Sun* report continued. 'In addition, there will not be any fear of getting warnings or summons from the Department of the Environment for discharging harmful exhaust smoke into the air.'

For the Singapore launch in October 1998, the guest of honour was the president of the Automobile Association of Singapore, Gerard Ee, who posed next to Johnston for the *Good Morning Singapore* television cameras. Next to them was a man dressed from head to toe in a red PowerMax superhero costume. The organiser was Ian Robertson, who had been a salesman for Clegg's New Image International when Johnston convinced him to become his Malaysian, and later his South East Asian, distributor. Robertson paid Johnston about $70 000 for the distribution rights to his products, in the mistaken belief that Johnston, who first presented as the chairman of US Lubricants International, actually had the right to sell them.

Robertson had teamed up with a rich and influential Malaysian family to form a Malaysian-based company, TLC Fuel Conditioners (M) Sdn Bhd. It hired twelve staff, and spent hundreds of thousands of dollars buying an initial supply of stock of what was essentially a mixture of ferrocene pills and liquid products from both Chemplex and US Lubricants. Robertson also set up a distribution network across South East Asia, all on the basis of what he now admits was 'a three-line email' from Johnston. The email promised much but ultimately delivered little. 'I mortgaged my house for the business and I dragged my wife into it,' Robertson says. 'In the end it cost me everything, including my sixteen-year marriage.'

The problems began when Robertson found it difficult to get a reliable supply of the PowerMax products. When he ordered something, it often arrived several months later. Meanwhile, he lost clients and the bills began to mount up. Things went from bad to worse when Robertson's rich but increasingly frustrated Malaysian partners decided to do a little checking up on Johnston. They visited Chorney in California and discovered that the Vanuatu-based US Lubricants International bore no relationship, apart from Johnston, with the American-based US Lubricants. They also found out that Johnston owed Chorney a lot of money, which explained the intermittent supply of some of the products. 'Their next call was to the Commercial Crime Squad,' Robertson recalls.

At first, Robertson's Malaysian partners thought he was part of an elaborate scam and the police wanted to lock him up. When he tried to call Johnston to have him explain the situation, his calls were ignored. Robertson barely avoided jail and was forced to refund all of his business partners' investment. He says he left the country 'a beggar', having lost his marriage and about $250 000. 'I know I shouldn't say this,' says Robertson, who has since become a born-again Christian, 'but I do not think that man should be allowed to walk the earth.'

Though the profit margin on the Chemplex products was remarkable by any standard—Johnston was getting the pills for cents and selling them for dollars—before 1998 came to an end he had decided he no longer needed the Grebes.

By then, Johnston had met Geoffrey Lee, a wealthy Singapore businessman, at one of the revival-style meetings in Malaysia. The Lee family is best known for its ownership of the Singapore Peace Centre, two gigantic eighteen-storey commercial and residential towers. Johnston sold Lee the same exclusive rights to the pills and liquids that he had previously sold to Robertson, and had Lee register another series of companies called The Lubricants & Conditioners Pte Ltd and Global Lubricants and Conditioners (GLC) Pte Ltd.

Lee had been convinced of the merits of Johnston's products by an unscientific trial conducted on the ferrocene pill in September 1998 by the Productivity Standards Board of Singapore. The trial involved driving a four-year-old Rover sedan through city streets without taking into account simple factors like traffic conditions and the time it took to complete each journey. Nevertheless, it too joined Johnston's so-called box of evidence.

Johnston sourced a second-hand commercial pill press in Melbourne and had it installed in a garage at the Peace Centre buildings. He imported powdered ferrocene direct from China and had the powder pressed into pills and packaged locally.

Jim and Carol Grebe, the Chemplex company owners, did their best to sabotage his operations. They wrote warning letters to Johnston's customers claiming that the new tablets were made from 'a cheap industrial grade look-alike chemical' and that they would not dissolve in fuel.

'Because we cut off his source of supply he substituted what he decided was a comparable product and is now selling that . . . in the exact same packaging,' the letter to one customer reads. 'It is important for you to understand . . . [the product] has never been tested . . . and will definitely cause engine damage.'

Johnston sent a legal letter to Chemplex threatening defamation. But by then the Grebes had made another mistake. They had let Johnston in on their idea for an engine-cleaning machine they hoped would revolutionise the motoring world. Though merely a concept—it was drawings of pipes and fluids that swirled around more the Grebes' minds than in any actual engine—they recall the excitement Johnston felt as the possibilities sank in.

A machine that could service cars at the touch of a button would surely threaten the livelihoods of mechanics all around the world.

5 WANTING TO BELIEVE

It was a bleak Wellington day in June 1998 when Ray Whitham saw the advertisement in his local paper. It was headed 'Profitable Life Time Licensee Opportunity' and proclaimed that a well-established, multinational fuel-conditioning company was introducing an exciting new technology to the New Zealand motoring market, one that would be backed up by a nationwide advertising campaign. For an initial investment of just NZ$15 000 plus GST, the qualified applicant could get in on the ground floor.

Whitham was the last person you'd peg as a victim. He had spent fourteen years with the New Zealand police, mainly as a detective in criminal intelligence, and another fourteen years as a private detective, until recently as a principal of a small firm. In between were six years spent in sales and marketing, including an award-winning spell with Rank Xerox. But at fifty-three, Whitham was at a stage in life where he was looking to go into business for himself, something that would take him through to his retirement years.

Whitham ran through the details of the advert with his mate Steven Clegg, who had no relation to Graeme Clegg from New Image International. He was a mechanic by trade but was better known for his former glory days as an international motorcycle road racer. The two had met on the racing circuit, where Whitham, to add to his many other hats, was one of New Zealand's best-known motorcycle commentators. They decided to go along to the meeting and check things out for themselves.

'We met some people in Wellington,' Whitham says. 'We were very impressed because it was in the boardroom of a big oil company and it all had a good ring about it.'

Though noteworthy claims were being made for some of the company's lines—pills and engine fluids that made fuel burn more efficiently and reduced toxic emissions—what really excited Whitham and Clegg was another product.

'I was told they had something really smart they were developing,' Whitham says. They were building machines that could automatically clean your engine and, ultimately, they were going to be selling them direct to the public.'

The Revolutionary Power Purge System looked a little like an old-fashioned upright Space Invaders video-arcade game, with a number of pipes that connected to a running engine through which a series of fluids could be pumped in and out. It didn't matter how dirty the engine was to begin with, the result was a motor returned to 'as new' condition.

'There was input from the United States and we were told the Shell oil company was involved,' Whitham recalls. 'We looked at these machines and thought, shit, these aren't too bloody bad.'

Whitham and his business partner were presented with an exciting series of figures. Tens of thousands of second-hand cars, of questionable service history, were imported into New Zealand from Japan each year, they were told. Each new owner was a potential customer. They could profit twofold from the venture: they would make money selling the machines, and make even more money selling the Shell-manufactured flush-and-purge fluids that were needed to service the cars.

'On the original figures we were given, we were all going to be millionaires before the end of that year,' Whitham recalls. 'It all looked very good and the presentation was very smart. They told me not to worry too much about the pills and other products because they were going to be small compared to the flush-and-purge machines . . . We were told they were negotiating with Shell to introduce them into service stations and there were going to be businesses throughout the country. I must confess, I was quite impressed.'

The words that really stuck in Whitham's mind were those of the man who emerged as the brains behind the operation, the clean-cut Jehovah's Witness who liked to 'talk in telephone numbers', Tim Johnston: 'Let's crank this up and make some serious money and have some fun doing it!' Whitham had little idea that what he was buying into was a complex business pyramid that would eventually cost him his life savings and his home. He was like a human chess piece, being nudged by a master player.

Johnston was an accumulation of contradictions. His patter was that of a used-car salesman, yet he sold Ferrari concepts. He studied the Bible in the comfort of first class, but never questioned the morality of what he was doing or whose money he was spending. He had pinched the idea for the automated engine-cleaning machine from the Grebes, and taken it to Barry Barmby.

Barmby, a genial round-faced Kiwi-Canadian engineer with large rectangular tinted glasses, can no longer recall how the introduction came about. But he does remember the lure, and

FIREPOWER

it's a memory tainted by bitterness. Barmby was promised NZ$5000 a month in wages and a 10 per cent share in the new venture that would be formed to sell the machines. 'He [Johnston] has ruined I don't know how many lives,' Barmby says. 'One of his lines was, "If you give me some cash, I'll double it". And that attracted a lot of people.'

Johnston's main source of money about this time was from an investor called Ian 'Lex' Forrest, an accountant recently retired from the giant pharmaceutical firm Johnson & Johnson. Forrest was looking for ways to increase his hard-earned nest egg and a merchant banker friend—someone he described as a sort of professional fixer—had introduced him to Johnston. It was during the early harebrained years of the dot-com boom and easy fortunes were being made around the world from ideas hatched in home garages. Johnston spoke convincingly to Forrest about his plans to float his engine-cleaning machine company on the NASDAQ, the secondary stock exchange in the United States favoured by the ludicrously successful new technology companies. 'He could sell ice cream to the Eskimos,' Forrest says. 'There is no doubt about that.'

Forrest pumped about NZ$200 000 of his retirement fund into a company called TLC Manufacturing and Design Ltd in the expectation of a fivefold return. But Auckland was no Silicon Valley and the new TLC was simply a room at the front of a grey-coated former broom factory at 32 Hill Street, Onehunga, now a panel-beating shop next to a 'Magic Stone' company.

It was here that Barmby eventually cobbled together the Model 802. It had five knobs and a number of impressive-looking features, including expensive Festo components, yet Barmby was under no illusion. It was simply a prototype, something that would need a lot more work and at least twelve months of extensive road-testing. But Johnston had other ideas.

58

While Barmby was in the workshop, Johnston was out organising investment seminars in hotel rooms across the country, designed to whip up demand for franchisees in the new venture.

'He had big rah-rah meetings and conferences and the like where he made all kinds of outlandish statements,' Forrest recalls. 'It was pyramid selling. He was pretty good at getting people all supercharged up.'

Johnston had Barmby's prototype machine replicated at a factory owned by the Exclusive Brethren, a subset of the Christian evangelical movement that would later leap to prominence in New Zealand after it was linked to the resignation of National Party leader Don Brash. The factory provided about twenty of the machines, but the sect never got paid by Johnston. Nevertheless, its leaders declined to answer queries on the matter.

Johnston had these new machines painted in bright colours, dominated by yellow to match the logo of the giant oil company Shell. Shell had accepted a contract to make the fluids used in the apparatus, and Johnston seized upon this and later portrayed it as a type of joint-venture arrangement, claiming to investors that Shell was seriously considering buying him out.

'Shell actually fed us a line that [it] would help market the machines,' Barmby recalls. 'But when you looked at the contract all it said was that you couldn't use anyone else's fluid in the machine. There was nothing there to say they were obliged to sell [the machines].'

The contract with Shell led to several meetings with senior Shell officials in Australia, one of them in Melbourne where Johnston addressed a gathering of Shell distributors. Barmby especially remembers the Melbourne trip because Johnston turned up in an expensive tailor-made suit, all ready to play the role of the big entrepreneur, yet he didn't have the money for a trolley at the airport, or for the expensive meal he insisted on eating at an upmarket restaurant later than night. Barmby, who had to pay for the trolley and for the meal, also recalls a second meeting in Adelaide at a Shell subsidiary that was considering making the machines. But, again, nothing eventuated. In any case, Barmby says, the machines weren't ready and should never have been put on sale in the first place. 'Tim was more interested in the story, not in whether the machines worked.'

Ray Whitham, the former policeman who answered the newspaper advert, was oblivious to the background. He registered Lube-Tech Dynamics Ltd with his business partner in November 1998. They then entered into a licence agreement with a company called TLC (NZ) Ltd to market and sell the fuel pills in the greater Wellington region. One month later they entered into a second agreement with another seemingly related company, TL Chemplex Automotive Group Ltd, to market and sell the colourful machines. Whitham was informed through a company brochure handed to him by Johnston that TL Chemplex Automotive Group Ltd had been formed in 1990, 'bringing together the technology and manufacturing facilities of Tested Lubricants and Conditioners Inc, United States Lubricants International and later Chemplex Automotive Group Inc'. In reality, records from the New Zealand companies' register show that Johnston had registered the company only four months earlier, using an ownership structure involving an entity called TL Chemplex International Inc based in Port Vila, Vanuatu.

Whitham signed leases on six machines. Initially, they were exciting times for the former policeman. Each day he and his business partner would draw up a list of mechanic shops to visit where they would give free demonstrations of the mechanical wonders. They would hand out samples of the pills and talk up the merits of carrying them as a retail product. The business plan forecast sales of five of the machines within the first ninety days of business and two more units per month after that. Total annual turnover was projected to be $901 000, giving a net profit of $219 000.

The pair was told they could also expect to sell $340 000 worth of pills and injector cleaners in the first year, with each of these products also providing a handsome return on their initial investment. They were informed that the various TLC entities were in negotiations with major oil companies, including Shell, and with K-Mart and Repco Auto Parts to have the pills stocked in service station outlets and major chain stores across the country. Johnston drew up plans for an extensive radio advertising campaign, incorporating a superhero figure called Mr Dipstik—an employee who was required to walk up and down outside mechanic shops across New Zealand in a flapping cape.

'These projections were very conditional upon a promised comprehensive marketing support package being in place by the end of January 1999,' Whitham later wrote in a note to his lawyer. 'And of course by TLC conducting itself as a responsible business partner.'

But with Johnston, things were never that simple.

By April 1999—more than four months into operations and at a point where he was projected to be selling the machines like hot cakes—Whitham had sold just one, to a Holden dealership in Wellington. It would take him the rest of the year to sell another. The promised blanket advertising campaign never eventuated. And none of the major service stations or chain stores seemed to be interested in the pills.

'We told them from the outset that the equipment would need to be marketed, that the equipment would not sell itself,' the note to Whitham's lawyer continues. 'The fact that the marketing support did not eventuate was gross irresponsibility, bordering on fraudulence.'

A second factor weighing on the business was the machines themselves. They would work once, maybe twice, at best three times, before breaking down. '"It's coloured yellow because it's a lemon" has become a common catchcry in several Wellington workshops,' Whitham's note continued. The machines kept popping their seals, spraying fluid over both operator and vehicle.

The third element in the progressive destruction of Whitham's business was the bewildering passing parade of suppliers, contractors and logistics support personnel brought to him by Johnston. Within the first few weeks of starting up business, Whitham was informed that the people he had originally been told to work with 'had become persona non grata' despite the fact that only weeks earlier these same people 'had the best products on the marketplace'. Whitham counted numerous investors or suppliers who went the same way. Chemplex, the California-based fuel pill manufacturer, was the first. Another was the company that Whitham had originally bought his pill franchise from: TLC (NZ) Ltd.

TLC (NZ) Ltd was associated with the Perry family, one of whom, Edwin Perry, later became a prominent Maori politician. The Perry family had bought into the pyramid at an earlier stage than Whitham, paying more than NZ$100 000 for the rights to sell franchises for the pills in twenty-five New Zealand territories for NZ$15 000 each. The Perrys had happened upon the opportunity through their earlier involvement in a multi-level distribution scheme run by an associate of Johnston. But after the initial high-profile launch of the fuel pills at the Solway Park Hotel in Masterton in early 1999, nothing much happened. Edwin Perry says the marketing support promised by Johnston never eventuated. His family still has thousands of the unsold pills.

Another distributor who went by the wayside about this time was Graeme Drummond, a former speedway driver, who thought he had purchased the exclusive right to the TLC range of products for the Auckland region. Whitham recalls Drummond suddenly went from being 'TLC's smartest operator', according to Johnston, to someone who 'couldn't be trusted'. Drummond, for his part, says that shortly after he set up business he found that Johnston had sold a similar franchise to another person—one that covered the entire North Island of New Zealand, including Auckland.

'He would sell someone the rights to his products on an exclusive basis, and then go right out and sell the same thing to someone else," says Drummond, who estimates his losses at about NZ$40 000. 'The thing I found was that all of the contracts were just bits of paper. None of them seemed to be legally binding. There was little point in pursuing it.'

And nobody did.

Another of Johnston's customers about this time was Ken Gracey, who had worked previously as one of his salesmen. Johnston sold Gracey a line that he had powerful contacts in Ford and Holden who were going to guarantee the success of his new engine-cleaning business. He claimed the giant car manufacturers were going to remodel their new vehicles so that the machines would become essential to the servicing process. 'He convinced me that this was really going to happen,' Gracey says. 'I wasn't the only one. All his investors in New Zealand were going "wow!".'

Gracey was told to return to his home town, Melbourne, to set up a franchise network. But Johnston wanted $200 000 up front for the rights. Gracey didn't have that kind of money, so he turned to a friend. He convinced Don Spiteri, a small oil merchant from Dandenong in the outer suburbs of Melbourne, to travel back with him to New Zealand. There, Johnston pulled out a spreadsheet showing that with so many services per day at so much profit per service, the two men stood to make millions. Spiteri eventually bought two engine-cleaning machines for $26 000 each. He and Gracey registered TLC Oil Corporation in Australia in March 1999 and began marketing the machines throughout Victoria. The initial signs were promising. They had no trouble placing the machines at two big city dealerships in Melbourne, so they arranged for three more machines to be sent over. They painted the TLC logo above Spiteri's workshop door, complete with an American flag and the words 'The Pollution Solution'.

'We got a big map out and divided the state up into regions,' Spiteri recalls. 'Mate, he is first class, believe me. He is very good at building you up . . . We were going to make so much money he [Johnston] was already working out ways to hide the money overseas. He puts so many things in your head. And then, bang! He cuts you loose.'

According to Gracey, Johnston arrived unannounced in Melbourne one day and demanded that unless he was handed a majority share in the franchise under a new agreement the pair would not be supplied with the special oil that was needed in the machines. Spiteri contacted his solicitor. But that was when the machines started breaking down—and when Spiteri collapsed, and needed open-heart surgery.

Despite his poor health, Spiteri pursued Johnston through his solicitors, but ran into problems when it became difficult to determine the trail they should follow. 'They kept changing the name of the business,' Spiteri says. '[We] tried to send letters and they changed the names.' Spiteri—who still has the faded TLC sign above his door and a broken-down Model 802 gathering dust on a shelf—spent $3000 on legal fees before giving up. 'I said to my lawyers, stop, because you could go into a deeper hole,' he recalls. 'In the end I called it a business experience.'

* * *

Meanwhile, things were going from bad to worse for Whitham. In August 1999, he discovered that the nationwide rights to the engine-cleaning machines, including his Wellington region, had been sold to a former car salesman called Dean Owens. To deepen insult, Whitham was offered a job by Owens' new company, marketing the very products he thought he owned the rights to.

'To be perfectly honest, I should have opted out months and months before,' Whitham recalls, as he explains why he accepted the offer. 'But you get to a point in a thing like this and you are still seeing the benefit of some of the products, and there were certain aspects about it I liked and still had faith in. I was hanging on by the skin of my teeth financially and so long as there was always a bit of light at the end of the tunnel I kept stupidly thinking, we might be able to turn all this around. More intelligent people might have pissed off long ago, but you are in so far and you think while you still see a chance you might as well go into hock again, and sell the house, and we just might be able to pull this off.'

Owens' new company, Advanced Lube Technology Ltd, set off at a swift pace, setting up trials of the machines in the large Ford dealership where Owens used to work. The company also convinced the New Zealand army, which was getting ready for a peacekeeping role in troubled East Timor, to try the device on one of its ageing personnel carriers.

The one-off army trial went well, but by then the entire Johnston network was in chaos. And there were further malfunctions, this time in the demonstration machines that had been placed at the Ford dealership.

Whitham remembers the last time he saw Johnston. It is recorded in his diary—8 December 1999—and etched even more deeply into his memory. It was a hot, sticky day at the former brush factory that served as Johnston's headquarters, but the atmosphere inside was cool. The audience included the principals of TLC and a number of nervous investors.

Johnston, fashionably dressed in boat shoes and walk shorts, was pacing up and down before a whiteboard. The business was clearly in trouble but he was acting like a tin-pot general who still believed he could take over the world. He hardly drew breath as he talked up a series of drawings and diagrams that outlined TLC's plans to expand across Asia, and even into Europe. 'It was one of those strange days,' Whitham recalls. 'I remember thinking, what sort of a fairy tale is this?'

At the back of the room, waiting patiently, but growing more anxious by the hour, was a man who had purchased a franchise to sell the pills and liquids in the northern region of the North Island. Whitham had never seen him before, so he inquired politely if he was a new investor. The man explained he had most of his savings tied up in TLC and he had some concerns that Johnston had promised to clear up in person. That was why he was there.

As Johnston continued to outline plans for new packaging, he acknowledged the man and indicated he hadn't been forgotten but requested his patience because there was so much to get through. 'I always remember that,' Whitham recounts. 'He carried on talking.' The meeting broke for lunch and resumed with the man still waiting.

As the afternoon wore on, Johnston apologised to the increasingly distressed investor but again assured him he hadn't been forgotten. 'We will get to meet, don't worry,' he said. A short time later, he shot a glance at his watch and a fretful look at the gathering. He explained he 'just had to dash' down the road to pick up his kids from school, that he'd be no more than a few minutes. As he reached for his car keys he again acknowledged the apprehensive visitor, promising they would meet as soon as he returned.

But Johnston drove straight to the airport and caught an international flight to Perth.

Over the next few years, he would waltz from near poverty to inhabiting a series of multimillion-dollar mansions around the world and mastermind the greatest swindle in Australian history. It would be on a scale that was almost unimaginable, and involve everyone from the Australian prime minister to the United States Senate; from foreign spies to high-flying diplomats; from business leaders to international arms dealers; and from the KGB to the Australian Trade Commission.

6 A NEW BEGINNING

The public warning came four days before Christmas Day 2000. It was unusual for a state government department to step so quickly into the public spotlight to alert consumers about defective products—the prospect of litigation made them cautious—but such was the fuss caused by the Fuel Magic pill, a little brown capsule that promised fuel savings of up to 42 per cent, the West Australian Ministry of Fair Trading felt obliged to react. It secretly bought some of the products and commissioned tests on them by the Engineering Design and Consultancy Centre at the University of Western Australia. A chemical analysis showed the 1-gram pills were comprised simply of ferrocene, and tests found they 'produced no measurable reduction in fuel consumption and could have even worsened' fuel efficiency.

Much of the commotion over the pill had been caused by the national current affairs television program *Today Tonight*. Petrol prices were again on the rise and the show featured the pills—priced at $2.50 each—as a possible solution. The segment garnered enormous interest from consumers. But the pill sellers then made a blunder. Milestone Marketing began advertising its wares with the slogan 'As seen on *Today Tonight*', which prompted a second, more critical story from the tabloid show.

That was when the Ministry of Fair Trading got involved. On Thursday, 21 December 2000, the Commissioner for Fair Trading, Patrick Walker, issued a press release warning motorists about the false claims made for the pill. 'People naturally want better fuel economy,' he said, 'but consumers need to take any claims of improved fuel-efficiency with a grain of salt.'

The ministry prosecuted Milestone Marketing, and almost three years later, on 31 October 2003, it finally trumpeted its success. But by then the media had lost interest and there was little fanfare as the four directors of the company pleaded guilty to thirty-two charges in court. 'The magic fuel pills were without the performance characteristics, uses or benefits claimed for them,' said magistrate Jeremy Packington as he fined the directors a total of $24 200. This included the costs incurred by the ministry over the thirty-four months it took to get a resolution.

One of the directors of Milestone Marketing was Mal Emery. Today, he is hailed on the internet as Australia's mail-order guru and an authentic business genius. He is the author of the self-promoting fliers 'Eight Best Ways To Still Make A Fortune From Scratch In Australia Today' and the equally impressive 'How To Turn An Ordinary Business Into An Extraordinary Business—The 9 Indisputable Laws Of Speed Wealth'. The fliers tell you how to own and develop an extraordinary business by working from home, and include the following advice: 'I believe you will never make anywhere near as much money owning a business as you will selling a business'. Emery should perhaps have taken his own advice before dealing with Tim Johnston.

Emery and his fellow director in Milestone Marketing, Lang Lefroy, were introduced to Johnston through Graeme Clegg at New Image International, whose colostrum-based health products they also sold.

Johnston presented them with a suite of test results that, unknown to them, were drawn from his personal Pandora's box and dated back to 1977. Much of this 'proof' was also contained in a 'technical manual' for the fuel pill that dates from this period. The manual runs for over ninety pages and is a mixture of pseudo-technical gobbledygook and plain nonsense headed 'For A Cleaner Future, TLC—The Pollution Solution'. The pill, it says, 'can be used as a power booster, it is environmentally friendly, it reduces carbon deposits and it maximises fuel economy thus reducing the cost of operation'. The manual includes extracts from a scientific paper on the chemical ferrocene that was presented to an international motoring conference in Detroit in 1990. The paper had nothing to do with Johnston or his companies, but—like the video of Dr Douglas from Queen's University, Belfast—Johnston misrepresented it and made it his own. The manual also references a respected German testing institute called TUV, drawn from the same scientific paper; and, for some comic relief, makes claim to figures and graphs said to be at the back of the document, which don't actually exist if the reader bothers to look.

As always, Johnston relied on the fact that people usually see what they want to see and don't seek out the detail. In this way he succeeded in the same way that most confidence tricksters do: by playing on those two ancient human weaknesses—ignorance and greed.

The claim that the Fuel Magic pill got a fuel saving of 42 per cent was based on another report that appeared in Johnston's manual, which stated that in February 2000 a Nissan Motors service manager in the Philippines, Angel Gonzales, achieved the reduction by using the pill in his pickup truck. Milestone Marketing had no idea that the test was in fact carried out by New Image International, the pill pressers, and that Gonzales then went to work for the company. Lefroy says he went to the WA Ministry of Fair Trading and, unaware of its origin, asked if he could use the Philippines' report. He claims he was given verbal permission to do so. 'Then they came after us for false advertising,' he says. 'It cost us a lot of money in lawyers' fees. We were arguing for years.'

Milestone Marketing was prosecuted, but the authorities failed to take the next step and inquire where the products were coming from. And so passed the chance to kill the farce that was about to unfold.

Johnston had been planning his exit from New Zealand long before that last meeting at the former brush factory in Auckland.

In July and August of 1999, he helped form a business in Perth called TLC Manufacturing and Development Australia Pty Ltd. In September 1999, he extended the labyrinth and registered TLC Automotive Pty Ltd. Both businesses were waiting for him when he stepped off the plane.

His early business partner in Perth was Mike Smith, a fellow Jehovah's Witness who installed ATMs in large department stores around the city. Smith, who was unaware of the circumstances that brought Johnston to Perth, had been a shareholder in one of Johnston's New Zealand pill-selling companies dating from 1995. He was also the former co-owner of a small Perth-based company that had sold the Techni-Lube liquids from about 1993 until about 1995.

The new TLC was a tiny operation, existing out of three rented rooms in Ogilvie Road, Mount Pleasant, which were owned by another, unconnected, member of the church; and later at an industrial unit at 4 King Edward Road, Osborne Park, after an alleged dispute over unpaid rent.

During this early period in Perth, Johnston seemed to be living on a personal financial edge. A removalist firm was chasing him for the unpaid relocation bill, and later the owner of a caravan park pursued him over some bounced cheques used to fund a modest family holiday. But Johnston still managed to attract money. One investor around this time was a rich and genial American called George Measel, the owner of a chain of Mexican restaurants. Measel was impressed by Johnston's grand plans to float on the Australian Stock Exchange and he invested $50 000—a sum he is still owed. Measel's involvement had convinced Ken Gracey, the former salesman who had been burned trying to sell the engine-cleaning machines in Melbourne, to return to the fold.

When he was still based in New Zealand, Johnston had flown to Perth and asked Smith if he knew anyone locally who could replicate the engine-cleaning machines. Smith directed him towards his friend Dave Tate, a Yorkshire-born businessman then in his early forties. They arranged a meeting and, as he had no mechanical knowledge, Tate says he brought along Frank Collier, a former English bobby who liked to dabble with his own backyard inventions. The two Englishmen were so convinced by Johnston's sales patter they decided to form a company to make the machines. 'Tim came over and the figures were good,' Collier, now in his fifties and a prison officer, says. 'We were going to make hundreds of these machines and we were all going to be really rich, you know. So I just got caught up in it, same as everyone else.'

But Collier, a trained toolmaker, was unimpressed at the sight of the apparatus he was supposed to replicate. 'They sent over a machine from New Zealand and I pulled it apart,' he recalls. 'I mean, it was just horrendous, the money that was spent on this machine that didn't work—it was unbelievable . . . when I figured out the circuits I thought, well, this is an absolute nonsense, whoever designed this wants shooting.'

So Johnston commissioned the two Englishmen to redesign the machine on the understanding their newly formed company would be responsible for all future production. The investor who put up the money to back the project was Dr Jeremy Foster, a prominent Perth dentist. He advanced more than $80 000 into both the English pair's machine-making business and into Johnston's entities, all of which he eventually had to write off. 'I was not in a position to lose that money,' Foster recollects. 'It just about killed me financially.'

But Johnston's main benefactor at this time was Len Mijat, a wealthy property developer and a fellow member of the Jehovah's Witness church. He took pity on Johnston and agreed to go guarantor on a second-hand car because he was so broke. 'He had about twenty credit cards and they had all maxed out,' Mijat says. 'He seemed to be living from week to week.'

Mijat had met Johnston by chance through a relative who was one of Johnston's new employees. The relative wasn't being paid his wage because there was no money, so Mijat kicked in $50 000 'to get the business over the line'. Very soon, the $50 000 had turned into $100 000, and Mijat found himself paying the wages of the relative. It was like being sucked into a vortex. The tale Johnston spun Mijat was that he was a former senior TNT executive who had been hounded out of Australia by unidentified criminal elements. In New Zealand, he had acquired the rights to the fuel pill and, together with a senior executive from Ford, had developed the engine-cleaning machine, before running out of money just as business was about to take off.

Johnston claimed he was on the verge of signing a series of massive contracts with the Communist government in China to clean up Beijing's pollution problem in preparation for the

2008 Olympic Games. Once these contracts were bedded down, he intended to float his business on the Alternative Investment Market (AIM) in London, a stock market that features small speculative companies. (The lightly regulated AIM has historically been considered something of a Wild West for investors. Speculators are left mainly to themselves to separate high-risk companies from those that are just plain risky. For this very reason, it is popular with exploitative financiers eager to cash in on the latest stock market fashion.)

Alarm bells began ringing for Mijat after he hired a lawyer to investigate the licensing agreements for the pills and the machines. At first, Johnston assured investigators he had all the documents needed to patent the products. But the countless excuses soon wore thin. The final straw for Mijat came when he flew to Melbourne to talk to Don Spiteri, the small oil merchant who had teamed up with Ken Gracey to sell the yellow engine-cleaning machines and lost his money. 'After I heard what he had to say I couldn't get out quick enough,' Mijat recalls. 'The silly part of it was that I fully believe it could have been a viable business if only he had tried to run it properly. But he never had any intention of doing that.'

Though Tate and Collier had a working machine designed and built by about March 2000, they claim they were forced to mothball the operation because Johnston failed to make any of the agreed initial payments. They hired two shipping containers and locked the machines away.

Johnston got around the problem by offering Tate a job as the general manager of his business. Though the wages were low, Tate accepted on the understanding that he would later get equity in the grand plans Johnston outlined. 'He is a chronic user of people, a consummate liar,' Tate says now. 'If there were two stories to tell, one the truth and one a lie, he would always go for the lie. It was almost as if he wanted the world to find out.'

Johnston didn't mention the mothballed machines. Months passed and they remained locked away in the shipping container. Then in August 2000, Tate's mother fell ill and Johnston immediately offered to pay his fare back to the United Kingdom to see her. Tate was impressed, thinking it exceedingly generous. But no sooner was he out of the country than Johnston contacted Collier, his former partner, and sold him a line that Tate had given away the secrets of the machine and he had better follow or risk being left empty-handed.

'That's how he got his hands on all the designs, when Frank joined up,' Tate recalls. 'I came back three weeks later and knew we had been done.'

Though logic told Tate to leave, he needed the job. Just as had happened in New Zealand, there was little desire by anyone involved in the business to confront the reality that Johnston's promises might be nothing more than that.

'It was all about the short term,' says Collier. 'Get investors' money and then move on.' They knew it wasn't right, but Johnston always had an answer for every hesitation, a balm for every moral concern. 'He was such a good talker and so convincing,' Tate says. 'I was on the brink of leaving on three occasions, and each time he brought me back.'

Rather than confronting reality, the employees wanted to believe in the world Johnston was creating for them and they set out to find evidence to keep their hopes alive. As long as there was even the slightest chance that it just might be real, they wanted to believe.

'I am a cynical guy and my shutters would be up, but by the time he finished talking I would be all positive and ready to go again,' says Tate. 'He was just so good at evading things, and he would spin such a good story for whatever the occasion.'

Johnston was also good at telling people he was going to make them rich—very rich. But even Johnston could not always escape reality. In May 2000 his past caught up with him when three of his former New Zealand partners—Lex Forrest, Barry Barmby and a South African engineer called Gavin Barnard—arrived in Perth unannounced.

'We essentially came over to terminate his employment,' says Forrest, the retired Johnson & Johnson executive who lost most of his life savings. 'Technically he was still CEO of our company back in New Zealand, but we hadn't heard from him in months.'

By then, Forrest had discovered that Johnston had used about NZ$200 000 of Forrest's investment to pay off some personal debts. But rather than chase Johnston for the money, Forrest made the mistake of first tackling the bank. He claimed the cheques should never have been cashed without having at least two signatures on them, and had only ever had Johnston's signature. Johnston had apparently befriended a female teller at the bank whom he would target every time he wanted money. The matter dragged on for years before Forrest lost his claim against the bank. He then went to the police. But by then too much time had passed, making it a difficult matter to investigate.

'We did want to question him [Johnston],' Elaine Hautau, a forensic accountant with the fraud squad in Auckland admits. Her interest centred on 'questionable payments' that were made by some of Johnston's companies to entities registered in Vanuatu. But when Johnston could not be traced the investigation ended.

The visit by his old New Zealand business partners prompted Johnston to construct a new labyrinth. In August 2000, he registered his first Firepower entity—Firepower Oceania Pty Ltd. The origins of the Firepower name are rather mundane; it was simply an allusion to 'firing up your power'. Three months later, he added a company called TPS Firepower Pty Ltd. The letters TPS stood at various times for The Pollution Solution or Transport Pollution Solutions, references to his previous engine-cleaning business. Johnston extended the maze by taking on new investors and registering three other interrelated companies: TLC Engine Care System Pty Ltd, in turn owned by another new entity called TPS Group Pty Ltd, and TPS Technologies Pty Ltd, which owned Firepower Oceania. There were now seven Australian entities, each with its own complicated ownership structure, but TPS Firepower would emerge as the dominant player.

Much as he had done in New Zealand, Johnston continued to travel, spruiking the qualities of his products right across Asia and trying to convince middlemen to purchase his franchises.

He did have a customer in China, as he had told Len Mijat, but it wasn't the Communist government wanting to clean up Beijing. It was Steve Yu, a Hong Kong businessman with good business and political connections on the mainland. Yu helped organise a series of trials with the government-owned Beijing and Shanghai bus companies. The trials, according to Johnston, were spectacularly successful, with one bus returning a massive 30 per cent fuel saving. On the basis of the results, Yu ordered US$200 000 worth of the pills and liquids, and spent another US$100 000 setting up a series of distributorships and advertising the products throughout China.

But customers soon began complaining that the pills didn't work and business quickly dried up. Yu then commissioned his own independent tests. In contrast to Johnston's trials, they found no fuel saving. This came as no surprise to Ken Gracey, the salesman Johnston had employed to help conduct the original trials. He revealed that halfway through the test drive with the bus that showed a 30 per cent fuel saving he paid the bus driver to pull into a service station. The other good results, he says, could be explained by the fact that they picked the oldest, dirtiest buses they could find and effectively gave them an old-fashioned service before adding the pills or liquids.

When Yu attempted to contact Johnston to tell him his woes, Johnston refused to take his calls. To compound the damage, Johnston had earlier convinced Yu that he needed him to urgently return some of the fuel pills that had been shipped to China in loose form to fill an immediate order. Though Yu had paid for the pills and they belonged to him, he organised to have them packaged in China and freighted back to Johnston. When he sought payment for his work, these calls were not returned either.

The pills Johnston had had packaged in China made the usual rash of fraudulent claims: that they had been tested by 'The Engineering Society for Advanced Mobility, Land Sea Air Space' and by another body called 'SAE International'. Not only are these two names for the same organisation, they are taken from the scientific paper on the chemical ferrocene that was presented to the international motoring conference in Detroit in 1990. A third reference to the German testing institute TUV was also drawn from the same scientific paper.

Yu sought legal advice over his dealings with Johnston but was told it would be difficult and costly for him to pursue an Australian-based company for damages. He was still getting over his loss when only weeks later he was astounded to see a range of similar products suddenly appear for sale in China. Johnston had gone and sold them to someone else.

In October 2000, Johnston asked Tate if he knew anyone locally who could replicate his liquid products—the suite he had brought back from New Zealand and which he had originally purchased from Chemplex and from US Lubricants. Johnston claimed he had misplaced the formulas.

Tate introduced him to Peter Matthews, a chemist and inventor and the owner of a small oil-blending plant in Perth called Gold Leaf Enterprises. Tate recalls that Johnston handed over a plastic unmarked bottle of liquid and asked Matthews if he could reproduce it. Matthews opened the bottle, sniffed the product and immediately identified it as coming from the US Lubricants plant in California.

Proving that history is often a series of accidents, Tate says Matthews then marched over to a shelf, pulled down one of his own products and handed it to Johnston. 'Why are you using that, when you could be using this?' Matthews asked.

He had just handed Johnston the final piece of his big concept.

7 FOREIGN SHORES

The controversy over the Fuel Magic pill back home sharpened Johnston's focus abroad. He returned to Russia, where he had supposedly convinced the sprawling Russian Railways network to try his liquid product in one of their trains. Russian Railways is a giant state monopoly whose network is the second largest in the world, spanning eleven time zones and handling 80 per cent of all Russia's transportation needs. By itself, it accounts for 3.6 per cent of Russia's annual gross domestic product. Johnston claimed the trial was overseen by a scientific research institute funded by Russian Railways, and if the fuel saving that was achieved on the one locomotive was applied to every train it would save Russian Railways between US$23 million and US$100 million a year.

But there was a major hole in the story. When the experiment began in July 2000, Johnston was still selling the old Techni-Lube merchandise he had brought from the United States. By the time it ended six months later, the product being used had morphed into something called FP4000, the name he gave to the liquid that had been handed to him by Matthews, the Perth chemist. Nevertheless, he claimed the Russians were so impressed they were going to rewrite their fuel specifications to include the use of FP4000 in all locomotive diesel fuels. The person who was going to write the requirements for the 'new fuel' was Professor Evgeny Kossov, a department head with the Russian Railways Research Institute in St Petersburg.

Johnston claimed Kossov would also recommend FP4000 for every locomotive across Eastern Europe, and the combination of these events would ensure multimillion-dollar annual contracts and the financial future of TPS Firepower. A number of reports—written by Kossov in Russian—were added to the Pandora's box, but Johnston never disclosed that he was paying Kossov to prepare these reports and would continue to do so for a number of years. In this respect, Johnston was mirroring his first adventure in Russia with Professor Rozenblit from the Kharkov State Academy of Railway Transport of the Ukraine— the man in the open-necked shirt and over-sized glasses who stared out from his New Zealand brochures.

Johnston was also in India. In May 2001, he arrived in Bangalore and presented himself as the head of the TPS Group, a company based in Australia that was interested in setting up a multimillion-dollar manufacturing plant for its products. He claimed TPS was a conglomerate that sold its PowerMax products in ninety-one countries, and that it had the support of the 'Shell Motor Corporation'. His promotional material played to the international fashion of the day by declaring his PowerMax pill was 'to your car what Viagra is to mankind'. 'Like the blue wonder drug that revolutionised male healthcare across the world,' the material reads, 'PowerMax promises a major breakthrough to a cheaper, cleaner transport system and thus a purer world.'

The Karnataka regional government, which subsidised Johnston's trip in the hope of attracting jobs, organised for tests to be conducted on some decrepit and ancient blue buses belonging to the Bangalore Metropolitan Transport Corporation. Though they failed to record any fuel savings, a triumphant Johnston claimed a whopping 70 per cent reduction in emissions. He immediately declared to the local media at a press conference that within 'ten to fifteen months' he would set up a $10 million industrial plant that would cater to the local market as well as the exports sector.

The trip to India had been organised by Johnston's new partner in the region, an Indian-Malaysian businessman called P. Mugunthe. But later that night Johnston secretly met with Mugunthe's business rivals to try to cut a separate 'exclusive' distribution arrangement for India. They dined in the hotel paid for by Mugunthe.

Johnston convinced the Indians of the same mind-boggling logic he applied to every new investor. Rather than simply approaching a respected testing institute in Australia or the United States or Europe and subjecting his products to rigorous scrutiny, he told them the only way to truly examine their qualities was during the everyday workload of the vehicles or machines being tested. The demonstrations of his products followed a pattern set by Gracey, his salesman, and involved a routine very different from the highly scientific standards that are applied at respected testing centres. Factors that would normally be taken into consideration during a laboratory test—such as traffic conditions, load and the condition of the engine being tested—were dispensed with. Typically, an old vehicle would be filled to the brim with diesel and taken on a 100-kilometre run through suburban streets. From this highly variable standard, a calculation would be made about how much fuel the vehicle used. The next stage involved washing the engine out using the engine-cleaning machine and a series of strong chemicals. The oil filters were changed. Only at this point would the pills or liquids be added. Any subsequent improvement in a second 100-kilometre journey would be put down entirely to the pill or the liquid.

Collier, the former English bobby, had been sent to India to act as a technician for the trial. He now found himself being sent to various parts of the world on similar missions. In March 2002, he was sent to Pontianak, the capital of the Indonesian province of West Kalimantan on the island of Borneo, to oversee a trial on a diesel generator belonging to PLN, the troubled and financially stricken Indonesian government-owned electricity board. The trial had been organised by another of Johnston's overseas partners, a local businessman named Tanto Adi Pramoko, who had family in Perth. But every time Collier attempted to measure how much diesel the generator was using, he found his efforts being sabotaged. It soon emerged that the locals were stealing diesel to heat their homes and didn't want measurements taken. Three months later, the trial still hadn't been completed, but Johnston once again declared the operation a triumph, claiming a fuel saving of 6.3 per cent. He also used the trial to maintain that the Indonesian government-owned electricity company was using his products. He had made similar assertions in relation to the earlier trial, claiming that state transport groups in India were big users of his products.

Johnston also had a presence in Thailand. In January 2002, another of his overseas business partners organised a trial on a Hino truck and a Mercedes bus both owned by the Thai Department of Defence. Johnston claimed a 16 per cent fuel saving and soon began to boast that his products were being used by the Thai military, though there is no evidence that the tests led to any ongoing business relationship. The trial did, however, trigger a memo from the Australian embassy in Thailand to the Australian Trade Commission, the arm of the federal government that assists Australian companies to export to other countries. This simple note, drawing Austrade's attention to TPS Firepower, set off a chain reaction that would be felt in Australian diplomatic circles for years to come.

TPS Firepower began applying for and receiving grants from the Australian government under the Export Market Development Grants Program run by Austrade. The scheme was an initiative of the Howard government, designed to encourage small and emerging Australian businesses to bring their products to the rest of the world. But in its early years—until the legislation changed in June 2006—it was rather too generous in that a company didn't have to actually export anything to qualify for taxpayer dollars; it just needed to show that it intended to export. The grants were, in fact, reimbursements of the expenses spent in the previous year by the company in trying to develop its overseas markets. One expense Johnston costed back against the Australian taxpayer was the consultancy fee for Kossov, the scientist promising to rewrite the fuel specifications for Russian Railways.

TPS Firepower would eventually get $394 009 in grants.

Government endorsement and Johnston's optimistic talk of giant overseas contracts soon drew the attention of people like Michael van Rens, a former Channel 7 journalist turned businessman, a prominent racehorse owner and identity around Perth. He helped manage the Strategic Capital Superannuation Fund, a private retirement trust favoured by 488 wealthy members of the Perth social establishment.

Van Rens essentially made his money by taking other people's money and punting it on companies that were getting ready to list on the stock market. Many were small technology companies or mining and exploration companies, some of which were based overseas. Van Rens sat on the boards of some of the companies he invested the money in, and many turned out to be spectacularly successful. Others were not.

The problem with van Rens was that he didn't always play by the rules. When the Australian Prudential Regulation Authority later seized control of the superannuation fund in April 2003 it found it wasn't licensed to take contributions from the public. It had also failed to lodge audited annual financial statements with the regulators since mid-2000—pretty much since its formation. The financial watchdog later discovered the fund could only account for $13 million of the $24 million said to be under its management, and it launched legal action that eventually saw van Rens barred from the superannuation industry. But that was all in the future. At this point, van Rens was still master of his own peculiar universe and he invested about $100 000 of the superannuation fund into the TPS Group, which in turn owned TPS Firepower.

Van Rens belonged to an obscure network of wheelers and dealers that spanned the globe—from Australia to Canada to the heart of Eastern Europe. One of these was Perth-based Quentin Ward, a former bankrupt who, from 1995 until 1998, was barred by the Australian Securities and Investments Commission from dealing in securities or giving investment advice. He too would assume a key role in the unfolding saga.

Perhaps the best-known member of the van Rens worldwide network was Vasile Frank Timis, the man London's big financial institutions would soon come to know as the Gusher. Timis was born in Communist Romania in 1947 and there are various accounts of his escape to Perth from the brutal dictatorship of Nicolae Ceauşescu at the age of sixteen. One story has his father shot by a police death squad. In another his father is blown up. Timis' escape was sometimes a swift exit and at other times a barefoot march to safety.

The *Sunday Times* in England reported in May 2005 an account of his escape. 'I escaped from Romania in 1979. I walked from Timisoara, a town in the west near the Yugoslav border, all the way through Yugoslavia to Trieste in Italy. It took 42 days. We crawled for six nights to get over the borders so we didn't accidentally walk on top of a border guard,' the newspaper reported.

Timis migrated to Perth as a motor mechanic, but ended up working on mining sites. In the early 1990s, he was twice convicted for possession of heroin with intent to supply but escaped a jail sentence. Shortly afterwards, he returned to Romania and acquired some of the biggest and richest gold assets in the world for what the local newspapers described as a scandalously low US$3 million. Timis set up a Jersey-based company called Gabriel Resources and in 1997—with the help of investments secured in Australia by van Rens—floated the gold assets on the Canadian Stock Exchange. Early participants got a handsome return.

But the company that really put Timis on the world stage was Regal Petroleum, founded in November 1996 and floated on the AIM in London in 2002. Regal was a combination of Timis' oil and gas interests in Romania and the Ukraine, many of which were also obtained controversially according to critics in his home country. Regal was a perfect example of what can happen when investors—even those with the best advice that money can buy—value dreams over common sense.

Regal's love-to-hate relationship with London's financial sector began in September 2003, after it acquired nearly 60 per cent of a Greek oilfield. Timis began to boast that Regal had struck so much oil in this field that the underwater pressure was in danger of destroying the drilling platform and the lives of those working on it. The oil reservoir at Kallirachi was vast, he gushed, anything up to a billion barrels, one of the biggest finds in Europe. In London's financial district the smart money was already on the story, driving Regal's share price up above 500 pence, and putting a market value of more than £500 million on the company, making it one of the most highly capitalised on the AIM. Large institutions, including Merrill Lynch, Commerzbank, Artemis and Schroders, joined an army of private investors and bought into Timis' vision of creating 'a significant oil producer within Europe', the *Sunday Times* reported.

But in May 2005 the bubble burst. The City was stunned to learn that despite all the hype, despite all of Timis' loud confidence, 'the flow rates achieved from the Kallirachi well were minimal and deemed to be non-commercial'. In short, the well was a dud. Shares in Regal, already hit by a series of delays and setbacks since the initial boast, fell to 94 pence. The shock waves travelled far and wide—to the big institutional investors such as Henderson, Fidelity and Goldman Sachs, which backed a £45 million fundraising at 390 pence in April 2005; and to Evolution, the broker that had arranged that share placing. Shares in Evolution fell 10 per cent as investors speculated about the damage to the firm's reputation.

There were calls for the Financial Services Authority to investigate, amid allegations that investors had been conned. Eventually, AIM market officials were forced to overhaul their entire regulatory structure. But back in Australia, many of the early investors in Regal who had bought in through van Rens—including those in his superannuation fund—made a killing after getting out early.

Some of these gains would be rolled over into Johnston's entities.

Before then, however, another new player entered the mix.

Trevor Nairn, a Perth chartered accountant, ran into Johnston one day in late 2001 when dropping his children off at school. Johnston introduced himself and they got talking. Johnston wondered how he could, as he often put it, get his business 'to the next level'. He was, Nairn says, the most persuasive fellow he had ever met, the kind of guy 'who would punch you in the face and you'd end up apologising for it'. The two men ended up sitting down together at Nairn's kitchen table, mapping out a way to bring TPS Firepower to the attention of the world. Their plan involved targeting large users of fuel, such as mining and transport companies.

Nairn was a savvy businessman who had figured Johnston for a bumbling individual with a great product but little commercial sense. He had no way of knowing that he was already talking Johnston's language—that of the big concept. Nairn travelled to Russia to meet the man who claimed he was going to write FP4000 into the fuel specifications of the Russian Railways. He found Kossov to be an agreeable character, even if he didn't understand a word he said. Nairn organised, through Austrade, to have the Russian Railways test translated into English, at a cost of $100 per page. It appeared to show promise.

Nairn next met Matthews, the chemist, and was convinced by his credentials. He was prepared to gloss over the fact that Matthews was owed $298 000 for two container loads of FP4000—some 32 000 litres—that Johnston had said would be needed to fill a large order from the Indonesian power company that never materialised. Faced with being stuck with the unsold goods—far more than his small business could possibly carry— Matthews' very future was tied to Johnston whether he liked it or not.

Nairn was no fool. He could see there was money to be made if Johnston's stories about pending large contracts in Russia and Indonesia were true, and he was keen to be part of it. He was also convinced—after trying the liquid product in his own car—that the product worked. In this respect, he was the same as everyone else who got involved. But Nairn had a harder business edge than Johnston's other investors. More than most, he was determined not to lose. He took over the day-today running of the company, and both he and his stockbroker friend Phil Grant became the biggest new investors.

Nairn imposed a cost-cutting regime that curtailed Johnston's extravagance and instituted a number of changes that attempted to put TPS Firepower on a proper business footing. The company moved from $100 000-a-year premises at Osborne Park to $30 000-a-year offices at a government-owned technology park in the outer Perth suburb of Bentley. Nairn's arrival also added a sense of momentum and urgency that proved difficult to decelerate. By then, many of the early employees like Tate and Gracey had either left or been sacked, and with them had gone much of the key historical knowledge that future backers might have preferred to know.

Nairn identified Matthews, the chemist, as the company's biggest asset. He also knew that unless TPS Firepower owned the intellectual property rights to Matthews' products it didn't have very much. In August 2002, he hired Matthews as a consultant chemist on $100 000 a year. As part of the deal to give TPS Firepower and its related entity, the TPS Group, the rights to his products, Matthews was promised a percentage royalty on any future sales of his liquids. The agreement promised to deliver him several million dollars.

There was another pressing reason to tie up the rights to Matthews' liquids. A new player had arrived on the scene: a Singapore-based Chinese businessman named Li Hai Dong who wanted to float a public company on either the Singapore or the Hong Kong Stock Exchange to sell the liquids, pills and machines into China, Indonesia, Malaysia and Thailand.

Dong was what could be best described as a Capitalist Communist, and had business contacts right across Asia. He was also the youthful president of APR Norinco International, better known as China North Industries Corporation, the Chinese government-owned arms manufacturing company—a firm sanctioned by the United States in 2003 for selling missiles to Iran. It was Dong who had organised the Firepower products trial with the Thai military that had sparked the note to Austrade.

In August 2002, the same month the agreement with Matthews was signed, Dong established a company in the Cayman Islands called Firepower Holdings Limited. The new entity was split into 500 million shares. Dong explained this was because of the Chinese belief that it was better to own lots of cheap shares than just a few expensive ones. He said the shares would be easier to sell this way, and he arranged for a logo to be designed for the new company that featured a fire-breathing dragon.

Under the arrangement negotiated between Dong and Nairn, TPS Firepower was to receive a royalty for all products sold through the Cayman entity after it listed. TPS Firepower, which was owned by the TPS Group, would also retain the rights to the products in Australia and New Zealand. Yet Nairn had little intention of selling anything in Australia. If things went the way he expected, the TPS shareholders had only to sit back and watch the money roll in.

But it never did. For reasons that are still unclear and unable to be verified, by early 2003 Dong had decided he wanted nothing more to do with Firepower. He simply handed the Cayman entity over to his Australian business partners and the TPS investors, with all of its 500 million shares. Johnston's big concept was nearly dead.

8 GAINING CREDIBILITY

An unlikely saviour came in the form of the Australian Trade Commission.

In April 2003, John Finnin, a dark-bearded giant of a man, was headhunted from the beverage company Foster's Group for the role as Austrade's regional director for Europe, the Middle East and Africa. He took up the job three months later. As one of only four regional directors in Austrade, Finnin stood near the very summit of an organisation that spanned 142 locations in 64 countries and employed more than 1000 staff, many of which, like him, were based overseas. His job, which involved elevated dealings with diplomats and foreign regimes, afforded him a top-secret security clearance from the Australian government.

Finnin's brisk and meticulously presented exterior belied his upbringing in rural Ireland. His parents had been obliged to seek the permission of the Catholic Church for him to attend the country's most prestigious university, Trinity College Dublin—once the exclusive domain of the Protestant ascendancy—as a scholarship student. Fluent in French and Arabic, Finnin had emigrated to Australia with his wife and young family, settling initially in Perth where he ran a small tourism business, and then moving to Melbourne, where he helped turn around the fortunes of a government-owned train company. Finnin and his wife had since separated, and from the early days of his Austrade appointment he adopted a punishing schedule of flights and meetings across his vast portfolio. At one point, he spent just twenty-seven nights a year at his new home in Frankfurt.

Seemingly everywhere he went in those first few months, Finnin kept bumping into Firepower. The company had been mentioned in Austrade dispatches from Thailand and Russia, and when he visited Romania, Firepower was there too.

Johnston's connection to Romania had been forged through the van Rens network in the form of George Teleman, a consultant to Timis in Regal Petroleum, the company that would claim to find vast amounts of oil off the coast of Greece. Teleman was a former diplomat for the Romanian government based in Singapore, and had links, albeit indirectly through his business partners, to the Romanian intelligence community. Teleman became the 90 per cent owner of a subsidiary based in Romania called Firepower Romania SRL and a director of another Hong Kong entity, Firepower Enterprises. His key contribution to the unfolding saga was his role in having some of Johnston's engine-cleaning machines manufactured by the Romanian government's arms manufacturer, RomArm, in a complicated deal involving the British arms dealer, BAE Systems.

BAE Systems was in the country because in early 2003 the British government had sold two clapped-out warships to the Romanians for the scrap metal price of £100 000 each. The frigates, the HMS *London* and HMS *Coventry*, were built in the 1980s but the Romanians were led to believe they were still serviceable and were convinced to spend £116 million refurbishing them with new guns and electronics. The contract, of course, would go to a British firm, in this case BAE Systems—Britain and Europe's biggest arms dealer.

A common practice in such transactions is what is known as an offset agreement. BAE Systems was required to 'offset' a percentage of the contract by either sourcing goods or services from Romania or by bringing some other benefit to the country, for instance in the form of new technology. Since there wasn't much the British company wanted from a country that was still bleary from decades of autocratic rule, BAE Systems was quite happy for Johnston to step in. BAE Systems accepted the notion that Firepower's engine-cleaning technology was a form of radical whiz-bang know-how because that fulfilled the requirements of the offset arrangement. The deal was worth about £75000 to TPS Firepower, but was even more valuable to BAE Systems in the form of offset credits.

Though there is no suggestion that the arrangement was anything other than a normal business transaction, the background to how BAE Systems found itself in Romania would eventually become a major political scandal both in Romania and in Britain. The Serious Fraud Office in London would investigate allegations that payments of up to £7 million were made to corrupt Romanian government officials—using offshore accounts—to secure the frigate deal. Two people were arrested over the matter.

But for Johnston it was simply a gift that kept on giving. Not only did he get his machines made for next to nothing, he was able to add a sense of mystery about Firepower's relationship with BAE Systems, a powerful global conglomerate. Austrade, which had also helped broker the deal, sent a letter of congratulations from the then Australian trade commissioner to Romania, Jacqueline Davison, who reported to Finnin in his capacity as regional director.

Finnin decided to find out more about Firepower, and in early 2004 had lunch in Perth with Nairn and Johnston. Johnston was at his charming and effusive best, and, after obtaining Finnin's business card, followed up the lunch with a steady stream of phone calls and emails. 'I thought he was charismatic, I thought he was friendly,' Finnin would later tell the ABC *Four Corners* program. 'I thought he was a terrific businessman, a lot of charm, and was taken in by him, very much so.'

Finnin says he had no reason to doubt Johnston's credentials because TPS Firepower was already receiving export market development grants. He knew the grant process was rigorous and that dispelled any doubts as to Firepower's legitimacy. But he now admits that the scrutiny done by Austrade was not what it should have been. 'You will, in any large organisation, get companies that slip below the radar,' he told *Four Corners*. 'But you could honestly quite describe it [the scrutiny] as inadequate.'

Part of Finnin's job at Austrade was to pay special attention to a select number of Australian firms of his own choosing. At the time he had a catalogue of about twelve, some of which were large trading companies listed on the Australian Stock Exchange. These were termed 'key clients' and each was afforded particular support from the regional director. Firepower was soon added to the list.

Finnin had arrived as an outsider, and he immediately began to clash with Austrade's traditionally staid and conservative world. He felt that trade with Russia was being neglected, in line with the political view from Canberra at the time. The long-reigning prime minister John Howard was in power and he tended to take his lead from his ally, the United States president George Bush. Both leaders viewed the then Russian president Vladimir Putin, a former KGB operative, with distrust. But Finnin was determined to make Russia one of his biggest priorities, and he asked another outsider to make it happen.

Gregory Klumov had only been an Australian citizen for nine years when he found himself posted back to his native country as the senior trade commissioner to Moscow in July 2003, a role ranked just below that of ambassador. His bridge to Australia had come through Monica Attard, the award-winning ABC radio journalist and future host of *Media Watch*. They had met and married during her time in Russia as a foreign correspondent, and in 1994 he had accompanied her back to Sydney, where he worked in a variety of private and government roles before joining Austrade. The couple later separated. Klumov's great capacity was his ability to sell, and he returned to Russia at a time when Australian exports there had markedly dropped, from about $2 billion a year to about $300 million a year, following the collapse of the Soviet Union. Wheat, wool and coal contracts had dried up and there was a general sense of unease about even visiting the country. The perception was that Russia had been overrun by crime. Klumov saw his new role as a go-between for Australian businesses, big and small. The opportunities were not confined to big business, he told the *Sydney Morning Herald* in October 2003. 'If they [small businesses] talk to us, we'll find them agents, partners and distributors.'

It was a situation that was ripe for Johnston to exploit. At a time when few Australian companies were venturing into Russia, Klumov saw Firepower as an opportunity, a chance to fulfil his mission. In February 2004, he helped Johnston sign his first real distribution deal in Russia—at least in his modern guise of TPS Firepower—with a small Moscow company called the Irbis Group. He had introduced the two parties and acted as a witness to the agreement.

In typical Johnston fashion, the arrangement was complicated. The Russians were asked to sign an agreement not with TPS Firepower but a Hong Kong-registered company called Firepower Enterprises Limited, the same entity that had entered the contract with BAE Systems in Romania. Firepower investors were told that the Irbis Group was being brought in to close the massive impending deal with Russian Railways on the back of the impressive trial overseen by Kossov of the Russian Railways Research Institute. Significantly, the date of the trial had changed. It had been moved a year, from 2000 to 2001.

The Irbis Group didn't actually sell anything but that didn't stop Johnston talking up the deal. The impending contract with Russian Railways now became the central feature of his every sales pitch and, like a good fisherman's yarn, the prize got bigger with each new telling.

'I subsequently used some of the facts and figures that were being used by Firepower at the time,' Finnin told *Four Corners*. 'Russian Railways, over 20 000 locomotives burn 9 billion litres of fuel annually. You know, €180 million contract, and I used that in presentations to my own board at the time . . . we talked it up . . . senior members of the Russian government were entertained at our ambassador's residence in Moscow. So how much store did I put in it? I believed it to be factual.'

On the surface, the distribution agreement with the Irbis Group was indeed impressive. The company agreed to a schedule of purchases of Firepower liquid and pill products that ran to several million dollars over a three-year period. But the agreement was never enforced, because making sales was always secondary to Johnston's main game.

Finnin says Johnston was already getting something more important from Austrade—the sweet smell of authenticity. 'We introduced them [Firepower] at very senior government levels both within Australia and overseas,' he told *Four Corners*. 'I think it gave them another level of credibility, another level of legitimacy whereby they were able to say that they were being supported by the Australian government, which, in essence, they were.'

One of Johnston's business partners from that period, who declined to be identified, recalls that Austrade never asked for any proof of sales. And it wasn't just in Russia that the red carpet was being rolled out. It was all over the world. 'Mostly they [Austrade] would host us at events such as dinners at the local ambassador's residence,' the former business partner says. 'This would be great from Firepower's perspective because if you wanted to meet someone in a particular company you got Austrade to invite them. Most people would be impressed . . . it would give great credibility.'

He names Firepower's contact in the United Kingdom as Alison McGuigan-Lewis, the senior trade commissioner to London and now senior trade commissioner to Washington. In Poland it was Malgorzata Hill, the trade commissioner to Warsaw. In Russia, apart from Klumov, it was Nina Mitropolskaya, Austrade's senior business development manager. 'I attended numerous Austrade functions at various embassies and the ambassador and Austrade representatives would always do a fantastic job of promoting them. Everyone would then automatically assume they [Firepower] were on the level.'

Firepower presented a perception of success, but such perception was expensive. Away from the limelight, Johnston spent most of his days sitting in the Florian coffee shop, now called the Merchant Tea and Coffee House, in the Perth suburb of Applecross. The company was consuming about $100 000 a month in wages and overseas travel, and Nairn and the latest group of shareholders were nearly $1 million down. Sales were negligible, other than on the internet where the pills were offered on obscure trading sites like Mango Universe; and the existing investors were reluctant to tip any more money in.

The solution came in the form of what is known as an 'information memorandum', a device that allows a company to sell a percentage of itself to affluent people known as 'sophisticated investors'. Information memorandums are usually a precursor to a full stock market float and the shares are usually sold at a sharp discount of their perceived value. The advantage of information memorandums is that they allow companies to raise capital without having to go through the rigorous process involved in satisfying the full requirements of a stock exchange listing. Financial regulators expect rich people to have the wherewithal to do their own due diligence.

The shares offered for sale through the van Rens network were in Firepower Holdings Limited, the Cayman Islands entity handed back by Li Hai Dong, the Chinese arms dealer. In 2003 and again in early 2004, helped by the perception of Australian government support and the fuzzy connection to BAE Systems, the company sold about 50 million shares—or 10 per cent of those created—at 5 cents each, which notionally valued the company at $25 million. The $2.5 million raised was used to pay down loans from Nairn and other investors and to provide the capital needed to get the company ready to list on the AIM.

The vast majority of the shareholding remained in Johnston's hands.

Johnston would work a roomful of diplomats talking about his religious faith and the importance of integrity. But the information he was feeding his new investors bore little resemblance to the truth. It was all blue-sky promises of big contracts and difficult-to-verify assertions.

A newsletter from this period, dated June 2004, claimed NATO had given its seal of approval for Firepower's products, as had the 'British Ministry of Defence' and the Australian defence attaché in Washington. Johnston claimed his distributor in Italy had just achieved an 18 per cent saving for the Italian Fire Brigades; in fact, this was a trial on a single vehicle belonging to the fire department in Forli, a small city of about 110 000 people near the birthplace of the Fascist leader Benito Mussolini. Tests on two trucks in Belgium that hauled milk and soft drinks became trials with the national Belgium milk bottler and Coca-Cola. A trial on a tourist bus in Istanbul was presented as a trial on a transport fleet. The newsletter implied Firepower was about to test its products on London's distinctive red double-decker buses and on London cabs. In fact, New Image International, the company still supplying the pills to Johnston from New Zealand, had given some of the pills to a handful of cab drivers in the English capital.

But perhaps the biggest claim came under the headline 'Australian Government'. Johnston said that Firepower had been 'selected by the European office of Austrade as one of only ten "Rising Global Businesses" to be supported through the Austrade global network'. The newsletter went on: 'Firepower activities within Austrade will be coordinated by John Finnin, Deputy Consul-General and Regional Director, Europe, Middle East and Africa. This is a very significant development as it gives the company access to foreign governments at a Government to Government level and the extensive network of multinational corporations with whom Austrade has an existing relationship.'

It was about this time, in mid-2004, that Johnston began to compile a Firepower company profile. What was eventually produced was dated September 2004 and headed 'Performance Technology For A Better Planet'. All the information in it was based on what Johnston told his staff.

The 45-page document painted a picture of a Cayman Islands-registered conglomerate far removed from the reality of a tiny operation in a shared industrial park on the outskirts of Perth. Firepower was said to have access to technical knowledge that was being ignored by some of the biggest companies in the world. It propagated the conspiracy theory that the major oil companies were deliberately withholding information about Firepower's products in order to sell more fuel, even though they knew the products could help stop the pollution of the planet.

'The fundamental premise behind Firepower products is that the fuel produced by the major oil companies has failed to keep pace with the requirements of modern engines, or the expectations of society in relation to emissions,' the company profile said. 'Despite the technology being available, economic and other pressures prevent the major oil companies from applying it to the fuels they produce (why would they want to add a product which reduces fuel consumption?).'

Though Firepower had no factory, no trucks nor much of a staff, the document stated that the company 'manufactures a range of hydrocarbon-based fuel conditioners and high technology machines', each of which had been 'comprehensively tested by several world leading independent testing institutes'.

These products were said to enhance engine or boiler performance for petrol, diesel and heavy oil users, 'providing substantial fuel saving, significantly reduce harmful emissions [and] reduce maintenance costs and increase equipment life'.

In an apparent contradiction of the conspiracy alluded to earlier, Firepower was said to have contracts with Shell and that its products had been used for fourteen years by various unnamed military, bus companies, car workshops and trucking companies around the world.

'In January 2002, the Australian government became in-volved as a result of a trial of our products with the Thai military,' it stated. 'This became the first of a number of government to government meetings in a number of countries, with the Australian government endorsing and recommending Firepower products and technologies at a diplomatic level.'

Austrade was said to have introduced the company to the British Ministry of Defence, the United States Defence Department, the president of Romania, the Russian railways minister, the minister for transport in the United Arab Emirates, the Tianjin provincial government in China, and the United States Environmental Protection Agency.

Under the heading 'Current Prospects', the document claimed Russian Railways was about to commence buying Firepower products and that this would lead to a rollout by other railways across all of Eastern Europe. Kossov, the man developing the 'new fuel' for Russian Railways, was quoted, claiming a need for 17500 drums of FP4000 a year.

The Russian Railways contract alone was said to be worth US$50 million per annum, and there were also claims of potential contracts with the Italian and Russian electricity monopolies, the Russian military and PLN, the Indonesian state-owned power company. There were other implied business deals in Italy, Switzerland, Monaco, Brazil, Turkey, the Gulf States, the United Kingdom, Belgium, China, India and Romania.

The document would help propel Johnston from his then bare-bones existence in a rented Perth abode to sudden and extreme wealth.

9 THE EMPEROR'S NEW CLOTHES

The mystical value of the intellectual property rights of Johnston's products now formed a new canon within Firepower.

Presumably recalling the issues that arose the first time around, Johnston convinced people there was no need to seek patents, arguing that to do so would risk handing rival companies the secret formulas. Instead, Firepower would have the constituent parts of the liquids manufactured in different countries; they'd only be brought together when ordered by a customer. Comparisons were made with the secret sticky black substance added to plain soda to form Coca-Cola. 'The actual formulations are held offsite in a secure environment with restricted access,' Johnston stated.

When those with knowledge of chemicals pointed out that anyone could simply have the formula broken down, Johnston deflected their doubts, replying, without any irony, that Firepower had only three good years to make lots and lots of money before the copycats moved in. The best way to protect the company, he continued, was to target powerful people for joint-venture partnerships in foreign countries. In India, for instance, one of the directors of the company appointed to distribute the Firepower products was 'a retired Rear Admiral from the Indian Navy, allowing him to introduce Firepower products to the Navy at the appropriate level'. These powerful figures, Johnston said, would earn a healthy profit margin on the products and therefore would have a compelling incentive to battle the pirates. The bigger and uglier the joint-venture partner the better.

Johnston also implied that Firepower had a large research and development program that was constantly evolving new formulas. The truth, like the stories about powerful contacts in India, was rather more modest. Recorded minutes from the expansively titled 'Product Development meetings' from mid-2004 show that some of the work was being done by the company's bookkeeper, Nigel Parker. Parker, another Jehovah's Witness, would trial various formulations in his private vehicle and then report back to the meetings. On one occasion, a 1-litre sample of liquid was provided to Parker's father so he could test it on a trip to the remote northern town of Broome.

The large batch of FP4000 that Matthews had made in 2002 for the big Indonesian order that fell through—now finally paid for, thanks to the capital raised from the information memorandum—was shipped in drums to rented storage units in Europe, Asia and St Petersburg in Russia. It would last for years.

Some was used for a trial on two dump trucks in use at a subsidiary of Russia's largest coal producer, Kuzbassrazrezugol. Trucks 97 and 100 were randomly chosen for the test, which involved using a plain measuring ruler to determine how much diesel each was consuming. The trucks were driven around for three days using the FP4000 product and, without any accurate account for variance, a calculation was made about how much fuel the Firepower product was saving. Johnston would later claim it was a saving of 40 per cent. And not just for those two trucks. The saving, he said, was made across the entire Kuzbassrazrezugol operation.

It was in this heady mixture of fantasy and optimism that momentum for a stock market listing re-emerged. In October 2004, Johnston told investors that 'the continued excellent results of Firepower's technology in the areas of reduced emissions and improved fuel efficiency' had led to interest from all over the world. The business, however, was being hampered by Perth's distance from Firepower's principal markets. 'Whilst we have achieved these positive results,' he wrote in a company announcement to shareholders, 'we have not been able to follow up these demands and fully capitalize on the interest that has been generated.' Johnston announced that Firepower had hired the corporate finance division of KPMG, one of the four biggest auditing firms in the world, to advise on a strategy going forward and to assist in optimising Firepower's 'true value worldwide'. It would also pursue a listing on the AIM. 'Whilst it is too early to give clear indications on the potential value and timing of this IPO [initial public offer], the company feels from a strategic point of view and with the assistance of KPMG, that this is the correct course of action.'

Johnston named David McDougall, KPMG's corporate finance director, as the man who would lead the company to the promised listing. 'Over the next three months the members of the board of directors and Mr McDougall will be travelling to various countries and regions to discuss business and strategies with our partners, staff and Australian government officials.'

In November 2004, McDougall—a Brisbane-based partner in KPMG with over twenty-five years of experience in capital raising and valuations—accompanied Johnston on a trip to London and Dubai, where they met representatives from

KPMG's British office to talk about the listing. One month later, KPMG in Russia was asked to help establish a Firepower entity in Moscow.

KPMG's involvement stirred renewed interest from the van Rens network. Financial advisors wanted the chance to sell more shares to their clients before the listing, and at a higher price than the original 5 cents each. Johnston, who had no other income except through Firepower, had powerful reasons to comply with their wishes.

But behind the scenes, problems were emerging. Matthews, the chemist, decided to walk away, having long given up on the $2.5 million in royalties he had been promised two years earlier. He put his chemical-blending business, Gold Leaf Enterprises, up for sale. Johnston also had another issue. Nairn, whose tight rein on Johnston's excesses had caused tension, opposed the sale of any new shares until the company was truly ready to list.

So Johnston got rid of Nairn.

Johnston had lined up a replacement for his former chief executive long before Nairn departed. The new man, Gordon Hill, had been police minister in the state government of Brian Burke, the notorious West Australian state premier who was imprisoned for seven months in 1994 after being found guilty of cheating on his travel expenses. Hill, an affable personality who was then in his early fifties, had largely escaped his former association with Burke and had served successfully in later state governments, including a stint as minister for mines and fisheries. After twelve years in parliament, he resumed practising law and had built a solid reputation as a company director.

In about August 2004, Hill was engaged to do some legal work for Firepower, after being recommended by van Rens. On one of Hill's visits to Perth from his home in rural Western Australia, Johnston offered a trial of his products, including the engine-cleaning machine, on Hill's six-year-old Land Rover Discovery. Hill was apparently so impressed with the results that he pulled over to the side of the road halfway back and rang Johnston to express his amazement. Within weeks, he had joined the company. One factor in Hill's decision—apart from Firepower's apparent association with the giant British firm BAE Systems—was Johnston's professed religious beliefs. Hill had fond memories of former neighbours who were also Jehovah's Witnesses, whom he'd found to be honest and well-meaning.

Johnston set about ensuring that Nairn, who was still a major shareholder in various entities, became isolated. Nairn remained a director of TPS Firepower, so in December 2004 Johnston registered another new company, Firepower Operations Pty Ltd, which took over the day-to-day running of the business in Australia. The move further muddied the ownership structure, given that there were now numerous investors in numerous earlier Australian-registered companies, all of which retained an interest in Johnston's self-proclaimed and mystical intellectual property.

In February and March 2005 the ownership structure became even more convoluted when a fresh round of share selling in the Cayman Islands entity took place, this time at 20 cents a share—four times the price paid the previous year. The selling was done through a group of investment advisors linked to the van Rens network. They included Quentin Ward, the former bankrupt from Perth whom ASIC had once banned from giving investment advice. Documents show that by 11 March almost $5 million had been deposited into a National Australia Bank trust fund administered by Hill's legal firm, Gordon Hill & Associates.

But the real beneficiary was a British Virgin Islands registered company called Green Triton Limited—the company that was selling the shares. Johnston controlled Green Triton. The money was quickly transferred from the National Australia Bank account in Melbourne to a UBS account in Singapore. Johnston was suddenly a multimillionaire.

The shares sales were unusual in a number of respects. They were mainly to so-called 'mum and dad' investors, scattered across the country and overseas. Under normal investment rules, the company should have produced a company prospectus, a disclosure document under the Australian Corporations Law that is registered with the corporate watchdog ASIC. But Johnston got around this by offering the shares to the licensed financial advisors using the old information memorandum, claiming that because they were transfers of existing shares, as opposed to new shares, there was no need to issue a prospectus. The investment advisors—part of the van Rens network—were then encouraged to hawk the shares to their customers in return for a commission. The commission was often on top of whatever fees the investment advisors normally charged their clients, and was not always disclosed to the purchaser.

The small investors were told they were being let in on the chance of a lifetime, a golden opportunity to get in early like the big investors usually did. They were shown the company profile drawn up by Johnston's staff and told that Firepower would list in London later that year at about $2.50 per share, which represented an enormous return for their 20 cent per share investment. So enamoured were some customers that they told their friends and families, who also invested. They were made to feel like members of a secret club. A few weeks later, some of the investors were posted certificates that looked as if they'd been typed up on a home computer.

Johnston received most of the money that was raised, then lent some of it back to Firepower for its everyday operations, which in turn gave the impression that the company was making sales. Very soon, he wasn't just the majority owner of Firepower, he was also its biggest creditor.

Hill had an early warning about what life would be like at Firepower when he was told to go to England in early 2005 to meet with the then British prime minister, Tony Blair. The London gathering was organised by David Slack, Firepower's partner in the UK and a man who claimed to have powerful connections with the British Labour Party and within the British establishment. Slack had teamed up another Englishman, Dave Booth, to form a British-based company called Firepower EMEIA [it stood for Firepower Europe, Middle East, India and Africa] with the aim of selling Firepower's products through the internet. They worked out of the offices of the giant international London-based law firm Bird & Bird, which drew up some of Firepower's contracts. The connection to the British Labour Party was through Slack's friend, Hamish Sanderson, a Bird & Bird partner.

When Hill turned up to his meeting with Blair at Grosvenor House, one of the largest and most famous luxury hotels in London, he found Firepower had simply bought tickets to a Labour Party fundraiser. There were thousands of people in the room, including Finnin, the Austrade director, who had also been misled. Hill nevertheless managed to shake hands with Blair, and an image of this moment adorned a second newsletter in June 2005 that Johnston sent out to his new shareholders under the misleading heading: 'Meetings With British Government'. The caption on the photograph read: 'At dinner with the British Cabinet'.

By now Johnston was a constant fixture at Australian diplomatic functions around the world.

Finnin had been instrumental in organising a special function at the sumptuous private residence of the then Australian ambassador to Moscow, Les Rowe, where senior officials from

Russian Railways were wined and dined by Firepower. He then arranged for Johnston to be introduced to Rowe's successor, Bob Tyson. Johnston wrote to shareholders in the June 2005 newsletter that the new ambassador to Moscow 'commended Firepower for the superb job it has done in Russia in developing exciting export markets' and that he had expressed his commitment to work with Firepower during his term. Tyson would be as good as his word.

At the same time, Johnston was claiming in the newsletter that the British government had 'offered enthusiastic support for manufacturing in Britain' and that 'first export orders have been sent internationally from our British manufacturing base'. He was lying. Firepower had simply commissioned a small amount of blending to be done by a firm based in Wales. 'In my view it [Johnston's statement] was downright misleading,' a former senior member of Firepower says. 'It implied that we were involved with some kind of government-approved or government-sponsored production in the UK, which just wasn't true.'

He goes on: 'In fact, I was at the Labour Party event the night that infamous photo of Gordon Hill was taken with Tony Blair. They had not been speaking—many of us shook hands with him—Gordon was simply in the right place at the right time to get snapped. What stunned myself and others was the resulting article that went out to shareholders which was less than economical with the truth about the situation.'

But thanks to the lack of oversight at Austrade, and with the help of two powerful figures like Finnin and Klumov, the momentum was with Firepower. The meeting with Bob Tyson led to an invitation. Firepower was asked to become one of only three inaugural sponsors of a new annual trade show being planned by Klumov to try to boost trade between Australia and Russia. 'Australia Week In Moscow', scheduled from 10–15 May

2005 at the upmarket Radisson SAS Slavyanskaya Hotel on the banks of the Moscow River, was advertised by Austrade as 'a unique opportunity' for Russian companies to meet potential Australian-based partners.

In the lead-up to the event, Johnston was taken on an Austrade-funded roadshow to Sydney, Melbourne, Brisbane, Adelaide and Perth, where he was one of the guest speakers advising Australian business leaders how to retail their products into Russia. Firepower, which was selling nothing, was hailed in an Austrade press release in February 2005 as an 'exporter case study'. The other speakers at the meetings were Klumov, the Russian ambassador to Australia, Leonid Moiseev, and Austrade's senior economist, Tim Harcourt.

The other inaugural sponsors of Australia Week In Moscow were BHP Billiton and the Russian mining giant Rusal, each of which also paid $80 000 for the privilege. The contrast with Firepower could not have been more startling. BHP Billiton was the world's largest diversified resources firm, with 35 000 employees working in more than 100 operations in more than twenty countries. Rusal was one of Russia's biggest companies, and had recently made the largest single investment in the southern hemisphere by taking a $400 million stake in Gladstone-based Queensland Aluminium. Firepower didn't have a factory or a mine; it was a fairytale.

Yet when Austrade was asked by Russian state television to nominate an Australian company that could feature on the local equivalent of the *Today* show, it chose Firepower. Cameras were dispatched to Perth in the middle of the Australian winter to film Johnston diving into the cold waters off Cottesloe Beach and to capture his commanding presence in Firepower's modest boardroom. A segment entitled 'A Day in the Life of a Successful Australian Business' later appeared to 80 million Russians each morning of the trade show.

Johnston was so grateful for all the help he was receiving that he pulled Finnin aside and offered him free shares in Firepower. When Finnin declined the gift, Johnston persisted. He said he could set up a blind offshore trust fund that would hold the shares for Finnin's children. Finnin again declined the offer, and on 12 April 2005 he formally reported the matter to his boss, Peter O'Byrne, the head of Austrade. And yet no alarm bells rang out.

Significantly, Firepower had by now become known as the more lofty-sounding Firepower Group. 'Firepower Group is an international company providing effective solutions for users of liquid hydrocarbons, ranging from the private motorist up to large industrial organizations, transport companies and large-scale power generators,' Austrade told the Russians in a briefing pack handed to exhibitors.

Australia Week In Moscow was opened by the Australian head of state, Governor-General Michael Jeffery. About thirty small and large Australian companies took part. Jeffery's visit to the Firepower stall was recorded and quickly relayed in a newsletter to shareholders under the heading: 'Government supports Firepower in Russia'.

At the conclusion of the trade fair, Hill, the former state police minister and now a Firepower director, headed to London to meet some of the people he hoped would help with the listing on the AIM. He knew his first job would be to win support from a nominated advisor—known in the financial industry as a 'NomAd'. The NomAd helps with the listing, in return for a fee. Assisting in the negotiations was Eileen Carr, whom Hill had met when they worked together at Goldstar Resources, an Australian-based exploration company. Carr was an accountant and a member of the Sloan Fellowship program at London Business School. She ran a corporate consultancy business in London that specialised in providing advice to British and international companies on AIM listings.

This excursion to England was the beginning of an on-again, off-again dance with banks and brokers that would continue for years. 'The meetings in London generated a great deal of enthusiasm and excitement amongst the experienced London stock market community,' Johnston gushed in the June 2005 newsletter to shareholders. 'KPMG together with a British firm with considerable experience in public floats will now work towards preparing the required information with a view of the company's European business listing late this year or more likely early 2006.'

Subtly, the time frame for a listing had moved back. And behind the scenes, an even bigger move was underway. As May 2005 came to a close, Johnston moved the Firepower mother ship from one tax haven to another, from the Cayman Islands to the British Virgin Islands. At first, the only apparent difference between his new entity, Firepower Holdings Group Limited, registered on 2 June 2005, and the old Cayman entity was in the name—the tiny insertion of the word 'group'. But it would later be alleged in the Supreme Court of Western Australia that in moving the domicile of the company Johnston neglected to bring all of the old shareholders along. Nairn, the former chief executive who had fallen out with Johnston, directly—or indirectly, through his wife—owned millions of shares in the Cayman entity. He appeared to own none in the new entity. His stockbroker friend and fellow investor Phil Grant would also later claim in court that his millions of shares had been left behind.

The situation was repeated for some smaller investors who had bought in through their investment advisors only months earlier. Some people were given certificates saying they owned shares in the Cayman entity; others got certificates saying they owned shares in the British Virgin Islands entity. The truth was, nobody really knew who owned what.

Hill, who organised the move to the British Virgin Islands, argued he was simply following advice that Firepower needed to be incorporated away from the Cayman Islands in order to be more acceptable for a London listing. The shares had not disappeared, he explained, but had been put aside in the name of a trust account. That was a matter for legal argument. But in moving the furniture, Johnston achieved what he wanted to achieve. As people scrambled and searched for their shares, nobody stopped to question what they were buying in the first place.

10 LITTLE HELPERS

With Firepower relocated to the Caribbean, Johnston was on his way elsewhere.

In May 2005, the Australian high commissioner to Pakistan, Zorica McCarthy, brokered a meeting between Johnston and the powerful Pakistani foreign minister, Khurshid Kasuri. Johnston's pretext was that Firepower could save the country US$500 million a year in its energy bills, and he carried with him an eight-page report on the wonders of his products that included newspaper clippings of his previous exploits in neighbouring India with the ancient blue buses of Bangalore.

Relations between Australia and Pakistan had never been better. Concern over the country's perceived military dictatorship had been conveniently pushed to one side over a common desire to combat the growing threat of international terrorism. Back home, the Australian government was preparing for the first ever visit by a Pakistani head of state, President General Pervez Musharraf, and there was much talk of greater economic cooperation.

Johnston told the Pakistani government he wanted to build a US$35 million manufacturing facility in the port city of Karachi to service South East Asia with its cutting-edge technology. If the Pakistani foreign minister had looked closely at Johnston's eight-page presentation, he would surely have noticed in the newspaper clipping headed 'Now, Viagra Pill for Automobiles' that Johnston had also promised to set up a manufacturing plant in India to cater for the same market four years earlier.

But at this point, Firepower appeared to have a similar status in diplomatic circles to companies like BHP Billiton, whose vast and real investments in Pakistan usually ensured the Anglo-Australian giant got a seat at every important gathering between the two countries. Now the BHP representatives regularly found themselves sitting next to Johnston.

When President Musharraf visited Australia in June 2005, Johnston was one of the honoured guests greeting him in the Great Hall of the Australian parliament building in Canberra. The printed invitation for the gala function came directly from the prime minister, John Howard. Firepower reproduced the invitation in the June 2005 newsletter to shareholders under the disingenuous heading: 'Meeting with Prime Minister John Howard & President of Pakistan'.

The day after the Parliament House reception, Johnston attended another function at the Sheraton Hotel in Sydney, organised by the Asia Society. He was invited because Firepower was a sponsor of the event. Johnston again greeted the Pakistani leaders and, after politely listening to Musharraf speak frankly about the challenges and opportunities in the region, the rebuilding of Afghanistan and problems in the disputed territory of Kashmir, he secured an invitation to return to Pakistan.

That same day—16 June 2005—Firepower Global Developments Limited, a company Johnston had registered in Singapore, signed a 'memorandum of understanding' in Sydney granting a Pakistani company called Alpha Associates the option to become Firepower's Pakistani distributor. To exercise the option, Alpha Associates had simply to purchase up to US$25 000 worth of liquids, pills or engine-cleaning machines.

Johnston followed up the invitation to return to Pakistan three months later. In September 2005, he was an honoured guest of the Pakistani government and met with the federal minister for petroleum and natural resources, Amanullah Khan Jadoon, and the environment minister, Tahir Iqbal. He also met privately with President Musharraf, and presented him with a A$30 000 ceremonial dagger he had purchased in Australia.

PakTribune.com reported on Johnston's 'worldwide activities in the energy development field' and his claim that Firepower products were extensively tested and used worldwide by industry, power generation companies, the railways, in the agricultural sector 'and in the armed forces of Australia, New Zealand, Russia, Thailand and Indonesia'.

Johnston circulated newspaper clippings collated by Austrade to the financial advisors selling his shares, and they in turn circulated the clippings to existing and potential new clients. These included a clipping from Pakistan's *Dawn* newspaper with the heading: 'Australia to set up petroleum plant'.

'Hi everyone,' begins an email from Johnston, dated 10 September 2005 and with the *Dawn* clipping attached. 'Below is one of many newspaper articles about the Firepower trip to Pakistan where we met with President Musharraf last Monday. The meeting was excellent and the President and Pakistan Ministers have welcomed Firepower's technology in Pakistan and offer their full support. The meetings were televised for several days and received Nation wide [*sic*] coverage.'

Though, strictly speaking, Pakistan was outside Finnin's sphere of responsibility, Johnston had insisted he be allowed to tag along, on the understanding that Firepower would be invoiced for his business-class airfares and five-star accom-modation. Finnin says he was horrified to later learn that Johnston ignored the bills and Austrade never insisted that the invoices were paid, leaving the Australian taxpayer to pick up the expense.

The charade continued in November 2005 when the Australian prime minister, John Howard, made his own historic visit to Pakistan and met with his counterpart, Shaukat Aziz. In a formal ceremony carried out in the full media spotlight of both countries, which High Commissioner McCarthy also helped organise, the two leaders witnessed the signing of six agreements and memorandums of understanding for bilateral cooperation. The accords included the establishment of a joint scholarship program and an agricultural pact between the two countries, and plans for better police cooperation. A fourth covenant involved BHP investing US$120 million to expand a large gas field, and a fifth granted the Australian copper company Tethyan the rights to explore for minerals in northern Balochistan. The sixth agreement witnessed by the two prime ministers was Firepower signing the same memorandum of understanding with Alpha Associates that had been signed in Sydney five months earlier. A photograph featuring Howard and Aziz at the signing ceremony—like two feudal lords holding court—adorned the next issue of the shareholders' newsletter. It carried the mandatory deceptive headline: 'Prime Minister witnesses Firepower agreement with Pakistan Government'.

Just fourteen days after the signing ceremony involving Prime Minister Howard, which she had helped organise, McCarthy, the Australian high commissioner, bought 200 000 shares in Firepower for 10 cents each, after being offered them by Johnston. McCarthy says she had 'no reason to believe' the price she paid was unusually low. She correctly points out that the price of Firepower shares at the time was in a constant state of flux. Yet on the same day she bought her shares, she also bought 10 000 shares for her two daughters and paid the full advertised price of 50 cents a share. Even at the higher price, McCarthy probably figured she was getting a bargain. By this point, the rumours were that when Firepower listed, each share could be worth as much as $7 each. On the face of it, McCarthy and her daughters stood to make more than $1.4 million from her modest $25 000 investment.

Johnston's sudden wealth triggered an immediate lifestyle change. By the middle of 2005 he had separated from his wife, Sandra, and was in another relationship. He moved out of the rented family home in the middle-class Perth suburb of Booragoon and into a luxurious bachelor pad at Cottesloe Beach. He began to dye his hair, and frequently splashed out on luxury vacations—for instance, flying himself and his two daughters business class to Los Angeles, where they visited the set of the television show *Desperate Housewives*, then went to a concert in Houston, Texas. The airfares alone were nearly $40 000.

He used some of his millions to purchase an opulent mansion on the Indonesian island of Bali, in a beachfront resort favoured as a holiday destination by the Hollywood movie star Mel Gibson. He flashed an ultra-exclusive black American Express card and began to travel with bodyguards during his frequent trips to former Soviet-controlled countries—trips that included stopovers in $750-a-night hotels in Dubai.

Around this time, Johnston reconnected with Peter O'Meara, his old schoolfriend and rugby teammate from Brisbane. The two became central figures in a loose social circle of friends that became informally known as the 'Queensland Club'. The group included an Assistant Commissioner of the WA police force and a prominent newspaper editor. O'Meara had recently arrived in Perth as chief executive of a new Super 14 rugby union franchise called the Western Force. Only months earlier, Perth had surprised many people by beating Melbourne for the right to host a team in the world's best rugby competition. The city had long been considered a one-game town, obsessed with the tempestuous tribal rituals of Australian Rules football. It had little or no rugby tradition. Heading up the new Western Force Super 14 franchise was O'Meara's first job as a full-time sports administrator, but he saw the job as a stepping stone towards his real target. He wanted to be chief executive of the game's elite administrative body, the Australian Rugby Union (ARU), a coveted position he had applied for and failed to secure two years earlier.

But first O'Meara needed to build a successful team. And that wasn't easy. The rules of the competition capped the wages of the players he wanted to hire. Without being able to offer extra payments, he had little to persuade a good player to relocate to the other side of the continent, to a city that many felt didn't appreciate the finer points of the game. So O'Meara decided to break the rules. Together with the chairman of the new club, Geoff Stooke, and with the passive endorsement of the Rugby WA board, the Western Force made secret arrangements with the commercial representatives of six Wallaby players: Brendan Cannon, Matt Henjak, Scott Fava, Cameron Shepherd, Lachlan MacKay and Nathan Sharpe, who would be the new club's captain. Western Force promised to secure the players paid employment with one of the club's sponsors in addition to their regular income. The club then went further and guaranteed to pay the players the agreed amounts if the employment fell through, which was what occurred in each case except that of Cannon. Some of these secret payments were worth up to $400 000 a year to the players, although there is no suggestion that the players themselves knew the protocols were being broken.

The transactions would later create headaches for the new club, including the need to hide the payments from the ARU or risk sanctions. But the immediate benefit was that six top-line players had been hired. More significantly, the club had shown it was willing to splash around money, a fact appreciated by the powerful player agents that lurk behind the professional game.

Johnston walked into this world in May 2005 when O'Meara introduced him to club officials and around Perth's business community as a self-made millionaire. Johnston was described as a former industrial chemist for Shell who had invented a number of oil-based concepts that he was now selling internationally. He was, it was said, a man with money to burn. Firepower was signed up as an inaugural sponsor of the new club, with Johnston promising at least $300 000 a year for three years to have his company's dragon logo stitched onto the sleeve of the Western Force shirt. It was the same logo that Li Hai Dong had commissioned for his company. Johnston inherited it when Dong returned the company and its shares back to Johnston. Though no formal contract was ever signed—Johnston complained he was too busy—he left nobody in doubt over his ability to pay. In early July, he stunned an audience at a gala function held in honour of the team's new sponsors by paying $30 000 for one of the club's new shirts.

In this way, Johnston took his first tentative steps into the world of Australian sport.

A number of other people gathered around Johnston at this time. One was Warren Anderson, another character from the haze of Johnston's distant past. According to Johnston, the politically connected property developer had maintained a friendship with Johnston and his wife, Sandra, over the previous two decades, since the time of the events recounted in the Gyles Royal Commission into the Building and Construction Industry. Now he began to take an interest in Johnston's business. But Anderson's version of events is that he did not meet Johnston until about March 2003, after Sandra—who he knew from years earlier in Sydney—knocked on his front door and reintroduced herself. She later introduced him to her husband.

Documents tendered to the Federal Court by ASIC state that on or about 2 June 2005—the day that Johnston registered his new Firepower mother ship in the British Virgin Islands—some 40 million shares in the new entity were transferred to Anderson's company, Owston Nominees No 2 Pty Ltd. Anderson was later made a director of the British Virgin Islands company, though he says he only acted as a director for a short period. Company records from the British Virgin Islands show him as a director for six days in August 2006. Other records show Anderson signing himself as a director in 2007. Anderson would later tell the *Australian* in June 2008 that he had been employed by Johnston in 2004 as a 'consultant' to fix unspecified 'problems'. He told the newspaper he had also been employed to protect Firepower from predators Johnston said were trying to gain control of the company's intellectual property. 'He [Johnston] was surrounded by sharks and approached me and said, "Warren, can you help me?"' Anderson told the newspaper. 'I said, "I'll have a look at it", and he gave me a big bunch of shares.'

One of Anderson's first moves was to approach the barrister Les Stein, who at the time worked in Sydney as a consultant for the large law firm Freehills. Anderson offered Stein the job as Firepower's legal advisor. Stein, originally from the United States, is one of Australia's most highly regarded planning lawyers and litigators. A former professor of law at the University of Western Australia, he was once the chief judge of the Town Planning Appeal Tribunal of Western Australia and chief counsel for the Sydney Metropolitan Strategy, a body set up by the New South Wales state government to decide the future expansion of the city. Stein was politically connected in ways that Anderson, whose famous friends tended to be on the

Labor side, wasn't. He had served at the Town Planning Appeal Tribunal from 1994 until 1998 with the Liberal Party's rising star Julie Bishop, then federal minister for ageing and soon to be minister for science in the Howard government. The two were close personal friends.

Stein had represented Anderson in some of his property deals and had recently been engaged to help advise him on a proposed residential project at Fernhill, his sprawling Blue Mountains farm. In selling Stein on the merits of Firepower, Anderson convinced him of something so extravagant Stein figured it must be true. Anderson said Firepower had products to ease the world's reliance on oil, products that would save the environment, products that were so good they were going to make everyone they came into contact with extremely wealthy. Stein told associates it was presented to him as the chance of a lifetime. Not only would Firepower be saving the planet, it had the potential to be bigger than the world's biggest company, Microsoft.

According to Federal Court documents, when Stein signed up on 2 August, Johnston transferred 15 million shares in Firepower's British Virgin Islands entity to Stein's company, Sattvic Pty Ltd. Stein would later explain that he paid 1 cent for each share by issuing a promissory note at the time of the transfer.

Apart from his competency in the field of urban planning, Stein also had an interest in the global industry of carbon trading—a relatively recent approach used by some governments around the world to control pollution by providing economic incentives for reducing toxic emissions. The concept is that authorities set caps on the amount of a pollutant that can be emitted, and companies are then issued with permits allowing them to pollute to those levels. Industries that need to increase their emissions have the option of buying pollution credits from those who pollute less. In effect, the buyer is paying a charge for polluting, while the seller is being rewarded for reducing emissions by more than was required. Stein could see that if the stories about Firepower's pollution-reduction capabilities were true, there were enormous possibilities in the area of carbon trading. But it is unclear what steps he took to ensure the stories were true.

A third presence during this period was an American called Don Klick, whom Johnston had been introduced to through Austrade's Dubai office. Klick was a decorated Vietnam War helicopter pilot who worked for DynCorp International, a United States-based private security contractor that receives the vast majority of its $2 billion annual revenue from the US government for services in countries like Iraq, Bolivia, Bosnia, Somalia, Angola, Haiti, Kosovo and Kuwait. DynCorp's pattern is to hire former Central Intelligence Agency operatives to supplement its other staff, then contract them back to the US government. It is reportedly linked to at least fifty subsidiaries and satellite companies across the United States and around the world, some of whose ownership and connections cannot always be traced.

Klick, who joined Firepower in October 2004 on the promise that he would get 10 million shares in the company, was heavily connected in Washington and could count former General Colin Powell, then the US secretary of state, as a personal friend. Johnston liked to imply Klick was a former CIA operative, but like many of Johnston's stories there is nothing to suggest that this was true. Klick was, however, able to open doors, and he introduced Johnston to another of his friends, a Washington-based lawyer called Jim Wholey. Wholey is a prominent Republican campaigner who co-chaired Lawyers for Bush-Quayle in 1988, and was a member of the White House transition team when the first President Bush was elected.

He served for seven years as a senior staff member in the US Senate. He was also an administrative assistant and legislative director to Senate Republican leader Bob Dole, where he handled trade and telecommunications issues for the Republican leadership.

Firepower paid Wholey's Washington-based company, the Blackship Group, more than $30 000 a month to lobby to have Firepower products used by the US military. This led to Johnston later claiming to have addressed representatives from the US Senate Committee on Armed Services, where he said in late 2005 a tentative interest was expressed in using the products. But an email from Wholey explains that the claim was not true. 'At one point through my contacts, arrangements privately had been made for Committee staff to organize a testing of the product by and for the US military (a key potential market)— but it never came about due to inexplicable foot-dragging, failure to follow up, and general unresponsiveness on the part of Tim Johnston and his team. To my knowledge, Tim was never presented to any senior US government officials, and certainly not by me. God knows I stood ready to do that, but he could never be relied on actually to turn up. In retrospect, perhaps, I should be thankful.' In any case the Americans insisted that any consideration to use the products would be contingent on having the products tested by the Environmental Protection Agency. Despite showing great initial enthusiasm, Johnston seemed surprisingly unwilling to allow this to be done.

Klick remained in Dubai and was given the grand title of Firepower's president for international business. His job included flying around the world as the public face of the company, and it was he who attended the staged signing ceremony in Pakistan witnessed by Prime Minister Howard. In August 2005, Klick also flew to Malaysia as part of an Austrade-organised 'Environment Industry' trade mission to that country. Eight companies from

Australia met senior members of the Malaysian government. But the entity that Klick represented—a company called Firepower International Pty Ltd—didn't exist. Johnston had simply made up the name. Nobody in Austrade had bothered to check.

Meanwhile, Klick's former employer, DynCorp, was casually added to a list of other major US companies that Firepower was said to be developing a relationship with. They included the defence giants Lockheed Martin and Raytheon Systems, the Fortune 500 engineering company Fluor Daniel, and Halliburton, the oil company associated with the US vice-president Dick Cheney. It all sounded fantastic but none of it was true.

Johnston was playing on the other side of the old Cold War fence too. In Russia, the person running his operations—such as they were—was Andrei Vaslilyev, who was ex-Russian Special Forces or Spetsnaz. (Spetsnaz is a general term that can refer to any elite or special-purpose unit in Russia that is under the control of the military or the Federal Security Service, the successor of the KGB.) Vaslilyev had once worked as a contractor for Australian Defence Industries where, coincidentally, he had worked with Klumov, the senior trade commissioner to Moscow.

'You have to remember, it was like the Wild West out in Russia at that time,' a former senior Firepower official explains. 'I remember meeting many of them [people contracted by Johnston] in Moscow and St Petersburg, including Sasha "Small", who was about 5 feet 10 inches tall and about 8 feet wide and looked like he could break you in pieces without breaking a sweat. He was highly decorated from the war in Chechnya.'

Johnston was muscled up everywhere.

11 MR BIG

Rumours about Firepower began to swirl around Australia's investment community. The company was said to be signing massive contracts across the globe, with Johnston encouraging these rumours by spreading disinformation in his newsletters to shareholders. He said Firepower was negotiating to supply liquid fuel conditioners to Russia's police, to state-owned energy producers, to regional government departments and to the Russian Railways, where the first bulk orders were now 'expected September 2005'. He estimated the annual value of these government contracts alone at nearly $400 million.

Johnston said in the same newsletter to shareholders in June 2005 he had been invited by the prime minister of Tatarstan—an oil-rich state inside the Russian Federation with a population about the same size as Sydney's—to perk up the octane content of the nation's petrol and help enhance the quality of diesel products from a new refinery that was due to open in early 2006. About 5500 drums of Firepower products would be needed in Tatarstan, Johnston said, another $45 million in annual sales.

The shareholders were also told in the newsletter that Firepower had unspecified multimillion-dollar agreements in Indonesia, Kazakhstan, in the Ukraine and in Kyrgyzstan, a small and heavily indebted Central Asian republic bordering Kazakhstan.

Most investors probably couldn't spell the names of these countries, never mind be in a position to verify the claims, and Johnston's stories need to be seen in the context of the time. Mineral-rich Western Australia was riding high on a once-in-a-generation resources boom and so was the Australian share market. Commodity prices were at an all-time high and doubling every year, along with the cost of houses—at least in Perth. It wasn't too dissimilar to the dot-com boom of the late 1990s, with stories aplenty about people who'd got rich over-night from investing in small nickel mines. And given the quality of the people who surrounded him, Johnston's stories had an air of believability. The date for the float was put back again, but the fantasy was getting bigger. Not only would Firepower list one part of itself in London but Johnston now told shareholders that Firepower might also list other parts of the company elsewhere. It was, after all, a Group.

Shareholders were presented with an ambitious diagram said to represent Firepower's global structure. It outlined a plan for four head offices—in London, Perth, Dubai and Moscow—that would service fifty-four countries around the world. 'The company has been approached by large US and Arab companies to support our business and investigate with their support the opportunities to list our Middle East/African/Asian business on the exciting new Dubai stock exchange,' the June 2005 Firepower newsletter states. 'This area is fast growing for our business and many great opportunities are opening for our company as word of mouth covers the region about our successes. We will continue to negotiate, examine the best options for our shareholders and keep you fully informed of developments.'

Much of the fantastic talk about large contracts in Russia and countries associated with the former Soviet Union could be traced to the help Johnston was getting from Tyson, the new Australian ambassador to Russia. In July 2005, Tyson approached Svetlana Orlova, the deputy chairman of the upper house of the Russian Federation, and trotted out Johnston's old line that Firepower was considering building a manufacturing plant in Russia. In return, he said, the company would need help from the Russian government in lobbying for the use of Firepower's products across the government and private sector. Tyson—encouraged by and no doubt relying on a brief from Austrade—painted a dazzling picture to the Russians about the wonders of Firepower. He said Johnston's products made it possible to markedly improve the technical performance of different types of engines, to reduce fuel usage by up to 20 per cent and cut emissions by up to 90 per cent. He said the products had been developed over forty years and had been proven in practice in fifty-four countries, including Russia, the United States, and in the Middle East and South East Asia. The products were said to be able to help Russia, its citizens, and people of other countries of present and future generations to enjoy an environmentally cleaner planet.

An Australian ambassador—especially one as experienced as Tyson, a man who had spent most of his career as a diplomat overseas should, at the very least, have double-checked his Austrade brief and the inflated claims it made on behalf of Firepower. But, considering where the message was coming from, the Russians took it all very seriously. Orlova dispatched letters to the country's deputy prime minister, Alexander Zhukov, and to eight government departments, including the ministries of transport, agriculture and defence.

Johnston used these contacts to offer free trials of his products to the various government departments; and then, where he could, made claims as a result of those trials. For instance, he claimed that on the back of successful trials on two vintage tractors belonging to the Russian Ministry of Agriculture, the department had ordered 4000 drums of Firepower liquids, a contract that would be worth $32 million annually. 'Firepower's Russian office is currently negotiating supply agreements with Railways, Agriculture, Federal Police, Energy and a number of other Regional and State departments,' Johnston wrote to shareholders in March 2006. 'The estimated value of these agreements is many millions of dollars.'

In reality, all Johnston was doing was going around signing memorandums of understanding with his distributors, just as he'd done in Pakistan in the agreement witnessed by Prime Minister Howard. A memorandum of understanding is very different from a contract or a sales agreement. It merely states that the two parties may do business together at some unspecified time in the future. The actual amount stipulated in some of Johnston's agreements was as low as $18 000, not the millions he talked about.

But to Johnston they were contracts. Big contracts. And by August 2005 the proposed listing was gathering pace. Meetings were set up with NomAds. Lawyers were hired. The only thing holding everything up was Johnston's own apparent lack of understanding about the requirements of a stock market listing. He was the only person who knew the true financial position of the company and yet he seemed strangely reluctant to hand over the information needed to get the company audited—an essential element of any listing.

In September 2005, though no prospectus had ever been issued, the share selling to mum and dad investors resumed in Australia at up to 50 cents per share. Between 2 September and 6 December another $5.4 million was raised, with the money again being credited to the British Virgin Islands-registered firm Green Triton Limited and deposited in a bank account in Singapore.

ASIC would later allege in the Federal Court that some of the shares sold during this period for between 35 cents and 50 cents each were sold by Anderson's firm Owston Nominees No 2 Pty Ltd, beginning in October 2005. The shares sold by Owston were sold through Ward, the Perth financial advisor who had once been banned from offering investment advice.

Documents indicate that the total amount of shares sold in 2005 exceeded $10 million.

Meanwhile Johnston continued to march new test reports into his private Pandora's box.

From about July 2005, he encouraged Firepower's new European head of operations, Guenter Nolte, to commission a series of tests on the Firepower products that would look good to the uninitiated. Nolte belonged to the van Rens network and had joined Firepower after resigning as chief executive of Regal Petroleum, the company that would be found just months later to have the shallow oil well off the coast of Greece, triggering massive losses on the AIM. Before joining Regal, Nolte had headed up the German subsidiary of Halliburton, the American oil company linked to former US vice-president Dick Cheney that Firepower had told shareholders it had an association with. Nolte demanded an impressive wage that, according to Finnin, eventually rose to €800 000 (then about $1.35 million) a year, the first of a number of high wages that Johnston was willing to pay to retain credibility.

Nolte took four products to the world-renowned German-based fuel-testing organisation Dekra: the Firepower pill, the FP4000 liquid, and related liquids called FP10 000 and FP1. But the tests were not to see whether the products reduced fuel consumption and cut emissions; they were merely to see whether fuel was still usable after the products were added to it. In other words, whether the products met local consumer standards. Though the FP10000 liquid failed the simple criteria of the test, the other results were posted on the Firepower website, alongside a panoramic photograph of the Dekra plant, under the heading: 'Firepower products meet German fuel specs'.

In November 2005, similar tests were done in Australia by the respected testing centre Intertek Caleb Brett. Again, the examination was not to see whether the products worked— i.e., reduced fuel consumption and reduced emissions—but to see whether Australian Standards were complied with once the products were added to fuel. The Australian results were similar to the German results: fuel was still usable when Firepower products were added to it. However, the Australian laboratory warned that the pills tended to leave sand-like grit from undissolved particles at the bottom of the fuel tank. In other words, the pills didn't fully dissolve and the grit had the potential to build up over time if people kept using them.

A third set of similar tests was conducted at the respected Southwest Research Institute in Texas but, again, the tests were not to determine fuel savings or emissions reductions. To determine that, Firepower instead headed to Belarus, a country of about 10 million people sandwiched between Russia and Poland. Here, in July 2005, the newly signed local distributor in the small town of Volkovysk claimed an almost 20 per cent fuel saving on a Belarusian train, and fuel savings of between 7.7 per cent and 14.7 per cent on two buses in the small city of Mogilev near the Russian border.

Firepower also went to Kazakhstan, which in recent times has become unfairly associated with Borat Sagdiyev, the fictional Kazakhstani journalist portrayed by British comedian Sacha Baron Cohen. In September 2005, the engine-cleaning machine was used on a bus in the city of Astana, the country's capital. After the FP4000 product was added, a 10.6 per cent fuel saving was claimed. But in a Borat moment, the following is included in the test report: 'The engine revolution counter at the moment of testing was not in working order. Measurement of the fuel consumption took place by use of the graduation scale on the calibrated container in the diesel engine fuel system cleaning apparatus.'

In November 2005, there was more success using the Firepower products, this time in a mine in Russia that appears to have been owned or run by the giant Russian steel company MMK. Four trucks were used in the trials. Their engines were flushed out using the engine-cleaning machine, then the FP4000 was added. The trucks appeared to run more smoothly after the additive, and good fuel savings were claimed over a four-day period. But MMK remained unconvinced. A report on the test suggested that 'for detailed and full determination' it would have been preferable to use more specialised equipment. It also said the change in the trucks' operations during different working shifts was not taken into account. 'We believe that for a more objective estimation of the diesel fuel conditioner FP4000 a longer trial period is needed.'

In December 2005, Firepower was back testing dump trucks in Kazakhstan, this time in the copper-mining town of Zhezkazgan (the site of a Gulag camp during the Soviet era whose history is recounted in Aleksandr Solzhenitsyn's book *The Gulag Archipelago*). Three of the four dump trucks used in the test showed a fuel saving. What confused everyone was that the fourth truck increased its consumption of fuel. Even the country mocked by Sacha Baron Cohen recognised that better tests were needed. But to Johnston, all results were worthy of saving. They could be used in such creative ways.

* * *

On 1 December 2005—with the new share sales well underway—Austrade drew up a formal contract for its continued services to Firepower.

The agreement was extraordinary in that it contradicted many of the earlier statements made by Firepower to its shareholders, and by Australian diplomatic staff to the governments of Russia and Pakistan. It is clear from the document that Firepower was not selling its products in more than fifty countries around the world. It was having trouble selling anything anywhere.

'Firepower's major hurdle in the CIS [Commonwealth of Independent States] to date has been the ability to convert strategic opportunities into contracts,' the document states. 'These include Ministry of Railways, Ministry of Agriculture, Ministry of Defence and others. Firepower requires Austrade to arrange for high-level introductions to companies and individuals who can assist the company in sealing these strategic contracts.'

But shareholders had been told that Firepower already had $400 million worth of contracts in Russia; that Russian Railways had been ordering products since September 2005; that farmers in Russia were ploughing their fields with FP4000 in their tractors.

Europe and the Middle East were, according to Austrade, also markets where Firepower had 'intensive need for assistance', particularly 'in the industrial sector where government plays a pivotal role'.

The document was, in fact, an offer by the Australian government agency to get Firepower up and running all over the world, using taxpayer-funded diplomats and ambassadors and Austrade staff. Under the proposal, Austrade would arrange 'government-to-government presentations' and offer letters of support 'to major companies/government departments'. Austrade personnel would also attend product presentations in an official capacity and 'host receptions for distributors and significant users of Firepower products'.

The Austrade regional director, John Finnin, was offered as a person who could travel with Firepower representatives to take part in high-level meetings and negotiations, to participate in telephone and video conferences, and provide business advice on strategies. The overall assignment would be coordinated and managed out of Russia by Klumov. In return for all of this, Firepower simply had to pay $190 an hour for Austrade's time.

The most farcical detail of the arrangement was the company name on the 20-page document: Firepower Group Pty Ltd. There was no such firm. Johnston as usual had made it up. Nevertheless, Austrade would eventually bill the phantom entity $180 000.

In the days leading up to the proposed alliance, Johnston was called to Moscow by Klumov to meet a man Klumov claimed could make all Johnston's problems in Russia go away. The Firepower entourage included Hill and Stein, and their final destination was a walled and guarded compound in the heart of the city where a set of opulent mansions housed the country's elite. According to the whispers that swept the party, one of them was the home of Mikhail Gorbachev, the last leader of the old Soviet Union. The person the Australians were meeting was probably better known to law enforcement agencies around the world than his supposed Nobel Peace Prize-winning neighbour. His name was Grigory Luchansky, a dual Russian-Israeli citizen who has, over the years, reportedly been scrutinised by Interpol, the British spy agency MI6 and policing authorities in several other countries. He has at times been banned from entering Canada and Britain, and was once denied entry to the United States for his alleged ties to organised crime.

Luchansky first came to public prominence in 1996 when he was the subject of a *Time* magazine investigation that made a number of serious allegations about him in relation to alleged criminal activity. He was named as the former head of a Vienna-based company called Nordex that, according to reports from American news organisations, was created in 1989 as a hard source of currency for the KGB. But apart from spending some years in a Gulag camp early in his life, Luchansky had never been prosecuted and he rejected the charges made by *Time* and that his incredible wealth was obtained by doing anything illegal. Though Luchansky was regularly seen with powerful people—he was once photographed at a White House fundraising dinner with then president Bill Clinton—the claims did not stop. He successfully sued *The Times* when the British newspaper reported that the CIA had described Nordex as an organisation associated with Russian criminal activity and when it repeated allegations that Nordex may have been involved in the smuggling of nuclear material out of Russia. The newspaper also accused Luchansky of being linked to one of the world's biggest money-laundering scams—an alleged plot to launder US$7 billion in organised crime proceeds through the Bank of New York. Luchansky has repeatedly denied all of the accusations made about him and there is no suggestion he was ever guilty. In refusing an appeal by *The Times*, the English courts held that the newspaper had no prospect of proving the money-laundering claim and that it did not attempt to prove the other accusations.

Luchansky might have seemed an odd choice for embassy staff to be matching up with an Australian company, but he wasn't just a powerful person in his own right; he also had powerful friends. He was close to the influential mayor of Moscow, Yuri Luzhkov, who in turn was allied to Putin, the Russian ruler. Luchansky also had strong business connections

Bill Moss (back right) with Tim Johnston (back left) on board a private jet on their way to Russia in late 2006. The third man (front left) is believed to be the mysterious Don Klick, the man Johnston liked to pretend was an ex-CIA operative.

Former Firepower CEO John Finnin (left) with Peter Holmes à Court at a Rabbitohs function on 8 November 2006. PHOTOGRAPHER: CRAIG GOLDING, FAIRFAX.

The commanding officer of the HMAS *Sydney* Guy Holthouse prepares to catch a ball during a photo shoot with the Sydney Kings players on board the HMAS *Sydney* in September 2006. PHOTOGRAPHER: TIM CLAYTON, FAIRFAX.

Brian Goorjian (left), coach of the Sydney Kings, with Firepower chairman Tim Johnston and team captain Jason Smith (right) pictured at a Kings function on 29 January 2007. PHOTOGRAPHER: WADE LAUBE, FAIRFAX.

Firepower chairman Tim Johnston (left) with Steve Waugh and Russell Crowe at Austrade's annual G'Day LA trade promotion in Los Angeles in January 2007.

Sydney Kings captain Jason Smith playing in the fourth game of the NBL Grand Final against the Melbourne Tigers on 12 March 2008.
PHOTOGRAPHER: JOHN DONEGAN, FAIRFAX.

Administrators Geoffrey McDonald (left) and Brent Kijurina of the firm Hall Chadwick prepare for the Firepower creditors meeting at the Sheraton Hotel in Perth on 31 July 2008. PHOTOGRAPHER: ERIN JONASSON, FAIRFAX.

Russell Crowe and Peter Holmes à Court arrive at the press conference following the voting-in of their new plan for the South Sydney Rabbitohs on 19 March 2006. PHOTOGRAPHER: ANDREW QUILTY, FAIRFAX.

in two of the countries Johnston hoped to do business in—the Ukraine and Kazakhstan.

The meeting at Luchansky's private residence was a lavish lunch attended by the Firepower representatives, some Australian embassy staff and about twelve of Luchansky's business associates. One former Firepower employee who attended the meeting recalls a general sense of bewilderment over what was supposed to happen next. But Johnston returned to Russia several weeks later, this time with Warren Anderson in tow. It was then, according to insiders, that the concept for a joint venture with Luchansky was floated.

12 CHANGING THE GUARD

The meeting in Russia spelled the end for Gordon Hill, Firepower's director. He resigned weeks later in frustration over the continued absence of sufficient financial information. Acquaintances say that Luchansky's reputation—deserved or not—also concerned him. But he didn't leave poor. Documents lodged in the Federal Court by ASIC show that when Hill moved Firepower from the Cayman Islands to the British Virgin Islands on 2 June 2005, some 20 million shares in the new entity were transferred into his company, Seaswan Holdings Pty Ltd. After resigning from Firepower, the documents indicate Hill began to sell his shares. By about April 2006, Seaswan Holdings had sold more than 2 million shares through various financial advisors for 50 cents per share.

It was about this time that existing shareholders were informed about another delay on the proposed share market listing. Johnston delivered the news in typical nonsensical fashion. 'Because Firepower is poised to complete very large contracts, if it lists after those contracts, it will have a value upon listing that will be greater than if it listed now and waited for the market to raise the share price,' he wrote in a memo to shareholders. 'The timing of listing is always complex but our top financial advice is to wait a little longer until the story of Firepower is not just a great story but is overwhelming.'

The truth was, the only thing Firepower was overwhelmed about was the level of detail needed for a London float. Eileen Carr, the London consultant, had emailed Stein, the former judge, in September 2005 setting out all the requirements. They included the need for audited accounts, a complete set of existing shareholders and details in respect of every sales contract that Firepower claimed to have. 'I can't understand myself why all of this information must be given,' Stein responded to Carr via email on 21 September. 'A full listing on the Australian exchange does not require this detail in respect of each contract. Must this all be done?'

Carr had drawn up plans for a restructure of the company that included Johnston as chief executive and the creation of an eight-member board to be chaired by an unnamed senior Australian public servant or a senior member of Austrade. 'To maintain offshore tax status, I would recommend no more than two directors be based in the UK,' Carr wrote in an undated three-page memo to Johnston sent via email in October 2005. 'The NomAd would require each director to complete a detailed questionnaire on past activities and would, more than likely, undertake an investigation of each director prior to listing.'

Carr's advice in the memo was based on several key assumptions. One was that the claims for the Firepower products were 'confirmed by an independent body'. She also said that the potential contracts and the company's business plan needed to be 'accepted as credible'. It soon became clear that Firepower was unable to provide that kind of detail.

Hill's departure—quickly followed by Carr's—signalled

an increased day-to-day involvement by Warren Anderson. Notwithstanding the delay on the stock market listing that had originally been scheduled for October 2005, Anderson's presence added a new urgency to the enterprise. Stein also got more involved. He began to advise on the signing of new distributors, and promising alliances were formed in India and in the Philippines.

According to Federal Court documents, Anderson resumed selling his shares through his company, Owston Nominees No 2 Pty Ltd, from the beginning of 2006, as did Johnston through his British Virgin Islands-registered company Green Triton Limited. During the first few months of the year, they sold millions more shares for between 35 cents and 50 cents a share. ASIC would allege in a statements to the court that a prospectus or a disclosure document was not provided to investors as required by law so that investors or their professional advisors had 'all the information they need to reasonably make an informed investment decision'. Those buying the shares came from all walks of life and most were acting on the advice of their various investment advisors—those who were offering the product for sale. They included journalists, retirees and public servants. All were made to feel part of a privileged society and, as word of mouth spread, more and more people wanted to join.

Some of the new shareholders were prominent members of the Australian military, who had bought their shares through Malcolm Phillips, a Canberra-based investment advisor. They included Air Chief Marshal Angus Houston, the head of the Australian Defence Force, and his wife, Liz; Rear Admiral Davyd Thomas, the deputy chief of the Royal Australian Navy; navy Commodore Kevin Taylor; and Errol McCormack, former head of the Royal Australian Air Force.

McCormack later got directly involved after he was engaged to assist Firepower to gain approval for the sale of its products to the Australian military. Klick, the man with the heavy

Washington connections, was flown over specially to meet with the Defence Science and Technology Organisation (DSTO) on 9 February 2006, where he explained the wonders of Firepower but failed to offer any proof. Follow-up data was promised and a second meeting set for 11 April. As the date approached, McCormack began to have doubts about the relationship. He had been promised a consultancy contract by Firepower but instead had been sent an agreement that would have made him a Firepower distributor. The company had also failed to send a single shred of evidence to back up its lofty claims.

'Let me assure you that Defence is approached by a lot of snake-oil salesmen particularly in the fuel additive business, with lots of promises and not much factual data,' McCormack wrote to Johnston on 28 March. 'Unfortunately, DSTO will start to doubt the validity of Firepower's claims if they are not backed up by reputable information.'

At first, Johnston didn't even bother to write back.

McCormack persisted. On 4 April he wrote again: 'Is anybody home? I will need to know by AM hours, Thu 06Apr06 whether you are serious about doing business with the Australian Department of Defence and willing to provide the information on your process . . . If you are not serious about dealing with the Department I will cancel the meeting with DMO/DSTO planned for Tue 11Apr06.'

This time Johnston did write back several hours later. 'Interesting question,' he said. 'Of course we are interested, it is embarrassing for us that we don't do business with them. We have just secured supply to all Croatian Military vehicles. We started and completed trials, demonstrations to eventually [*sic*] the first orders in 4 months.'

But there was no contract in Croatia. It was as false as Johnston's earlier claims that his products were being used by the Australian military. The bottom line was that Johnston simply didn't want to do real business, because to do real business would have meant subjecting his product to real scrutiny.

By the time the scheduled meeting date of 11 April had come and gone McCormack had given up chasing after Firepower, and he demanded that Phillips, the investment advisor, hand back the $10 000 he and his wife had invested in the company. He says he warned his friends to do the same, though he couldn't be sure they took his advice. 'Snake oil,' McCormack says. 'You can quote me on that.'

But to Johnston it didn't matter. By April 2006, he owned what was destined to become the most expensive home in Western Australia: a sprawling North African-themed cliffside property with extensive river views, on Chidley Way in the exclusive Perth enclave of Mosman Park. The mansion had originally been built during the 1980s for former high-flying Burswood casino boss Dallas Dempster, and it boasted five bedrooms, six bathrooms, two kitchens, a servants apartment and its very own ballroom decorated in eighteenth-century French style. Johnston converted the ballroom into a gym and home theatre.

Nothing in Johnston's life was ever straightforward, and so it proved with the house. The $8.85 million property was actually purchased by Anderson through his private company, Owston Nominees No 2 Pty Ltd and later transferred over to both Johnston and his wife, Sandra, who by then had reunited.

It is difficult to explain the mood behind the scenes during this period. For months, the bewildered Firepower entourage of about six low-level technicians and admin workers in the little office in the Perth industrial estate had watched Johnston come and go, from Perth to Europe, from Europe to Africa, from Africa to the Middle East, from one alleged staggering contract to the next. At first, these deals were treated with scepticism.

But over time, the line between a memorandum of understanding and a real contract began to blur, and Firepower's staff came to the conclusion that the sheer number of alleged deals and the quality of the people surrounding Johnston could only mean that he was operating on an elevated plane that they couldn't understand. Finally, watching Johnston work room after room of investors that often included lawyers, accountants and people who ought to know better, they became convinced that it must be real, and they began to see Firepower as investors did: a gilt-edged opportunity with plenty of room for everyone.

Each of these investor meetings—held in upmarket hotel conference rooms around the country—was hosted by one of a small network of financial advisors who were selling the shares. In Perth it was Quentin Ward, the former bankrupt who had once been banned from giving financial advice, and Michael van Rens, the person once prosecuted by the Australian Prudential Regulation Authority. In Sydney, it was one of their associates, David Armour, now believed to be overseas. In Adelaide, it was John Catt, a former Australian Rules footballer who was a friend to some of the country's best-known football stars. In Hobart, it was Tim d'Emden, one of the city's best-known financial planners. In Canberra, it was Malcolm Phillips, the financial advisor to senior public servants; and in Darwin, it was Tony Prentice, who sold the shares to his friends and business associates.

All of the shares that were sold were in fact share transfers from an existing shareholder—usually Johnston's company Green Triton. The financial advisors would apply for the shares, on behalf of their client, through Stein. In this respect, the former judge assumed the role originally occupied by Hill, the former police minister.

Those who purchased the shares were at the bottom of another Johnston pyramid. In return for promoting the shares, the financial advisors sometimes got kickbacks from Firepower in the form of free shares, something their clients, who had often paid for the advice in the first place, were not always made aware of. And because the shares were often sold to networks of people, the leaders of these networks were naturally obliged to keep the news about Firepower positive.

At these investor meetings, Firepower began to show a level of sophistication absent from earlier versions of presentations and company profiles. It was now according to an updated company profile a 'compelling story' framed by high fuel prices, and a company with a 'growing global footprint'. Rather than emphasising the actual trials on dump trucks and clapped-out buses, Firepower claimed that its product range had been 'tested by many independent testing institutes'. But beneath the sheen, it was the same old Tim Johnston. Firepower documents from this era feature all the old favourites: the personal testimonial from a US Coast Guard commander called Harold G. Reed claiming better fuel economy and a significant decrease in maintenance work; the letter from W.E. Becker, the 'general service manager' of General Motors Corporation, stating that using the Firepower products would not affect vehicle warranties. The New Zealand Automobile Association would have recognised both names—the same claims from the same people were made about the blue waxy pills being sold by Power Plan International in 1992.

Johnston's ability to dissolve the edicts of science and common sense was further evidenced in advertisements for the FP10000 product. He had only discovered the product three years earlier, but the promotional material claimed it had been 'used in all types of engines for 12 years' and had 'been used and tested in all of the major automobile models, Government agencies from around the world, and thousands of other commercial and private customers all with highly positive results'.

Another endorsement came from a test carried out by the Singapore Institute of Standards and Industrial Research on the Techni-Lube product, altered to imply that the test had been conducted on a Firepower product. If anyone had checked, they would have found that the Singapore facility by that name closed in 1996—four years before Johnston met Matthews, the inventor of the FP4000 product. Johnston figured, correctly, that nobody would bother checking; by pointing at the sky he stopped people from looking where they were going.

Firepower documents from 2006 regularly quoted 'recent independent studies' on the Firepower liquids done by Dr Roy Douglas from Queen's University in Belfast that showed Fire-power-treated fuels burned up to 30 per cent faster. 'This increased burn rate of a given fuel charge directly relates to an increase in economy, power output and a cleaner more efficient burn of the available fuel,' the documents stated. But these were the tests Douglas did in the mid-1990s using the US Lubricants products.

Even Dr Gennadiy Rozenblit, the elderly gentleman photographed beside the swimming pool in California all those years earlier, was dusted off and given renewed prominence for his notable research at the Kharkov State Railway Academy in 1996 on what were now referred to as Firepower products. Dr Rozenblit was said to have achieved a 9 per cent fuel saving.

In his statements to shareholders Johnston often liked to boast that Firepower's 'highly skilled team of research chemists and engineers worldwide' were continually redeveloping the company's products. But away from proper scrutiny, Firepower was lurching from one comical test of its products to another.

The liquids were tested on a steam train in Moscow. Firepower somehow reported a 5 per cent fuel saving. In South Africa, a test on a decrepit Mitsubishi car was presented on the Firepower website as conclusive proof that Firepower products had the ability to 'reduce atmospheric pollution at Johannesburg

International Airport'. The car was parked at the airport when the test was being done.

In Greece, the company's newly signed distributor conducted an equally anomalous trial on five local taxis. The drivers were encouraged to add the ferrocene pills to their fuel tanks and report back on their impressions. Seemingly without the aid of anything but their intuition, the drivers came to the remarkable conclusion that the pills cut 80 per cent of harmful emissions and gave them a 16 per cent fuel saving. 'With fuel prices at record high's [sic] this was a great relief for the taxi drivers that spend their life [sic] on the congested roads,' trumpeted Firepower's website promotional material.

But Johnston's finely tailored suits and incessant dollar-figure patter suggested he knew what he was talking about. When he launched into his silky PowerPoint presentations it was easier to float away on a cloud of goodwill and images of wealth than try to negotiate the complex maze that would have led to the truth. Yet it would only have taken a straightforward internet search to reveal the source of some of Johnston's complicated graphics and images. They were lifted from the website 'How Stuff Works'.

Firepower lacked substance, but Johnston had a plan. He would hire a new leadership team. And the man he had in mind was John Finnin, the Austrade regional director who had been enormously helpful in promoting the company and giving it credibility.

The courting of Finnin had begun with the offer of the free shares, which he had refused, and resumed in November 2005 when Johnston turned up unexpectedly in Frankfurt with Stein, the former judge, and offered him the job of chief executive. Finnin again resisted, but in April 2006 he finally relented.

Johnston proposed a remuneration package that any salaried public servant would surely have found hard to pass up: $500 000 a year in salary, a luxury Maserati Quattroporte motorcar, plus 6 million shares in Firepower. He was also given a $100 000 signing-on bonus. Johnston assured Finnin the shares would be worth up to $42 million once the company floated on the AIM. Tired of life on the road and attracted by the prospect of returning home to Melbourne, Finnin figured that if things went the way he expected he could retire after three years, richer than in his wildest dreams. But he didn't resign from Austrade until two crucial months later.

Johnston had already approached Klumov, the Austrade chief in Moscow who had also been enormously helpful in promoting Firepower and giving it credibility. He offered Klumov a similar deal to head up Firepower's Russian operations. He could pick and choose his own staff and retain his $120 000-a-year Austrade-funded luxury apartment overlooking the Kremlin. Klumov would eventually accept the offer, and take several office staff from Austrade's Russian operation with him, but again he did not resign from Austrade immediately.

Though there is nothing to suggest that Finnin and Klumov were anything other than pawns in Johnston's game, the fact that each was destined to join Firepower brings what followed into sharper focus. The sensational second Australia Week In Moscow trade show was a glittering occasion, held in the magnificent Manazh Hall next door to the Kremlin from 11–18 June 2006. Though thousands turned up to view the stands, Australia Week In Moscow would never again be repeated. But for now, thanks to the show's distinguished benefactors— the Australian taxpayer, the Queensland government and Firepower—the munificence extended to generous airfares and still more generous hotel rooms for politicians and journalists to attend from Australia. The Russian-Australian boxer Kostya Tszyu greeted the guests.

People get excited when money seems to be falling from the

sky. And though Firepower was still almost entirely running on investor funds, it continued to be the one company Austrade referred to as its shining star in the region. Firepower even had its own place on the Austrade website—under the heading 'Success Stories', where Klumov, who was about to jump ship to the company, was quoted as saying, 'Firepower Group is a wonderful example of the innovative thinking and advanced technology that Australian companies produce'.

Johnston was a visible presence at the trade show, surrounded by four burly Russian Special Forces bodyguards. The minders had been arranged by the Australian embassy after Johnston convinced everybody he was getting death threats from a Siberian crime syndicate. The threats had come, he said, after Firepower signed a deal reportedly worth 'tens of millions of dollars annually' with Russia's largest coal producer, Kuzbassrazrezugol.

'The threat came from Kuzbass, in Siberia, where we reduced fuel consumption [at Kuzbassrazrezugol] by 40 per cent,' Johnston told the *Sydney Morning Herald* on 16 June 2006. 'We've been selling a lot there and the people who had been supplying [the mining company] with diesel fuel weren't happy. I didn't get a Christmas card. They said: "Tim Johnston, you keep out of Russia, or else".'

Of course, there was no multimillion-dollar deal and there-fore no crime syndicate chasing after Johnston. The only link Firepower had with Kuzbassrazrezugol was the tests it had done on the two dump trucks working for one of its subsidiaries eighteen months ago. And yet nobody thought to challenge Johnston's story, which was repeated in other newspapers. 'In some places we have bodyguards from the time we get off the plane,' he told the *West Australian* the following day, 17 June. 'Engine makers don't like us either, because we can extend the life of injectors, fuel filters, manifolds. Why are they going to be keen to talk to us?'

Competing for attention in Moscow was then Queensland premier Peter Beattie, the guest of honour at the trade show. Beattie posed for press photos in Red Square and embraced Russia's second most powerful man, the formidable Yuri Luzhkov, mayor of Moscow, as if they were best friends. 'We should stop thinking about Russia as a commie country with crooks running around the place,' Beattie told the *Bulletin* on 28 June 2006. He was referring to the Russians.

Johnston paid particular attention to Beattie, and the attention was reciprocated because Luzhkov was a good friend of Johnston's new business partner in the country, Luchansky. After Johnston publicly claimed to have $1 billion worth of contracts for his products, Beattie began to openly woo him. 'The only thing wrong with Firepower is that they are not in Queensland,' he told the *Bulletin*. Johnston responded in the same article: 'We're considering moving some of our manufacturing to Queensland. The West Australian government has done nothing for us.'

Beattie invited Firepower to be a founding member of the newly formed Russian-Australian Business Forum, organised by the Queensland and Moscow City governments. It was co-chaired by Luchansky. The Forum would later run an event called Russia Week In Australia in September 2007, to coincide with the APEC world leaders' forum held in Sydney.

Johnston had arrived in Moscow at the same time as Beattie and they shared a police escort from the airport to their respective hotels. Johnston was travelling with his own small entourage that included some of the investment advisors who were selling his shares. The Moscow trip was part of an all-expenses-paid world tour that also took in St Petersburg, London and Dubai and included some of the finest restaurants and best hotels that money could buy. Those on the trip included Quentin Ward, the former bankrupt from Perth who would eventually sell $43 million worth of Firepower shares to his clients; Tony

Prentice, the financial advisor from Darwin; and Tim d'Emden, the financial advisor from Hobart. The entourage was paraded through the mayor of Moscow's opulent offices and they were observers at official trade talks between Australia and Russia. They were also guests of honour at an official reception for Firepower that was held at the taxpayer-sponsored private residence of the Australian ambassador, Bob Tyson. About sixty people attended the function. 'Our involvement was to meet and greet . . . and act as investors from Australia in the company,' d'Emden later wrote in an email to his clients on 28 June.

It was during Australia Week In Moscow that Johnston pulled off probably his single greatest deception. He had organised for a number of his newly found Russian contacts to appear at the show as prospective clients and he had them sit down and sign what appeared to be massive deals in front of the onlooking investment advisors and in front of Beattie and Austrade staff. One deal in Tatarstan was said to be worth US$600 million. Another—to supply the Moscow public transport system with Firepower products—was said to be worth US$9 million in annual profits. Other deals in Kazakhstan, the Urals, the Ukraine and with Russian Railways were equally mind-boggling.

'We have estimated approximate net profit on deals known to have been signed and agreed to in excess of US$600 million,' d'Emden's note to his clients continued. 'I must say that the excitement and enthusiasm exhibited by the MD of Firepower Tim Johnston is shared.'

Newspapers also fell for the stories. The *West Australian* reported on 17 June that Firepower had signed 'a $400 million deal with a group of Russian refineries, bringing the total deal pipeline to almost $1 billion'.

Within days, d'Emden and the other investment advisors were flooded with requests to purchase shares, and the price had climbed again.

13 THE BIG DISTRACTION

Professional sport in Australia is an astonishing phenomenon. Radiating out from the athletes is a complicated multi-billion-dollar industry, a world of unspoken codes and entrenched rivalries, where time is measured in seasonal calendars and end-of-game sirens; a world that rarely asks too many questions as long as you have the answer when they throw out the challenge that matters the most. It's the Jerry Maguire test: 'Show me the money!'

Johnston's foray into this world, which began at the Western Force, took him into a number of other sporting arenas, including the Sydney Entertainment Centre, the home of the Sydney Kings basketball team. Johnston started appearing in the Kings VIP box from about April 2006, after being introduced to one of the club's owners Bill Moss, the formidable millionaire head of the property division of Macquarie Bank, an institution that benefited more than most from Australia's decade-long economic boom.

The connection to Moss came through Warren Anderson, the politically connected property developer Johnston was in business with. Anderson had approached Moss to become the chairman of Firepower once it floated on the AIM, an offer Moss had initially declined but was not entirely dismissive of. He had, though, put certain conditions on his interest. 'I said to them upfront,' Moss recalls, 'I want a copy of your financials, I want a copy of your share registry and I want to have a look at your business strategy.' Moss was kept waiting for all three, but in the meantime Johnston latched onto the relationship.

At the time, the Sydney Kings was one of Australia's longest-running sporting enigmas. The team was the most successful in recent National Basketball League history; it had Australia's best coach, great players and an impressive home venue. But things weren't going so well off the court. Several years earlier, the business had to be rescued from receivership by a consortium of rich bankers and lawyers, one of whom was Moss. Since then, crowds had fallen by almost two-thirds. Chief executives and marketing managers came and went with the regularity of the seasons.

Johnston had little interest in basketball. He had barely attended three games when Moss asked him to be a sponsor. But Johnston recognised the opportunity, offering to pay $710 000 a year over three years. The deal was nearly three times what the Kings had hoped for. Firepower also compared favourably with the sponsor it replaced: a timeshare company that strained relations with the few remaining fans by assailing them with offers for their merchandise. Firepower didn't seem to want to sell anything. Johnston appeared happy just to socialise.

Johnston was used to being the big man in Perth, but Sydney was a bigger league and he liked the kind of people Moss introduced him to—like the millionaire Peter Holmes à Court, business partner of the Academy Award-winning movie star Russell Crowe.

In March 2006, Crowe and Holmes à Court had bought

the iconic South Sydney Rabbitohs rugby league team and they were eager to turn it from recent loser into future winner. Crowe's relationship with the Rabbitohs had long been the stuff of legend. He once paid $42 000 for the brass bell used to open the inaugural rugby league match in Australia in 1908, featuring his team, and made a gift of it back to the club. He flew over to games from Hollywood, and regularly brought fellow movie stars along, people like Tom Cruise and Burt Reynolds. 'Rugby league,' he said by way of explaining his passion to the Americans on the Jay Leno talk show in the United States in February 2008, 'is like you are running a marathon at pace while surviving thirty or forty small car crashes.'

It was at the Sydney Entertainment Centre that the idea of Firepower sponsoring the Rabbitohs was conceived, though it wouldn't be announced until later in 2006—on the Jay Leno talk show. At the end of this first appearance on Leno's show, Crowe pulled out the team's new shirt and displayed it to a live audience of millions. It had the name Firepower emblazoned across it: a company that had pledged a staggering $3 million over three years for the privilege. The figure garnered headlines around Australia because of its size. The Rabbitohs were, after all, one of the bottom teams.

The rationale, Johnston told colleagues, was that Holmes à Court had promised to introduce him to officials at Queensland Rail—he was a board member—and to a number of unnamed mining companies that might be willing to use his products. It is difficult to verify the claims because Holmes à Court no longer likes to talk about his association with Firepower. But at the time he said he had done due diligence before accepting the money. 'I am not a trucking or a train company,' Holmes à Court later told the *Sydney Morning Herald* in January 2007, 'but I have spoken to people who are, and they like the product.' But for a starstruck little boy like Johnston, Crowe was the real prize.

It was also at a Kings game that Johnston met Steve Waugh, the celebrated former captain of the Australian cricket team. Waugh was Macquarie Bank's 'ambassador' for a real estate project in India, where he is revered because of his altruism. At the time, Waugh was hoping for Moss's support for a Macquarie Bank-sponsored cricket academy in India. Johnston coaxed Waugh into a joint-venture arrangement to be the face of Firepower's fuel technology products in the country, with Waugh's charity promised a lucrative return.

There were broader concepts under discussion too. One was an ambitious plan for a world basketball league, sponsored by Firepower. The new tournament would blanket Russia and Asia with wall-to-wall television coverage, and feature several teams from Australia, including the Kings. It would compete with the North American juggernaut, the National Basketball Association. The concept actually belonged to Moss, who earlier that year had registered a company called World Basketball League Pty Ltd. One of his fellow directors in the proposed venture, which never got off the ground, was James Henderson, the chief executive of the Dynamic Sports and Entertainment Group (DSEG), a company that advises many of the biggest sporting brands in Australia on how to better market themselves. Henderson was also involved in the Australian V8 Supercar series, the self-proclaimed premier touring car category in the world, through the Tasman team. So Johnston offered $1 million to have two of his cars decorated with Firepower's fire-breathing dragon logo.

The largesse didn't stop there. By the end of 2006, Firepower was also sponsoring the surfer Mick Manning, the Australian Superbike Championship, the Porsche Carrera Cup, Nedlands rugby club, Tasman rugby union in New Zealand and the Tongan national rugby team. And DSEG had been hired to handle the major contracts. 'Tim had this idea,' one insider later explained to the *Daily Telegraph* in June 2008, 'that he was going to be the biggest sponsor in Australian sport.' Firepower's global sponsorship strategy, drawn up in November 2006 by the Dynamic Sports and Entertainment Group, outlined the spending of nearly $60 million in 2007 and 2008. There is no suggestion that DSEG knew what Firepower's real agenda was.

Nobody figured the truth: that Johnston simply wanted to create a grand distraction. By then—with the share sales continuing and the price of each share now at $1.33—he had taken a lot of money from a lot of people. And that was his dilemma: he had to appear so successful that powerful people would surround him and protect him when the inevitable questions began to be asked. He needed shareholders to point to their television screens and say: 'There, that's my investment.'

And he needed them to approve.

Firepower's generosity was nothing new in Perth. Six weeks into their inaugural season, despite the secret payments to players, the aggressive poaching from other teams and overwhelming support from Perth sports fans, the Western Force was doing badly on the field. It was already destined for the indignity of being the worst Australian outfit in the competition. So Johnston began to openly canvass the concept of buying some new players. Not just any players. One was Matt Giteau—the brightest star in Australian rugby in a generation. He was the player many people rested their hopes on for the forthcoming 2007 World Cup. The other was Drew Mitchell, another homeland luminary. Giteau played for Canberra and Mitchell for Queensland.

It was no surprise to Peter O'Meara—the Western Force chief executive—that Johnston wanted to do something extravagant. Since the old schoolfriends had reunited Johnston had been full of grand gestures. Like on Australia Day 2006, when he arranged for a giant flag to be dragged behind a light aircraft down the full length of the Swan River. The people of Perth take Australia Day as seriously as their sport and about 400 000 had gathered for the fireworks display. As a bonus, they saw the flag, with the Western Force logo emblazoned next to Johnston's fire-breathing dragon. Later, the $40 000 bill would land on O'Meara's desk.

By the middle of 2006, the grand plan to hire the big players was well underway. It was conceived over Sunday afternoon drinks at O'Meara's comfortable pad in the Perth beachside suburb of Cottesloe. At these informal gatherings Johnston would talk vaguely about how he would use the rugby players to promote his company in Russia, his biggest market; maybe even create an international rugby competition involving Asia and Russia. Nobody questioned the rationale. Nobody even knew the Russians played rugby.

O'Meara had talked openly about his admiration for Giteau and Mitchell, musing that with them the Western Force could go from being the worst Australian team in Super 14 to the best. He wasn't wrong. But O'Meara knew the rules of the competition. He could approach the players, there was nothing wrong with that, but he wasn't allowed to breach the competition's salary cap by luring them with the promise of extra payments from a team sponsor. It was decided that O'Meara would take the negotiations to the stage where the players were interested in moving to Perth. Then, so the rules wouldn't be broken, Johnston would take over. He would parade the players, their agents and, if necessary, their families through his imposing $9 million Mosman Park mansion. He would take them out on a boat. He would wine and dine them and introduce them to the concept of Firepower ambassadorships—an idea he had most likely lifted from Macquarie Bank. The players would become the public face of his company and they would be rewarded handsomely. Best of all, they didn't need to do much.

By April 2006, the Western Force had opened negotiations with Giteau and his then manager Greg Keenan. The best the club could do by way of extra inducement was to offer to rent a luxury unit for Giteau in Cottesloe, next door to the one occupied by his close friend and fellow Wallaby Matt Henjak. But then Johnston was wheeled out. The late appearance was deliberate, giving the player and his advisor little time to respond and therefore little time to do any proper checking up on Firepower. The offer Johnston made to Giteau was spectacular. He would be paid $1.5 million a year for three years—$4.5 million in all. It would later be hailed as the biggest deal in rugby union history and most observers were stunned by it. About half would be contributed by Firepower, with the rest made up from legitimate payments from the club and other sponsors. The secret twist was that Giteau could take his Firepower payments in either cash or shares in the company. Johnston explained the tax advantages of accepting shares and then watching the money multiply tenfold or more when Firepower launched itself on the secondary stock market in London.

Giteau was given only a few days to respond to a final offer that was made to him on Saturday 22 April 2006. He accepted it, and the signing was a coup in more ways than one. The player took the shares in lieu of some of the cash payments, figuring that if things went the way Johnston promised neither he nor his working-class Canberra family would ever have to worry about money again.

The club then upheld its part of the bargain. It leased the apartment next door to Henjak in May 2006, which sat empty for eight months, at a cost of tens of thousands of dollars, until Giteau arrived in December 2006. 'We went after Matt Giteau because he's such a great role model, and I can tell you in the case of Gits, it wasn't about money. He's a high-calibre young man,' Johnston would later tell the *Sunday Times* newspaper in Perth in March 2007. 'For him, it was about lifestyle; it was about a lot of challenges that he saw he could fulfil in the Force; it was about being with his mates; living in the same apartment block as Matt Henjak. It was the whole package.'

Drew Mitchell was next. He too was convinced of the advantages of being made a Firepower ambassador, with half of his rumoured $400 000 annual salary coming from the company. The two players shared Keenan as their agent, who was due a percentage of the overall contracts of both players. But, following an acrimonious split, both players would later allege in a complaint to the Australian Rugby Union that Keenan accepted undeclared side payments from Firepower to lure them west. Though Keenan had billed Firepower $50 000 for 'sponsorship consultancy advice', there is no suggestion that this breached contracting protocol.

Ryan Cross, another Wallaby, also joined the club about this time and he too was inducted into the Firepower ambassador program. But an attempt to lure a fourth Wallaby, the Waratahs' forward Alex Kanaar, was thwarted by the growing outrage of the other Australian rugby franchises. Not only was the Western Force once again stripping them of their best players, Firepower was changing the entire wage structure of the game. The approach to Kanaar, another player represented by Keenan, prompted an Australian Rugby Union tribunal that eventually fined the Force $110 000 (the amount was later reduced on appeal). The club was found guilty of negotiating with Kanaar when it was told it couldn't. The inducement to Kanaar included a potential offer of employment by Firepower worth $30 000 a year.

Some existing Western Force and Wallaby players were also inducted into the Firepower ambassador program, including Cameron Shepherd, Scott Staniforth and Scott Fava, and the team's coach and former All Blacks coach John Mitchell. Some of the deals included a share of Firepower's profits for any business they brought to the company. Johnston hired former Wallaby Adrian Skeggs to manage his growing band of ambassadors. Johnston also befriended the then Australian national coach John Connolly, who was preparing for the forthcoming Rugby World Cup to be held in France. Connolly was offered shares in Firepower to do work for the company; an offer that Connolly says he never acted on.

But it is now clear that at least some of the players or their agents didn't look too closely at what they were signing. At least one contract was with a company called Firepower Pty Ltd, an entity that had nothing to do with Johnston. Again, he had simply made the name up.

By June 2006, Johnston was arguably the most powerful person in Western Australian rugby and one of the most talked-about men in sport. The Western Force junior rugby academy was named the Firepower Academy in his honour, with the club forgoing a potential $100000 in naming rights sponsorship. A Western Force board member Russel Perry, a former employee of disgraced Western Australian entrepreneur Alan Bond, bought shares in Firepower. At the end-of-season party—a gala affair held at the giant Burswood Casino in front of about 1000 guests—Johnston insisted on an appropriate tribute. He sat like a beaming mafia don sipping his favourite drink, Bundy and Coke, as his teenage daughters were led down a red carpet under a blaze of bright lights by two mildly embarrassed Western Force players.

The guy who once couldn't get a game was now on top of the sporting world.

Despite all the hype, Firepower smelled in so many different ways. Though Johnston talked up the permutations and combinations of how he would use his sporting sponsorships to market his products, the only actual product for retail sale in Australia at this time was a pill being sold in Western Australia that bore the logo of the Western Force. It was, literally, made from mothballs. For some reason that is difficult to ascertain, Johnston had added the chemical naphthalene to the existing ferrocene in the formula for his product. Naphthalene is the white tar fumigant with the familiar smell found in wardrobes and sock drawers. Car enthusiasts have used it for decades as a homemade octane booster.

Johnston had announced to Firepower shareholders that Caltex and Ampol, two of the largest fuel retailer brands in Australia, had agreed to stock his products. But Caltex and Ampol had never heard of Firepower, until they received a query about Johnston's statement. It later emerged that Lance Burns, the Caltex 'business manager' quoted in the Firepower newsletter next to a photograph of a Caltex service station, worked for a tiny chain of fuel retailers headquartered in the industrial suburb of Welshpool in Perth.

Firepower's only actual distributors in Australia—aside from the service stations in Welshpool—were a marine store in Hobart and Peter Brown Auto Electrics, an unpretentious service stop in Darwin owned by Peter and Jayne Brown.

Peter Brown, who has since died, learned of Firepower through Tony Prentice, his investment advisor and friend and the person selling the Firepower shares. Brown had been persuaded to sign a memorandum of understanding for the exclusive rights to the products in the Northern Territory. Though Johnston presented the deal to shareholders as something very big, the practicalities were really quite small. Brown simply purchased $35000 worth of engine-cleaning machines, pills and liquids. The vast majority of the stock remains unopened and unsold today.

14 ORANGES AND LEMONS

Tim Johnston liked to divide people up into two groups: Oranges and Lemons. 'Those who didn't know him enough yet,' he called Oranges. They thought he was nice and sweet and juicy,' explains the former Firepower employee Ken Gracey. 'But those who really got to know him became Lemons. He left them bitter and twisted.'

Bill Moss, the Macquarie banker, was an Orange. In July 2006, he met up with Johnston in Milan, Italy and the two men travelled to Russia to meet a Russian scientist who was a world leader in cutting-edge experimental stem cell research into muscular dystrophy. Moss suffers from the hereditary muscle-weakening disease and Klumov, who still worked for Austrade at the time, had organised an appointment. The trip coincided with a dinner at the private residence of Grigory Luchansky, Johnston's influential contact introduced to him by Austrade, which brought together a number of Johnston's business associates from around the world. They included his newly signed partner in India, Adi Dubash, the rich owner of a giant maritime group; and Jan Bonde Nielsen, an associate of Luchansky's and the former owner of Wembley stadium in England.

Moss's three initial demands—a copy of the financials, the share registry and the business strategy—still had not been met. But before agreeing to the trip Moss had tried the pill in the fuel tank of his car and was convinced by it. 'The first day I put a pill in my car it worked,' he says. Other members of his family who tried it thought it did too. Now, faced with a roomful of equally impressive businessmen, Moss began to warm to Firepower.

'This guy sits down next to me and I said, "What do you do?"' Moss recalls. 'He replies, "I am the personal assistant to Putin".' Moss figured the Russian president probably had many personal assistants, but he questioned the man further and discovered he had flown directly from the G8 world leaders summit that had just concluded in St Petersburg, from a private behind-closed-doors meeting between Putin and United States president George Bush. 'I said, "How many people were in the meeting?" And he said, "Oh, just the four of us".'

Ironically, the other people in the room were probably looking at Moss in the same way. No one considered that Johnston might be playing them all, using one to impress another.

For instance, Dubash, the Indian businessman, probably didn't realise that the exclusive distributorship he had just signed in India was similar to that signed by another group of Indian businessmen eighteen months earlier. And there'd been two other exclusive distributors in India before that, including the Indian-Malaysian businessman who had organised the trials with the elderly buses in Bangalore. According to insiders, Dubash would eventually spend $300 000 setting up a sales network across India—hiring twenty-two full-time staff along the way—before giving up on the project without selling anything.

One of the previous joint-venture partners in India was an Indian-Australian businessman from Western Sydney, Agnelo Almeida, and his Indian business partner, Bharat Shah. They too spent hundreds of thousands of dollars marketing the liquids and pills only to see their business collapse after they had the products tested at the respected Indian Institute of Petroleum. The tests failed to determine any fuel savings or emissions reduction. Nevertheless, Johnston would later claim the products had passed with flying colours.

Moss should perhaps have twigged that things weren't quite right the morning after the dinner in Moscow, when he met privately with one of Luchansky's business partners and learned that the proposed joint venture with the Russians had stalled because nobody could settle on the wording of the agreement. Luchansky's team complained that they could get 'little sense' out of the company leadership. They'd thought they had an agreement in April, and again in June, and now it was being reviewed once more. Moss says he offered to help, and another revised agreement was nutted out in a matter of hours. He recalls Johnston being very grateful at the time. But it would be another twelve months before anything was signed.

Finnin was an Orange on his way to being a Lemon. The former senior trade official joined the Firepower enterprise in August 2006 and quickly discovered that things were not as they seemed from the outside. 'Every time I lifted a rock,' he says, 'another black cockroach would scurry out.'

The first thing he found was that an arrest warrant had been issued by German authorities for Guenter Nolte, the former Regal Petroleum chief who was heading up Firepower's German operations. 'The reason given for the issue of this warrant was a refusal or failure on his behalf to appear in court for affirmation in lieu of an oath regarding bankruptcy proceedings,' Finnin wrote on 3 August 2006 to Johnston and Stein, who was advising Firepower on legal matters. 'Chemical Trading [Nolte's company] has been acting and conducting business as Firepower Europe; Firepower Europe is not a legal entity . . . to conduct business in such a way can be perceived to be both misleading and potentially fraudulent.'

Finnin discovered the German operations were costing more than $100 000 a month and, despite what he described in a further email to Stein on 10 August as 'a myriad of tests' on trucks and buses across continental Europe, paid for by Firepower, nobody was buying any product. Nor was there any apparent accounting for the money being spent. Though Nolte protested that the arrest warrant was simply a misunderstanding over an unpaid electricity bill, more cockroaches came scurrying out.

One of Finnin's first meetings was in Perth with Johnston, Warren Anderson and a Sino-Indonesian businessman called Jopie Widjaja, better known for his business dealings with the family of the former Indonesian strongman President Suharto. Firepower already had two distributors in Indonesia, each of which thought their deal was exclusive. And here was Johnston trying to sign up a third.

But the biggest issue that Finnin identified was with the shareholders. 'I am gravely concerned that a number of shareholders have an expectation of a public float this November,' Finnin wrote to Kim Stokeld on 15 August 2006. '[It] is clearly out of the question, yet we appear not to be actually communicating them this.'

Stokeld had just been hired to manage the Firepower shareholder registry, which up to that point had been collated on Stein's computer using a database designed by his son. Stokeld operated from a postal address in Bondi Junction in Sydney and the shareholder register was only a sideline. She was also a busy management consultant and ran a company that offered mountain bike tours.

This scattering of full- and part-time staff across Australia and the world reflected the fractured nature of Firepower. Stein worked from his home in Sydney; Finnin from his new home in Melbourne; and Nolte, who headed the European operations, out of an office in a bus station in Celle, a fairytale German town near Hannover. The small number of Australian-based technical staff worked from the office on the industrial estate in Perth, while Johnston spent most of his time on first-class flights, in coffee shops, in expensive hotels or rented apartments in Sydney and London, and in his new Perth mansion. Internal Firepower documents show that the company's international air-fare bill for the 2005/06 financial year was $1.12 million. Hotel bills alone came to $322 962. To keep in touch, he handed his wife and two daughters Firepower company mobile phones. The bills for these came to a further $22 912, according to the 2005/06 financial documents.

The trials on the dump trucks and buses continued sporadically all over the world, but particularly in Europe and Russia. Collier, the former English bobby who had initially carried out the tests, had long since left the company and his role had been taken over by technicians based in Singapore and Bucharest, Romania. The trials themselves, however, followed the same tried and trusted methods that had little to do with science.

Ramli Bin Isnin, who worked out of his home in Singapore and who took over the work of Collier, earned $47 000 a year to fly at short notice to Johnston's potential new clients. There were always new clients, rarely any old ones. But Bin Isnin's real incentive was the promise of 1 million free shares when the company floated on the stock market in London. For that, he also had to act as gofer to Johnston during his many shopping trips to Singapore, where the Firepower money was banked. One day, Johnston spent $15000 on a watch and $20000 on a pair of shoes—almost Bin Isnin's entire annual wage on just two items.

The Firepower office in Bucharest—billed on the company website as the Eastern European headquarters of a global empire—was simply one room behind a blue-painted wooden door on the third floor of a near-derelict building on the outskirts of the city. The building, a five-storey former Communist government office block that has been broken up into tiny rented offices, is overshadowed by vast public-housing towers and its environs are patrolled by the wild dogs for which the city is notorious. Getting to the location necessitates a one-hour taxi ride and a journey in a vintage three-person elevator that complains floor by perilous floor before spitting you out into a dilapidated and darkened corridor book-ended by panes of broken glass. There wasn't even a sign to indicate that this was what millions of Australian investment dollars were buying.

By any of the generally applied criteria, Firepower wasn't a normal business. There were no factories, no trucks, no workers on an assembly line. Finnin, who was supposed to be chief executive, wasn't allowed to know the formulas for the products, where they were made or where they were stored. The level of secrecy was explained by the mystical value of the intellectual property rights to the products, said to be safely locked away in a vault, though the location of the vault changed depending on who was telling the story.

On 25 August 2006, Kim Stokeld, the keeper of the share register, replied to Finnin's earlier email where he'd expressed his concern over the mixed messages being sent about the float.

'The never-ending saga of the non-eventuation of the float is the bane of my life at the moment,' she wrote. 'Firepower has a tendency to keep everything to itself from a public perspective but then make announcements and quasi-promises which we can't fulfil at shareholder and broker meetings. The brokers tend to feed speculative theories to shareholders which then drives further rumour. This is all bad for our image and leads to unhappiness by our shareholders.'

Stokeld listed a raft of other concerns. 'I've found that since my existence has become more known, shareholders call me simply to reassure themselves that Firepower exists,' she continued. 'My attitude is that these people have invested money into the company and we need to treat them accordingly. This attitude needs to be shared . . . false promises just lead to dissatisfaction.'

But at the very time Finnin and Stokeld were expressing their concerns behind closed doors, further investor meetings were being held in small upmarket hotels around Australia, addressed by Johnston and Stein who talked up the prospects of Firepower and encouraged new investors to apply for shares.

Stein had recently returned from London, where he had re-engaged with a number of the NomAds who had originally expressed an interest in Firepower but had since been told, after the departure of Hill and Carr, that the company was to be funded privately. Stein had no trouble getting in to see them again. The London stock market was booming and the NomAds, who charged $45000 a month as a retainer and demanded fees of up to $500000 for a successful listing, were happy to listen to anyone who might pay them money.

But ASIC would later allege in documents lodged in the Federal Court that Stein had begun selling his shares in the company from May 2006, and that by August he had sold close to 2 million shares at prices between $1 and $1.40 each. The share sales were made through his private company Sattvic Pty Ltd and, according to the documents, most were sold through Tim d'Emden, the investment advisor from Hobart who had arranged for Stein to address his clients there. ASIC would allege that a prospectus or disclosure document was not provided to investors as is required under the law to allow them to make an informed investment decision. Stein says the financial advisors selling the shares were told about the need for a product disclosure statement and he was unaware that that advice was not followed.

Meanwhile, one of the companies Stein had met in London, now shooting for the business of listing Firepower, was Ambrian, a well-known NomAd company. Ambrian was told that Firepower wanted to raise capital of up to £50 million. It responded positively, saying that this could be done provided Firepower was willing to let it do a full due diligence. This meant having a look at the books and all of the company's contracts. It also wanted confirmation of the technical integrity of the products. From that moment on, Ambrian found the email exchanges slowed, decisions were delayed, responses were difficult to obtain.

Ambrian began to suspect something was wrong.

In Sydney, however, the Firepower sea of lies was calm . . . on the surface.

On 18 September 2006, the Sydney Kings—thanks to Johnston—spared no expense for the official launch of their new season. The club was handed over the 4200-tonne guided missile frigate the HMAS *Sydney* free of charge, which was berthed at the Royal Australian Navy's base at Garden Island, close to the world-famous Sydney Opera House. In the world of Australian sport there were bigger moments, but not many that could boast such a perfect setting.

In the months leading up to the event, Johnston continued to plant whispers about how he made his money. The technology he had helped invent. The clandestine contracts in Russia and Pakistan, and the hush-hush ventures with large oil refineries. Now his willingness to share that good fortune had brought his company to centre stage on a large boat in one of the most beautiful harbours in the world.

The ship was packed with journalists, sponsors and merchant bankers, who clutched drinks served to them by dark-suited sailors. Large basketball players in blue-striped polo shirts and baseball caps posed for photographs next to the ship's giant grey guns. The symbolism was strong: Firepower next to the firepower; the Kings next to the new kings of the sporting world. Johnston's employees swept from one person to the next, generating confidence. There was a sense that Johnston was a brilliant man. Some were describing him as the Bill Gates of the environment, and Firepower as the next Microsoft. The message was clear. There was no time to wait. Get on board, or lose out on the investment chance of a lifetime.

The optimism was not just in Sydney. It was across the country. In Adelaide it was particularly strong. John Catt, the investment advisor who was a friend to AFL stars, had sold shares to a bunch of them. They were all household names: Wayne Carey, the former all-Australian AFL captain, had invested $100 000; his father, Kevin, had invested $60 000; and the then captain of the Adelaide Crows Mark Ricciuto put in $175 000 in two parcels. Crows coach Neil Craig and his wife put in $30 000. Others who had collectively handed over hundreds of thousands of dollars included Adelaide players Brett Burton, Simon Goodwin, Rhett Biglands, former Crows forward Scott Welsh, radio broadcaster Anthony 'Lehmo' Lehmann, and former Crows and Sydney Swans player, *Big Brother* identity and Adelaide radio personality Ryan Fitzgerald.

The football players even had a secret game they played when interviewed on radio: they competed to use the word 'firepower'

FIREPOWER

in as many contexts as possible. It happened so often it began to be noticed, and drew comment in the *Adelaide Advertiser*.

The mood was optimistic in Brisbane too, where only weeks earlier Firepower had hosted a private function at the Sofitel Hotel for the Wallabies to mark the Bledisloe Cup rugby union match against the All Blacks. Johnston attended the function with his friends from the Western Force, including its chief executive officer, O'Meara. The weekend involved vast quantities of Bundy and Coke and much talk about the multimillion-dollar deals Johnston was securing in Russia.

And the optimism was obvious in Perth, where Johnston presented plans to Western Force officials for an ambitious rugby union super league based in Russia that would require his Firepower 'ambassador' players to give coaching clinics in Moscow. By then, Firepower was also a major sponsor of Russian rugby's governing body and Johnston was proposing to bring Russian players and coaches to the Western Force's academy—the Firepower Academy. Johnston boasted about how he was going to pump so much money into Russian rugby that within four years the country—long considered a third-tier rugby nation—would become a full member of the International Rugby Board and have a successful cross-border competition called the EurAsia Cup. It was nearly as odd as Johnston's other attempt at winning favour in Russia—by giving US$100 000 towards the refurbishment of the Pavlovsk Palace Museum, the summer home of the former Russian tsars, located near St Petersburg.

But as Johnston's employees swaggered across the deck of the HMAS *Sydney*, gushing about joint ventures with oil giants and a possible takeover by Macquarie Bank, they also unwittingly scripted the beginning of the end of Johnston's improbable tale.

* * *

174

Rod Allen wasn't a hard-bitten investigative reporter. In fact, as managing editor for sport at the *Sydney Morning Herald* he spent most of his time chained to his desk, dealing with the stories brought back by his reporters. At thirty-eight, he was younger than many of them, having joined a newsroom right out of school. But during and outside of work, Allen moved in sporting circles. He liked to spar with the boxer Danny Green to keep fit, and his clean-shaven head was a regular sight at many big events. For weeks, Allen had been hearing the rumours about the new giant on the Australian sporting scene. It wasn't the fans who were talking about Firepower; it was the very people who ran the games—the high priests and administrators of Australia's public obsession.

Allen looked at Firepower's website, which said it was working in a technical capacity with General Motors Holden. He listened to the stories about a supposed joint venture with Shell, and read press clippings that declared its products were being used in power generation, by railways, and even by the armed forces of Australia and New Zealand. He saw the photograph of Prime Minister Howard witnessing the signing of a deal in Pakistan. It was all rather intriguing. But he figured there was something about it that just didn't add up.

Allen and his chief rugby writer, Greg Growden, attended a private lunch with the then head of the Australian Rugby Union Gary Flowers, who explained that Johnston was making lots of money selling his pills to people who weren't even using them. They were just hoarding them in order to claim carbon credits. Yet when Allen went looking to buy the products, he couldn't find them anywhere. He wondered why a company would do so much marketing when people couldn't buy what they were selling. 'That was the thing I couldn't understand,' he says. 'I just couldn't make sense of it.'

At the end of the Sydney Kings event on board the HMAS *Sydney*, Allen, along with other guests, was given a bag of goodies from the event's sponsors. In it was a packet of the Firepower pills. They were about the size of a five-cent piece and looked like little bits of orange-brown cardboard. On the back of the packet was a testimonial from 'Joseph and Julie in Fiji' who claimed that if you put one pill in your petrol tank it would reduce harmful emissions and make your fuel last 12 per cent longer.

Allen cracked the packet open and carried out a little unscientific experiment of his own, using the Firepower pills in his family car. He came to the conclusion that they didn't work. He took the half-empty packet into the *Sydney Morning Herald*'s office and cast around for someone to make further inquiries.

It began the journey of investigaton that led to Firepower's end.

15 **RAINING MONEY**

Faced with having to produce evidence of an actual business in order to get a listing on the secondary market in London, Johnston changed tack.

In mid-2006, the most talked-about company in Australia was the Fortescue Metals Group, an enterprise whose share price rose spectacularly as it built a major iron export business by competing directly with the traditional industry giant BHP Billiton. Along the way, there was much scepticism about whether the company would ever succeed. But it did, transforming its billionaire owner Andrew 'Twiggy' Forrest from a rich man into Australia's richest man.

One of the people responsible for Fortescue Metals' apparently miraculous triumph was Peter Huston, the company's general counsel. Huston was a former partner in Deacons Lawyers who had established his own boutique legal practice in Perth, Troika Legal. It specialised in providing legal advice in relation to mergers, acquisitions and public listings. In about August 2006, Johnston met with Huston and convinced him to take Firepower to its proposed listing on the AIM. Johnston told staff that Huston was coming on board to complete the paperwork.

Huston received $20 000 a month, travel and accommodation costs, and his company, Mandalup Investments Pty Ltd, later appeared on Firepower's shareholder register as one of the biggest shareholders. Unaware of the history, Huston was soon treading the same worn path to London to talk to NomAds and brokers. He had no way of knowing that Johnston was handing out shares like they were Monopoly money.

One of the documents Johnston used to bring Huston on board was a more sophisticated version of the 'company profile' that had first been produced in September 2004. Now titled the 'Firepower Update Document', with the help of the accountancy firm KPMG it had grown to about eighty pages and would eventually reach ninety-two pages. KPMG, which was being paid $50 000 a month by Firepower, had continued to update it, using information supplied by Johnston.

'Firepower controls a suite of distinct products, that it is taking to market across a global distribution footprint,' the document began. 'Its compelling story is now framed by high fuel prices and its potential to generate value through emission reductions.' It listed Firepower's 'competent management' and 'world class product' as two key strengths, along with its 'strong track record' over a fourteen-year period. 'The Firepower product range has been tested by many independent testing institutes,' it continued. 'One of the key economic drivers for Firepower is the fuel cost saving generated by application of its fuel technology products that can result in potential fuel savings of up to 30 per cent.'

Johnston's cunning was evident in his ability to turn the lack of any actual scientific proof of his claims into an apparent advantage. 'To ensure that trials are properly conducted,' the document read, 'Firepower facilitates and pays for trials.' It went on to list everything from the experiments on the ancient Russian tractors to the remarkable intuition of the Greek taxi drivers as proof. One version even made mention of the fuel savings achieved on the steam train.

Also recounted were seven 'independent laboratory tests that have conclusively found fuel savings and reduction in emission levels'. The first four—the Southwest Research Institute in the United States, Dekra in Germany, the Hydrocarbon Development Institute of Pakistan, and the State Science Research Institute in Russia—had done no such tests. The three other institutions were Queen's University in Belfast (another reference to the 1995 trials conducted by Dr Roy Douglas using the old Techni-Lube products), the Indian Institute of Petroleum (the tests paid for by one of Johnston's many exclusive distributors in that country that showed no fuel savings or emissions reduction), and the Automobile Association of Singapore (the unscientific road trial conducted using the Chemplex pill almost ten years earlier).

The document contained other theatrical leaps in logic. Not only had the Firepower products the ability to reduce acid rain around the world (the line Johnston had stolen fourteen years earlier from Fred Chorney, the Californian chemist and Korean War veteran), they had a double economic benefit. Customers would pay money to buy them for their fuel-saving qualities, but Firepower would retain the rights to claim carbon credits on any emission reductions. The example used was that of Russian Railways, which was said to be saving $216 million a year on its fuel bills by using Firepower's products and delivering a gross profit to Firepower of $105 million a year. According to the document, Firepower stood to make almost as much again by trading the carbon credits created by the emission reductions on the locomotives.

It was the stuff of nonsense. But the claim was backed up by assertions that Firepower had the support of the Australian government, having been selected as 'one of only ten rising global business stars' for worldwide support by Austrade. And that it had 'strategic alliances' with parties such as BAE Systems, DynCorp, and the governments of Malaysia, Russia and Pakistan.

The document claimed multimillion-dollar contracts were in place all over the world, with companies from Coca-Cola in Belgium to the fire brigade in Italy, from taxis in Athens to shipping lines in Indonesia, and from Caltex and Ampol in Australia to the giant United States defence contractor Lockheed Martin.

It was utter fabrication, made all the more extraordinary by the fact that the document was compiled by one of the world's biggest accountancy firms, albeit with information supplied by Johnston.

The day after the function on board the HMAS *Sydney* in September 2006, Johnston bought a slice of the Sydney Kings.

The purchase of 10 per cent of the shares in the Kings ownership syndicate was made on behalf of Firepower for $250 000, though the shareholders themselves were never consulted about it. The purchase brought Johnston in as a partner to other members of the syndicate, people like Moss, the Macquarie banker; Harry Cousens, general manager of Dell Computers in Australia; and John Kench, who helped found the successful legal firm Johnson, Winter & Slattery, which would play a later role in the unfolding tale.

Johnston bought in at a time when Moss wanted to get out. Moss says he was getting ready for retirement—only months later he would resign from Macquarie Bank—and was keen to wind back on his business commitments. The Sydney Kings was different from the kinds of enterprises Moss was used to.

As a director of Macquarie Bank he made millions of dollars in his annual salary and bonuses, but each year that his syndicate owned the Kings it had lost an average of about $700 000. The reality was that being an owner of the Kings merely gave you the right to write a number of substantial cheques.

Though Johnston clearly had no real interest in the game of basketball, he immediately professed an intention of getting more involved with the Kings. He talked about how he was going to use the team to market his products in South East Asia and China, and how the Kings were going to spearhead his ambitious plans for a basketball league that would rival the American NBA. Everyone was excited, especially the players. Money was again falling from the sky.

'This guy has a tremendous personality. He's enjoyable and a good-looking guy and he can talk on a range of subjects,' Brian Goorjian, the Sydney Kings and Australian national coach says of Johnston. 'He told us the Kings were going global and that Australia would only be a small part of his plans.'

Team captain Jason Smith was told the team was going to be playing in Russia, China, Malaysia and Indonesia. 'He was very charismatic,' Smith recalls. 'He says what you want to hear.'

Another player, Russell Hinder, recalled the team being flown over to Perth for a barbeque at Johnston's stately mansion. 'It was gorgeous, overlooking the water, a $15 million home, you know,' he later told the ABC's *Four Corners* program. 'All the Western Force [players] were there. The former All Blacks coach John Mitchell was there, and it was all sort of glitz and glamour.'

By now Moss's partner, Lata Krishan, was also working as a consultant to Firepower after Johnston had professed his need for help in relocating the business to Sydney. In August 2006, Firepower began paying Krishan's company, Boston Management Services, $20 000 a month and the payments continued until the following May, though Johnston never did move to

Sydney. He preferred London, spending increasing amounts of time at the $10 000-a-week Mayfayre House executive apartments building in Mayfair. He liked to boast that his downstairs neighbour was the Hollywood actor Dustin Hoffman.

It was about this time that Johnston also hired the former Aboriginal rugby league star David Liddiard, another of Moss's associates. Liddiard was the executive director of the National Aboriginal Sporting Chance Academy, which had the backing of broadcaster Alan Jones, former prime minister Bob Hawke, Aussie Home Loans chief John Symonds, Qantas chief Geoff Dixon, and the chief executive of News Limited, John Hartigan. Moss and Liddiard had worked together on several indigenous causes. Moss personally invested in Gunya Tourism, a $1000-a-night indigenous experience with the Titjikala people near Alice Springs. In turn, Liddiard had helped Macquarie Bank with its ambitious plans to redevelop indigenous land. Johnston was learning the ways of influence and power, robed in the garments of charitable social networks.

When Moss decided to exit the Kings, he says some of the other syndicate members decided to follow. Under the rules, those who remained were offered the right to purchase the leavers' shares. 'That was a clause to keep weirdos and loonies out of the Kings,' says Moss, which, in hindsight, seems a little ironic. Prospective new owners were also interviewed and, according to Moss, it was at this point that Johnston stated his desire to buy out everyone. He wanted to become the sole owner of the Kings. 'I remember saying to him, "Tim, you don't want to buy this, it is the last thing you want to do",' Moss recalls. 'And his words to me were: "How many people in a lifetime get a chance to buy and own a national sporting team?"'

Johnston bought the Kings for $2 million, which he paid in instalments over the next few months. By about February 2007, he was the outright owner; and the National Basketball

League broke the rules of their own competition, which stated that the owner of a franchise needed to live in that city. The decision would ultimately bring the entire national basketball competition to its knees, but at the time selling to Johnston was good business for the syndicate. The deal gave a 500 per cent profit on the $400 000 that had been spent buying the Kings in 2002. But the tangible price was even higher, because the Kings had about $1.3 million worth of debt when Johnston took over, having failed to do proper due diligence. 'He bought a hole in the ground,' one former Kings executive reveals. Moss points out that Johnston was a full member of the old syndicate when he decided to buy the business and therefore would have been aware of all of the issues.

But money didn't seem to be a problem for Johnston, who by now had his sights set on the world of boxing. At the time, the Australian boxer Paul 'Hurricane' Briggs, the former World Boxing Council number one ranked light heavyweight, was getting ready to fight in Chicago against the world champion, Polish boxer Tomasz Adamek. They were scheduled to fight in the grand ballroom of the Hilton Hotel in Chicago, at an event organised by the legendary boxing promoter Don King.

Briggs was one of the feel-good stories of Australian sport. He was a former world kickboxing champion who had sunk to a life of drugs and crime. Self-loathing took him to the brink of suicide, but boxing saved him. Now, after a chance meeting between Johnston and Briggs's management at a function in Sydney hosted by the broadcaster Alan Jones, Firepower was offering to put bread on his table. In exchange, Johnston wanted Briggs to fight under a new moniker: Paul 'Firepower' Briggs. He wondered how much that would cost. Briggs's management set a fee of $100 000 but Johnston offered twice that. He said it could be paid in cash or in Firepower shares, which were worth $1 each now but would soon be worth up to $18 each when the company listed on the AIM. 'It was the easiest negotiation ever,' one insider says. 'There weren't even any performance parameters.' A mixture of money and shares was agreed on.

Johnston flew over a top-class sparring partner from America for Briggs; and, for the fight itself, flew Briggs and his entire entourage over to Chicago in business and first-class seats, including the masseur and the family babysitter, and put them up in five-star hotels. Johnston talked about how he would create giant boxing barns across the world, packed with people wanting to see a slugfest, and where Briggs would be the undercard.

By way of explanation, Johnston told his favourite tale of sitting in a hotel room in the Pakistani capital Islamabad when a Super 12 (the competition that preceded Super 14 rugby) game came on the television. 'There I was in Islamabad and there was Super rugby being televised all over the world,' said Johnston, later recounting the same story to the *Sunday Times* newspaper in Perth in March 2007. 'I thought: "Mate, these are my markets". For a reasonably inexpensive cost, we could get global coverage if we worked it well.' Sport, he said, could quite literally take his product around the world through sponsorship. Money was falling from the sky, apparently, and nobody was going to argue.

Briggs was invited to a Sydney Kings game and told to bring his family because Johnston's family would be there. Instead, he found himself mixing with a host of other sporting celebrities, also guests of Firepower. Briggs later told the *Daily Telegraph* he was pulled aside by a Firepower executive and told Johnston wanted to be Santa Claus.

Briggs got paid for about four months, then the payments stopped. 'I'm ringing saying "what are you guys doing to me",' said Briggs to the *Daily Telegraph* in June 2008. 'Then I got another month, and then I was chasing to get blood out of a stone, just a different version of the same crap.'

Johnston had lost interest once Briggs lost the fight in Chicago. He had another project consuming his time: dinner with the prime minister.

The first of what turned out to be three intimate dinners with John Howard came about through the then federal science minister and future deputy leader of the Liberal Party, Julie Bishop. Though Bishop knew Stein, her introduction to Johnston came about in late 2005 through Western Force chairman Geoff Stooke, who described Johnston as the person who was going to help put Western Australian rugby on the map. Stooke's prescience was more accurate than he might have wished for.

Johnston followed up the introduction by securing a private audience with Bishop—who happened to be his local MP—where he demonstrated his desire to become a major donor to the Liberal Party. That led to an invitation to a fundraising dinner in Perth in February 2006 that Prime Minister Howard also attended, having witnessed Firepower's staged signing ceremony in Pakistan just three months earlier. Johnston appeared at the fundraiser carrying a Western Force jersey with the Firepower logo prominently displayed. The Liberal Party backroom staff would later discover that Johnston hadn't paid for his ticket, but the matter wasn't pressed. With a crucial federal election looming in 2007, Johnston's repeated talk about becoming a major donor instead secured him a private invitation for a more intimate dinner with Howard and a group of Western Australian business leaders, which was where Johnston was heading when he returned from Chicago.

'It turns out he made no donations to the Liberal Party,' Bishop recalls. 'He was going to be a big supporter and he didn't pay for his ticket to the dinner [the fundraiser].' Nevertheless, Johnston later secured an invitation to a third dinner, this time also at the prime minister's official residence in Canberra, The Lodge, thus compounding the paradox of a serving federal science minister taking seriously a person offering a magic pill.

Documents indicate that Johnston's real game was to get access to the federal government's $500 million Low Emissions Technology Demonstration Fund, which had been set up by Howard to encourage the production of clean energy as an alternative to signing the Kyoto Protocol on climate change. 'We will need the active patronage and support of Julie Bishop in accessing these funds,' wrote Finnin in an email to Johnston on 25 October 2006. 'I would urge you to speak with Julie on how best we might approach a successful grant application.'

Johnston was clearly comfortable speaking with anyone.

In early October 2006, Kim Stokeld called Finnin to an urgent meeting at her home office. She set a box of uncashed cheques in front of him and explained they were from people who had bought shares; the cheques Johnston had not yet cashed. But more often, she explained, Johnston simply banked the cheques then forgot to issue a share certificate. At this moment it dawned on Finnin that Firepower didn't know how many shareholders it had. Stokeld had discovered that some of the paperwork had been lost, or had never been recorded in the first place.

Now Johnston was pressing Stokeld to hand over a completed list of shareholders to Peter Huston, the latest person who was going to make the stock market listing happen. 'I cannot stress the importance enough of Peter's role in our future IPO,' Johnston wrote to Stokeld on 25 October 2006. 'Peter is the link with KPMG and investors, Banks and NomAds. He is only as good as the information and support we provide.'

Stokeld flew to Perth and obtained what she described in an email to Finnin on 23 October as 'a jumble of unstapled paperwork thrown into a large box' by Gordon Hill, the former police minister who had resigned as a director of Firepower. It contained much, but not all, of the missing paperwork.

Meanwhile, Finnin embarked on a tour of the country, visiting each of the investment advisors to try to calm the hysteria and expectations. But Johnston liked the hysteria and he was anxious that Finnin didn't ruin things. 'Please act very carefully in Adelaide,' he had warned Finnin in an email on 22 September. 'Each time you make comments there is a huge ripple effect around Australia as your comments to date have been contrary to those of our directors.'

Any hope of a November float had long been abandoned, though this was not communicated to shareholders. The shareholders who had been in the longest started to complain. They were angry over the fact that they still hadn't seen any financials for the company even though one grumbled that he and others had been promised this information 'within three months' by Johnston at shareholder meetings in February 2006.

'I am a Firepower shareholder and I have introduced several other investors to Firepower,' the investor wrote to Finnin on 20 October. 'Together [with his friend] we have placed well in excess of 10 million shares and the majority of the people that we have introduced turn to us on a regular basis to get the latest on Firepower and news of the listing date. Unfortunately we are not in a position to tell them anything at all. It is both frustrating and embarrassing because we have painted a rosy picture of Firepower and its future potential but getting news and updates on company progress is like trying to get blood out of a stone. Forgive me if this sounds melodramatic, but it is absolutely true.'

Johnston reacted by spreading confusion. He began to talk up the value of the nonexistent carbon-trading arm of the company, claiming he had advice that it would soon be worth as much as the main body of the company. He argued that to list Firepower without taking that into consideration would be to undervalue the returns that were due to shareholders. 'They all [the brokers] feel we are ready to list by February/March [2007] subject to due diligence,' Johnston wrote to Finnin on 22 September 2006. 'However, we may look at alternatives as we have discussed. These include separating our green technology.'

Johnston also talked about creating a private market to trade shares in Firepower before the company listed, to allow disgruntled shareholders to offload their stock to someone else who was willing to buy them. That too, of course, was potentially illegal.

But by October 2006, Firepower had another pressing issue. Trevor Nairn, the former chief executive, was threatening legal action over the fact that his shares in the Firepower entity in the Cayman Islands, which were held through his wife, had not been transferred over into the British Virgin Islands entity. Nairn also pointed out that the mythical Firepower 'intellectual property' was actually owned by the Cayman entity. In effect, what he was saying was that anyone who had purchased shares in the British Virgin Islands version of Firepower didn't actually own the rights to anything, real or imagined.

Nairn had his lawyers write to the Australian Securities and Investments Commission (ASIC) pointing out that Firepower might be operating illegally in Australia. It wasn't the first time that Firepower had come under the gaze of the corporate regulator. In May 2006, Robert Northcoate, an accountant from Kalgoorlie, had smelled a rat when one of his clients, a retiree, wanted to invest his superannuation in Firepower shares. The shares were recommended by Quentin Ward, the Perth investment advisor who was part of the van Rens network.

'As a licensed advisor you are required to provide certain documentation—a product disclosure statement for a product; an information memorandum,' Northcoate later told *Four*

Corners. 'All of these things really outline what the investment is. They give the investor an opportunity to consider whether they really do want to invest some money in there. It identifies the risks. It maybe gives some financial sort of basis for balance sheets, profit and loss et cetera.' Northcoate said none of these were available for Firepower, so he lodged a complaint with ASIC naming Ward and alerting the corporate regulator to his suspicion that Firepower 'may in fact be a scam'. ASIC replied it was 'taking no further action at this time'.

ASIC took a similar, apparently soft line with Nairn's complaint, even though it came wrapped in the solemn tones and letterhead of Freehills law firm. The commission simply wrote to Firepower asking a series of questions in relation to the company's global structure. One of the questions was whether Firepower had conducted any fundraising activities in Australia and, if so, what was the extent of that activity. Firepower drew up a response on 10 August by Les Stein that it had 'conducted early fundraising world wide', including in Australia, but 'it has not done so for the last 12 months'. Though shares were being sold even as the words were being written, ASIC went away.

Nairn, however, persisted. About the same time that he had his lawyers write to ASIC, Nairn's wife lodged a writ in the Supreme Court of Western Australia alleging her shareholding in the British Virgins Islands Firepower entity had vanished during the company restructure from the Cayman Islands.

On 13 October 2006, Stein wrote a memo to senior Firepower management explaining that the lawsuit was an attempt to fish for information: 'Our advice from a senior QC is that there is nothing in this attempt,' he said. 'We are taking it seriously however and will defend it vigorously. As Firepower grows and expands, various people will seek to put pressure on us for their own ends. This is common for a company with the potential of Firepower. Rest assured, we will put our considerable resources into defending ourselves and seeking compensation from those who falsely accuse us of wrongdoing.'

Firepower engaged a Cayman Islands law firm—at a cost of US$100 000—to try to get around the issue.

16 ESCAPE ROUTES

Johnston couldn't afford to stay still. He began to canvass the idea of establishing new headquarters away from Australia. He talked about the tax advantages of the Dutch Antilles and Ireland, before settling on the idea of moving to Switzerland, to the old-world grandeur he was once unable to afford.

John Finnin, who was asked to make the move happen, turned to the Australian government for help, drawing on the services of Peter Rasmussen, from Austrade's Frankfurt office. Rasmussen was asked to set up a series of meetings with 'big end of town' tax experts and government officials in Switzerland who could give advice on how to escape Australia's tax regime. Austrade claimed a service fee for this, based on Finnin's old rate of $190 an hour.

'Our global head office, if you like, will be a Swiss company and not an Australian one,' wrote Finnin to Rasmussen on 25 October 2006. 'This will mean we will want to talk at a very senior level to the right people (eg: Richard Branson has recently set up the headquarters of Virgin in Switzerland, so who did he talk to, to facilitate this)?' The absurdity of a company like Firepower, with its little office in a Perth industrial estate and only about ten full-time employees, most of whom were scattered around the world, needing to match Richard Branson's Virgin conglomerate was lost on Austrade.

In Switzerland, it is common practice to meet with the local cantons—much like feudal regional governments—to negotiate a company's individual tax rate. The closer the company is located to the urban centres, the higher the rate, but the attraction is that the incentives compare favourably with most first-world countries. Finnin asked Rasmussen to set up introductions 'with individuals who have both the seniority and the authority to negotiate tax issues in at least three of the French-speaking Cantons'. He also said they would need meetings with lawyers and tax accountants: 'Once again I will want to speak to those entities dealing with "the big end of town", so to speak.'

Finnin spoke with a sense of bravado but he was in no doubt by now that Firepower was mired in problems, and he was anxious to bring in some expertise, hire some credibility. He was equally anxious to move the share registry offshore as quickly as possible, in case the regulators came knocking again.

'I have been fielding calls from some very disgruntled and indeed hostile shareholders. In all conscience, we cannot continue to let this happen,' he wrote to Johnston on 10 November 2006. 'I agree with you, many are immature and small shareholders with a limited understanding of how these things work. Nevertheless we cannot, leading into a listing, allow this hostility to grow. It will damage us all.'

Finnin also knew by now that there was no scientific proof to back up any of the company's outlandish claims. 'We cannot prove by any independent, recognised authority that our products do what we say they do!' he continued. 'Tim, I want to be clear on this and don't get me wrong. The product obviously works and I am as passionate and as excited as you are on what we are sitting on. Why else would we be getting the results we have achieved across the world in so many different environments? But our passion and enthusiasm won't be worth a pinch of shit in the marketplace.

'Leading into a public listing we will be expected to prove that our products do what we say they do. This proof will need to come in the form of an independent, internationally recognised and credible authority. It will need to say clearly, increased fuel efficiency, low emissions etc. Right now, right here, we cannot prove that!

'As an example, we say in our literature that we make the fuel burn better through greater atomisation. We have nothing to prove that . . . we say we achieve greater engine integrity and that our product will not affect seals, bearings, valves, etc. We cannot prove that.'

Finnin was equally scathing about the way Firepower did business, pointing out that the only thing the company appeared to do was expensive trials for customers, none of whom seemed to then purchase anything. 'There are a myriad of both lucrative, highly profitable and exciting "deals" that await us. However, having said that and whether we like it or not we are not closing those deals. There is a host of reasons for this . . . A key issue though is how we sell. To be absolutely frank the process isn't worth a lump of elephant shit. From the moment a customer presents themselves we have so far managed it badly almost each and every time.'

Up to this point Finnin had believed Johnston's tales about massive contracts in Russia and countries associated with the former Soviet Union. But now, as chief executive, privy to progress reports coming out of Russia, he could see there were no contracts. There was lots of talk about pending business, but no actual business.

In an internal email to a Firepower manager on 13 December, Finnin pointed out that a feature story that appeared in an earlier newsletter to shareholders about a pending deal with the Croatian military—the one Johnston was referring to when he emailed former Air Marshal Errol McCormack—was 'a complete fabrication'. The rest of the newsletter, he said, was 'full of promises that we have not delivered on, is misleading and overly optimistic'.

To make matters worse, the one pending contract that Johnston had referred to time and again—the gigantic deal with Russian Railways—had fallen through after it emerged that some of the trial results presented by Firepower had been faked. Finnin could see, in monthly report after monthly report, that there never had been any sales to Russian Railways. Nor were there any contracts in Pakistan, Romania, Germany and dozens of other countries that Firepower claimed to be doing business in.

Finnin's attempts to get answers were stymied by the fact that he was only ever allowed brief moments of access to Johnston. 'We'd get a few minutes in a lift, for instance,' Finnin reveals. 'Or he'd call you to a meeting in a coffee shop and there would be a passing parade of other people calling over, whom he had also arranged to meet. It was an impossible situation.'

The cold truth was also served up by KPMG, which pointed out Firepower's inflated sales figures in a report titled 'Register of Unresolved Issues' dated October 2006. 'For the 2005 calendar year Firepower was, in theory, entitled to expect at least US$19.27 million in distributor minimum purchase commitments. However Firepower's historical draft accounts . . . disclose a sales figure of approximately US$0.3 million.'

The complaints from Stokeld, the compiler of the missing names on the share register, were getting more insistent too. 'We are going to have a lot of questions to answer as to why we aren't reporting on our financial position, what's happening with the float etc,' she wrote to Johnston on 6 December 2006. 'There is a lot of rumbling going on.'

Johnston's emailed response two days later was flippant: 'Are you coming to the basketball Friday night, I will be there?'

Johnston was happiest in any sporting arena. In November 2006, he attended a function at Burswood golf course organised by the Western Force for its sponsors. There he bumped into a fellow sponsor, Ross 'Rosco' Graham, a knockabout multimillionaire businessman who had made his fortune in mining and renting out second-hand equipment to other miners. During the mining boom Western Australia was then experiencing it was a lucrative trade, yet Graham could see that it all might end and he was casting around for new opportunities. A few weeks later, he and his wife, Linda, found themselves meeting up with Johnston and his wife, Sandra, at the Old Swan Brewery in Mounts Bay Road, where Johnston sold Graham on his fuel efficiency myths.

'Johnston said words to the effect that: "My group manufactures an amazing product which increases diesel fuel efficiency and reduces emissions," ' Graham would later allege in a statement to the Federal Court in July 2008. He said Johnston explained how carbon credit trading would 'double the value' of his business once people understood the importance of carbon trading, and that 'Bill Moss from Macquarie Bank' was involved behind the scenes.

'I need someone to trust at the moment because there are sharks circling trying to take this business off me; it's such a great business,' Johnston continued. 'It will take me about ten months to get it to a float. I need 10 million dollars to sort the carbon credits side of things out and get it to a float.'

Graham outlined to the court his thinking at the time: 'I liked the concept of the "green" technology and the fuel efficiency and the cost savings and thought it would be a good business to invest in. I said words to the effect of: "I have those sorts of funds available."'

Graham called his financial advisor, Greg Coyle, a Kalgoorlie accountant, and arranged for a third meeting, at his South Perth home, involving Johnston and van Rens, the former television journalist turned businessman who had the amazing network around the world. 'During the meeting Michael van Rens and Johnston, but mostly Johnston, gave myself and Greg Coyle a summary of the business and of the Firepower products,' Graham told the court in his July 2008 statement. 'Johnston said words to us to the effect: "Each share is currently worth $1 but they could go to $5 or $7."'

Johnston explained how the quality of fuel in Russia and Indonesia, where Firepower did most of its business, was poor and that Firepower was 'just about to tie up' a significant number of contracts with refineries in both countries. Once those sales came through, Firepower would be worth up to $1 billion.

'I need $10 million to get the carbon credits sorted out to take it to a listing,' Johnston went on. 'My burn rate is about $1 million a month. I have other options. Bill Moss who is ex Macquarie Bank is prepared to back this. He is willing to be the chairman of the group and there are other big names like that who are interested, keen and watching the progress of the group. These people are circling me and I am worried about them taking the business over and away from me. I am in a vulnerable position and I need money to take it to a float.'

Based on little else, Graham pulled out his chequebook. By the end of December he had handed over $7 million, and $3 million more followed in February 2007. And that was just the beginning. Johnston then convinced Graham to enter a joint venture to sell Firepower products in Australia and New Zealand and in the islands of the South Pacific.

What Johnston failed to mention was that he had already entered into agreements that amounted to joint ventures with several other companies, including one called Techenomics International, to do much the same thing. The deal with Techenomics—an established distributor of speciality lubricants to the mining industry in Australia and Indonesia—had come about through Peter Richard, a stockbroker and financier with links to the NSW Labor Party. Richard had been a fellow exhibitor at the 2005 Australia Week In Moscow, where he first met Johnston.

Techenomics had conducted a trial using Firepower products on six dump trucks at the KPC coalmine in Indonesia, where it claimed to have achieved a fuel saving, and it was hoping to leverage those results to get Firepower products approved for use in other mines both in Indonesia and Australia. The company also hoped to sell Firepower products to the state-owned Sydney Ferries corporation and to local area councils in New South Wales, beginning with their use in garbage trucks owned by the Labor-dominated Canada Bay Council in inner Sydney.

Techenomics met with representatives of the deputy premier and New South Wales transport minister John Watkins on 6 September 2006 and presented the state government with a series of tests that allegedly proved Firepower's fuel-saving and exhaust-reducing qualities. 'Techenomics and Firepower have conducted many trials around the world to indicate the effective reduction of exhaust emissions in situations similar to Sydney Ferries,' the presentation read. But among the scientific reports presented was the one Johnston claimed had been done by the Singapore Institute of Standards and Industrial Research— the same institution that had closed down in 1996, four years before the FP4000 product had even come into being.

'We are waiting for the political minders at Sydney Ferries to take our approach to the next step,' Peter Richard wrote to Johnston on 3 October 2006.

The NSW government was still considering the proposal when the *Sydney Morning Herald* gave it a reason to think twice.

Between the meetings with Ross Graham, Johnston had visited Switzerland. The journey, paid for by Firepower, began in Sydney in early November 2006, where Johnston and his wife, Sandra, met up with Moss, his partner, Lata Krishan, and David Liddiard. Their first stop was Johnston's Perth mansion where they were scheduled to see the company's financials.

'I'd been asking for them a long time and Tim said, "Oh they are ready, we will see the guys from KPMG and we'll get them",' Moss says.

The accountants from KPMG arrived, but the report they handed over to Moss was not the kind he was used to. All of the vital information was missing. The words 'information provided by client' were repeated over and over again in the places where he would have expected details such as sales figures, company salaries and other basic financial information. Moss recalls: 'He [Johnston] kept saying: "Yeah, yeah that's coming, we are just trying to sort out a few bits and pieces".'

The stopover in Perth included meetings with Huston, the man in charge of the stock market listing, but what struck Moss was 'the mismanagement and the fact that everything was so disorganised'. It didn't stop him continuing with the journey though, which he said he began to treat as a kind of exploration—an opportunity to decide whether he wanted anything more to do with Firepower.

The party flew first class to Dubai, where they split up. Krishan, Liddiard and Sandra Johnston flew direct to Switzerland to inspect potential schools for the Johnston children if the move to Switzerland did go ahead. They visited the International School of Geneva, Collège du Léman and several French language schools, as well as French fashion, drama and photography schools. They also sought advice on the Swiss rental market.

Meanwhile, Johnston and Moss flew to Moscow for a second meeting with the scientist who had promised a potential cure for Moss's medical condition. Three burly bodyguards met them off the plane; Johnston, ever the oligarch, liked to have them shadow him whenever he was in Russia. The visitors were whisked off to the 34-storey Swissôtel, located on the worm-shaped island in the Moskva River and described by the *New York Times* as 'brash, elitist and staggeringly expensive'. Suites cost up to $2500 a night; whisky, almost $30 a glass. But, unknown to Moss, there was drama behind the scenes.

It was about this time that Johnston and Warren Anderson claim to have discovered that Stein had been selling his shares in Firepower. Johnston claimed Stein had sold up to 6 million shares by using a rubber stamp of Johnston's signature to issue the share certificates to mum and dad investors. Johnston and Anderson argued the money belonged to them, but Stein disagreed. He said he had taken independent legal advice and had been told he had every right to sell his shares, and that he had been given permission by Johnston to use his signature.

Johnston had arranged to meet with Stein in Moscow to talk the matter over. Moss, who was unaware of the background, was at a distance as the men met in the hotel's restaurant. But Johnston wasn't alone during the meeting. He was accompanied by a former Australian army major named Shane Drew.

Drew's company, Majestic Services, doesn't appear in the Perth phone book. Drew was officially described as a 'management consultant' to Firepower, but he advised on such things as security arrangements in Johnston and Finnin's homes, and was a discreet presence during some shareholder meetings. He was also available to fly halfway around the world when Johnston wanted a witness to a meeting.

Two days later—on 17 November 2006—Stein resigned from Firepower.

'At a meeting on 15 November at the Swisshotel [*sic*] in Moscow Shane Drew holding himself out as the agent of Tim stated that Tim no longer wanted me to give legal advice in the capacity of Corporate Counsel,' Stein wrote to Johnston and Anderson. 'With a hope of coming to grips with the matters in dispute between us, I would ask that no further statements maligning my character be made to any person in or outside Firepower. I am certainly keeping the affairs and issues of Firepower of which I am privy confidential and am making no statements that in any way reflect negatively on either of you or Firepower.'

Whatever the issues were, the dispute was never settled and Stein would refer in later emails to threats of legal action made by Anderson. He also claimed in emails on 21 February 2007 that he was under 'daily intimidation to meet with Warren and "pay back" money I don't owe'.

Ignorant of the inner workings of Firepower, Moss continued his journey of exploration, next accompanying Johnston to Dublin. The detour to Ireland had been presented as an opportunity for Moss to meet Firepower's European-based employees, but it soon became clear that the real attraction was that the Wallabies were playing Ireland at the Lansdowne Road ground. Johnston hosted the players and the team's management at the team's hotel after the game, splashing around money for everyone's amusement.

The largesse continued. On 20 November, Johnston arranged for a private jet, at a cost of $160 000, to fly him and Moss to Zurich to save them having to stop over in London. In Zurich they were met by private car, and it was at this point that Johnston decided they didn't really need to turn up to the meetings that Finnin had arranged with the heads of the cantons and the bankers.

Rasmussen, the Austrade official who had organised the meetings, had been instructed by Firepower to stress that 'as one of the five directors of Macquarie Bank' Moss was 'a serious player'. The Swiss did take Moss seriously and were treating him as a guest of honour. When Johnston and Moss failed to show up for their meetings what was close to becoming a full-blown diplomatic incident ensued. Finnin, who was on his way to London to interview a potential new marketing chief, took a series of angry calls. He tried and failed to get through to Johnston. The phone kept going to voice message. 'When I couldn't get through I immediately thought the worst,' he says. 'I thought their plane had gone down.'

Moss, who recalls thinking that it made sense at the time that Johnston would be checking out Switzerland as his base given that most of his sales were meant to be in Europe, says he had no idea there were meant to be so many meetings. He wondered at the time why Finnin kept ringing and why Johnston refused to take the calls.

Krishan, Moss's partner, eventually got a frenzied call from Finnin on her mobile asking why the meetings were cancelled. She had no idea what he was talking about, and tried to hand the phone over to Johnston, but he refused to take the call, using hand signals to indicate that he didn't want to speak to his chief executive.

Johnston's increasingly bizarre and unexplained behaviour began to cost. He returned to Australia to find that his newly appointed chief financial officer Mark Dwyer had resigned after only four weeks in the job. Dwyer was a former senior BHP executive and part of the team that Finnin hoped would give the company some credibility.

'I am extremely uncomfortable about an implied valuation of the Firepower Group of approx $700 million,' Dwyer's resignation letter on 14 December 2006 to Johnston read. 'The message to shareholders and stakeholders of "operating in over 50 countries"; "an emerging brand that is already a global leader" . . . give the impression that we are generating revenues at levels far above what we are actually doing.

'I do not believe that a valuation of this level is supported by net tangible asset backing, short to medium term earnings multiples or even best case cash flow streams of existing contracts. The majority of the value is based on blue sky.

'Tim, two of your most admirable attributes are your absolute passion for the Firepower business and unquestionable belief in the huge success that the company will be. By just talking to you about the business, one can't help but be infected with that enthusiasm and optimism. However, I believe that these attributes can hinder your ability to present a balanced picture of the associated risks and volatility of the business to shareholders and other stakeholders.

'The most recent proposed shareholder newsletter is an example of this whereby all current potential upside opportunities are laid out, but little detail of the level of business that the operations are actually doing now.'

But Johnston was unrepentant, telling a gathering of about 250 shareholders at the Perth Convention Centre that very night: 'Right now there is so much money available in the world for green technology we are being swamped with groups and consortiums just wanting to get a slice of Firepower.'

Listening to a recording of Johnston that day, it's difficult to understand how anyone could have fallen for his repetitive patter, but the mood in Perth was mostly jovial. Ward, the financial advisor who did the introductions, described Johnston as a trustworthy family man: 'He is a very genuine, very sincere, look-you-in-the-eye kind of guy.'

Johnston told his audience what they wanted to hear: 'We have major, major contracts in many countries . . . Major manufacturing plants in Russia are now buying our products without their own trials and simply due to the sheer weight of success by other companies already using Firepower. In other words, companies are asking for Firepower by name due to its reputation.'

He assured them the further delay in the listing was only to allow Firepower to take advice on how to best realise the value of its carbon-trading arm. 'We have taken advice from all sorts of experts in the field and these are the sort of household names that you would know, wanting to be involved with the company,' he said. 'Only a few weeks ago I was called to The Lodge in Canberra for a private dinner with the prime minister, for the prime minister to ask how we can affect the Australian government's vision on the environment.'

Meanwhile, Finnin—who had just lost the man he had chosen to be his chief financial officer—was exploring other ways to shore up the levee. As the year came to a close, he met with Professor David Siddle, the deputy vice-chancellor for research at the University of Queensland, and Professor Matthew Walker, the university's dean of education, to discuss 'cooperative research arrangements with the university including a potential Linkage grant and a Firepower Chair at the university'. The plan according to an earlier email from Finnin to Johnston on 25 October 2006 was to create a 'Chair in combustion research' at the university that would give Firepower some of the credibility it so badly lacked.

'There are significant Federal and State Government funds available to us if we approach it right,' Finnin wrote.

Both men knew by then that something else was approaching. For weeks, Johnston had taken calls and emails from the *Sydney Morning Herald* asking for an interview to discuss Firepower's products and its new role as the biggest sporting sponsor in the country. Initially Johnston agreed to cooperate and he requested that questions be sent to him in writing. Johnston, in turn, sent the seventeen questions to Finnin, asking for his advice. 'I am deeply suspicious of this individual's motives,' Finnin wrote back to Johnston on 14 December 2006. 'These questions are not focused in and around sport. In fact it reeks of a "muck rake" . . . these questions are hostile in nature and I do not like the tone one little bit.'

Johnston decided not to answer the questions, ignoring further attempts to contact him.

17 BEHIND THE CURTAIN

January 2007 was not a good month for Johnston. Eight days into the year, the *Sydney Morning Herald* published on its front page the first of what eventually would be more than sixty articles that, step by step, stripped away the Firepower deceit. This first article focused on the mystery surrounding the new big sponsor in Australian sport and questioned whether the company was everything it claimed to be.

Finnin was hauled back from Europe and wheeled out to respond. His mood at the specially convened press conference in Sydney on 11 January was defiant. He denounced the attack on Firepower's authenticity and claimed he got an extra 100 kilometres a tank in his Maserati Quattroporto by adding the pill. 'There are three consequences from using our product; increased fuel efficiency, in some cases by as much as 20 to 30 per cent; lower emissions, in many cases by up to 50 per cent; and reduced costs on maintaining plant life,' he stated calmly. 'Ultimately our customers are the testimony to the success and potential of that product.'

Going against all his doubts and what he suspected to be true, Finnin said Firepower's revenue streams were healthy. 'We can't cope with the amount of people knocking on our door at the moment wanting to use our product. There are legions of customers out there who are willing to say this product works . . . otherwise why would we be selling it?'

He tried in vain to compare Firepower to Coca-Cola, saying the company was not prepared to reveal its secret ingredients: 'There is a stack that high of test results that I can show you and I am quite happy to give to you, scientific proof. Tests conducted by Shell, tests conducted by Volvo, tests conducted by TUV who do all the testing for Mercedes-Benz, tests conducted by Southwest Labs in Texas. I am quite happy to provide that documentation to you.'

But, when pressed, he made a poor job of spinning the company line:

Finnin: It makes the fuel burn better through greater atomisation.
Journalist: How does it do that, what does that mean?
It sounds like gobbledygook.
Finnin: Well, it may sound like gobbledygook but it's our intellectual property rights and I'm not about to tell you what those are.

Johnston was in his opulent Bali hideaway when the first newspaper article appeared. He suddenly became difficult to reach, complaining in an email of 'Bali belly', which added to the chaos behind the scenes. When he eventually emerged, he lied. Via a temporary media spokesman he named the former brush factory owner Ross Johnston—his New Zealand business associate since the days of Power Plan International in 1992—as the co-inventor of the Firepower formulas, claiming he was an 'industrial chemist'. The Firepower machines, he said via the spokesman, were 'manufactured by BAE [Systems] in Romania'—a vain attempt to link the British company with the fraudulent Australian minnow.

In an email to a senior Austrade official on 11 January, citing 'vested interests behind the smear campaign', Johnston began to rally support among the people who were happy to take his money. As legitimate question after legitimate question rained down upon Firepower in the *Sydney Morning Herald*, and the questions remained unanswered, Johnston wrote to Anderson, also on 11 January: 'The support we are receiving from around the world has been fantastic and we are on the front foot and getting on with business.'

Johnston headed off to Los Angeles, having been invited by South Sydney Rabbitohs director Peter Holmes à Court to dine with his fellow director, Russell Crowe, at the annual G'Day LA trade function organised by Austrade. Holmes à Court had wooed Johnston in an email on 9 January, saying: 'It's a great way to meet Russell . . . the room is 1200 people, top tables US$10 000, honouring Russell and in memory of Steve Irwin, on our table are Russell, Cathy Shulman (producer of *Crash*, last year's Oscar winner for best picture), Brett Godfrey and his wife, CEO of Virgin Blue.' The night, he said, would be 'definitely fun, possibly fantastic but nothing can be guaranteed'. Also enjoying the Mulataga yabby salad, Australian grain-fed beef and water imported from the Snowy Mountains at the Hyatt Regency Century Plaza was the cricketer Steve Waugh, by now a familiar dining companion.

The *Sydney Morning Herald* articles—which Johnston was still refusing to respond to—were on the discussion agenda.

'I am very encouraged that there will be a response from Firepower on the SMH story,' Holmes à Court's email continued. 'I thought it was a largely unprincipled piece of journalism but the unanswered questions about Firepower certainly have everyone talking. Frankly, if the article is not answered it will have major impacts for us as a business. We have a major government department who is nervous and awaits the all clear . . . I am very keen to be able to answer people with the passion that I have felt towards your product since day one, all I need are the facts to tackle the claims . . . I look forward to going to bat for you . . .'

Fraud investigators talk about a psychological phenomenon that they commonly encounter in victims of deception. The average human being, they say, will often rather listen to further lies from those who have perpetrated the fraud than contemplate the truth. They will first look in every direction other than the right direction, because to consider anything else is often just too painful. This seems to have applied in the case of Firepower's shareholders; not knowing what to believe, they failed to organise, and allowed themselves to be swept along in the flood of competing and contradictory information. 'I recommend a press release or a statement from you or your new CEO to stop this fool,' wrote Rod Saxby, a shareholder from Tasmania on 6 February. 'Spread the news that the products do work!'

Two days after the first article, Johnston issued a statement to shareholders which quickly became public saying the *Sydney Morning Herald* article was 'poorly researched, misleading in several respects . . . furthermore and on legal advice it may indeed be defamatory of me personally'. He repeated Finnin's false claim at the press conference that the products had been independently tested. 'The full suite of Firepower products has been independently tested in Australia and other countries, both by industry bodies and by customers. These include Dekra, Volvo etc . . . the testing process is both detailed and complex, often resulting in lengthy technical documents. Tests are carried out to set specifications to determine a variety of different performance indicators of our products, such as fuel efficiency, low emissions, lubricity [*sic*], atomisation amongst many others. All tests indicate definite improvements in these areas the most significant of which are greater fuel efficiency and lower emissions from using Firepower products.'

The statement, and threat of legal action, was enough to scare most other media away.

'As you are aware there has been a planned and orchestrated attempt from the *Sydney Morning Herald* to discredit us,' Johnston wrote to staff on 23 January. 'Other media have demonstrated a more balanced approach, such as the *West Australian* [newspaper] and the Australian Broadcasting Corporation.'

Other than the *Sydney Morning Herald*, only the news website *Crikey*—in particular, its veteran finance and economics commentator Michael Pascoe—the website www.dansdata.com and ABC Radio's *The Science Show* followed the Firepower story with any gusto. Pascoe added to the chorus of unanswered questions that mounted as the *Herald* continued to investigate.

Meanwhile, Firepower engaged defamation lawyer Mark O'Brien from Johnson, Winter & Slattery—the firm started by Kench, one of the former Sydney Kings syndicate members. Four defamation suits were issued against the *Herald*, two by Johnston and two by Finnin.

Finnin announced the move in a statement to shareholders on 16 February: 'I would first like to tell you how deeply offensive Firepower's Chairman, Tim Johnston and I have found the defamatory and untrue statements recently printed in the *Sydney Morning Herald*,' he said. 'It started on the 8th January when the SMH published an article that implied Firepower is a sham fuel technology business. Not only was this insulting to our many hard working and committed employees, but also to the many shareholders who conducted their own due diligence before investing in Firepower.

'Had the SMH been more thorough in its research it would have spoken to the many major mining companies and governments around the world who have, after conducting their own thorough tests, purchased a number of Firepower products because they generate significant, sometimes dramatic, increases in fuel efficiency. We will vigorously defend the company's reputation and promote our many strengths. Unlike some of the articles that have been written, we stick to the facts and good science.'

But no amount of spin could prevent the realisation slowly dawning: behind the curtain, there was no wizard.

Wilkinson Media is located on the fourteenth floor of a building in central Sydney, with views over the Harbour Bridge. Three framed newspaper articles against a white wall shout the achievements of the firm's principals, Peter and Claire Wilkinson. 'Business in crisis?' the sales pitch goes. 'Wilkinson Media is among the new breed of public relations companies that can dig you out.'

Three weeks after the first negative newspaper story appeared, Firepower had failed to address any of the questions that had been raised about the company. Wilkinson Media was brought in to help. Peter Wilkinson, a former *60 Minutes* and *Four Corners* reporter and producer, came highly recommended by Moss. They had once worked together on a book about fraud, *Fraud Busters*. With the benefit of hindsight, the book's blurb might have been summing up Johnston: 'Fraud . . . is not carried out in dark alleys nor is it carried out by people wearing balaclavas or carrying weapons,' it goes. 'It is perpetrated by articulate, presentable, credible people.'

Wilkinson drew up a multifaceted strategy to defend Firepower. According to a draft communication strategy dated

7 February 2007, his company would 'develop a profile of Tim Johnston, showing he is not the shady character described in the SMH but a normal and successful Aussie'. To do this they would target sports journalists as a 'soft' entrance into some media organisations and, 'where appropriate', they would utilise Firepower's sporting assets to entice unresponsive journalists to briefings and meetings. 'Though a journalist may not trust Firepower they may trust Steve Waugh, Matt Giteau etc,' the strategy reads.

It also played into Johnston's own explanation that vested interests were out to get him. Under a heading 'Threats', it said: 'There are powerful vested interests opposed to Firepower's activities. These include oil companies, who want to sell more fuel, not save it, and engine manufacturers, whose profits come from spare parts. These opponents are global players with decades of brand recognition and far-reaching influence.'

What followed was a series of press releases with headings such as 'The Sydney Morning Herald Got It Wrong' and 'NSW Supreme Court Will Hear Firepower Defamation Case'. Most journalists went away, but the regulatory authorities didn't.

The first sign of trouble came in early February when the Western Australian Department of Consumer and Employment Protection launched an inquiry into the fuel pill. It was the same department that had investigated the Fuel Magic pill back in 2000, though nobody knew about Johnston's connections to that. The department did know, however, having done a chemical analysis on the Firepower pill, that both pills contained ferrocene.

'We will have the pill tested by an appropriate authority and then determine what action we will take once the results are in,' Mike Johnson, manager of the motor vehicles branch of the department told the *Sydney Morning Herald* on 5 February. 'The department is always concerned about extravagant claims made about the performance of products when those claims are not supported by anything other than testimonial evidence.'

The inquiry caused consternation behind the scenes, not least because Firepower had just secretly had its pill tested by the respected Dutch firm TNO as part of a scheme to counter the *Sydney Morning Herald* articles. But the pill had failed to show any fuel savings or emissions reduction.

Rather than inform the state government department about the TNO test, Firepower instead sent off a threatening letter questioning the department's assertion that the Firepower pill was 'identical' to the Fuel Magic pill. 'It is of serious concern to us that you appear to have made up your mind about the efficacy of the Firepower pill based on prior case history and a chemical analysis,' Finnin wrote on 17 April. 'Please be aware that any announcement that you make against the Firepower pill has the potential to cause irreparable damage for which we may hold you liable.'

Firepower then offered to commission its own test on the pill, to be confidentially carried out by Orbital Australia Pty Ltd, and undertook to furnish the results—good or bad—to the department. 'We firmly believe that the pill increases fuel efficiency and reduces emissions,' Finnin continued. 'There is no prejudice possible to consumers by allowing us to complete the tests.'

Presented with the opportunity to save on expensive testing, and avoid potential legal action for damages if the pill was found to work, the department accepted the offer. Firepower had just bought itself several valuable weeks. But the pill was never submitted to Orbital for testing. So confident was Firepower that the liquids did what Johnston said they did—and knowing from TNO that the pill didn't work—the company submitted the liquids for testing instead.

* * *

In early February, leaving Finnin to handle the mess, Johnston flew to South Africa to watch the Western Force play a series of games in the Super 14 competition. He took Ross Graham and his accountant, Greg Coyle, along for the show. At games' end, on 18 February, the three men joined up with Western Force CEO Peter O'Meara and, at Firepower's expense, caught a first-class flight from Johannesburg to Moscow, where they stayed at the hideously expensive Swissôtel. The pretext of the three-day tour was for the guests to get an overview of Firepower's Russian operations—essentially a luxury office near the Kremlin. But a highlight was dinner with Grigory Luchansky at the pricey Turandot restaurant, described in newspaper reviews as one of the world's most unusual dining experiences.

From the inconspicuous entrance, patrons enter a huge, white marble Italian courtyard, then a circular two-storey cavern large enough to accommodate winter gardens, frescoes and a Ming dynasty vase collection. Bewigged and costumed musicians perform classical music beneath a mechanical peacock that whirls and flops—a grotesque hi-tech copy of the Peacock Clock at the Hermitage in St Petersburg. The cuisine is a fusion of Chinese and Japanese under the direction of London restaurateur Alan Yau, of Hakkasan and Wagamama fame. The wine list features bottles from all over the world, including many *grand cru* options, such as a Château Lafite Rothschild at about $3000 a bottle.

Johnston liked to impress, especially when he was asking for money. And before the month was out, he had secured the remaining $3 million of the $10 million investment he'd asked of Graham.

Despite Johnston's business-as-usual front, all was not well back in Australia. Moss recalls that the *Sydney Morning Herald* articles came at a time when Johnston and Anderson were at war with each other, having fallen out over the status of the

Mosman Park mansion. Johnston had sold the mansion for a Perth record price of $16 million, almost twice what Anderson's company, Owston Nominees No 2 Pty Ltd, had bought it for. 'So he goes and sells and . . . next minute he says, "Oh, I've got a problem with Warren. The property is in Warren's name",' Moss says. 'Bottom line is, two of them had a huge fight over land, a huge fight over sorting out their affairs, to the point where Warren rang me swearing profusely: "I want to talk to that effing such and such, he won't return my calls".'

Moss, who had been offered and declined the option of 20 million shares in Firepower by Johnston, organised a dinner at the Hilton Hotel to broker the peace. 'By this stage I made up my mind I am not going near this company, it is a basket case,' Moss continues. 'I had dinner with both of them at the Hilton and I told them, it is a joke, you have no financials, I don't believe you have patents, your staff are hopeless. How can it be, if the product works and you got buyers for it and you got capital and you got money in the bank, how come you are not signing contracts?

'And I said, "my simple logic on it, guys, is that you keep telling me this company is worth a billion or half a billion dollars. From what I can see it is worth 10 cents a share". And I said, it is even worse than that. No one can run a company as bad unless you are deliberately trying to run it into the ground. Those words I said, I still believe.'

Though maintaining a public persona of defiance, Finnin was also privately at loggerheads with Johnston. His announcement at the press conference that Firepower was not yet committed to a market listing had not gone down well with shareholders. 'There is a wave of anger building on this issue,' Finnin wrote to Johnston on 31 January 2007. 'We have canvassed the potential to create a secondary market [for Firepower shares]. This is clearly a furphy. The ability to do this is constrained by regulations that are as onerous as a public listing, so why would you do it?'

He told Johnston that many shareholders were now expressing their suspicion that Firepower was 'operating a scam' and that 'perfectly legitimate requests from shareholders' were simply being ignored. 'Why are shareholder funds being used to sponsor high profile sporting clubs, institutions and individuals when we have failed to provide progress towards an IPO, failed to provide financial statements and failed to clearly address the strategy behind such sponsorships? We must clearly address shareholder resentment on these matters.'

Finnin then warned of 'a number of potentially damaging scenarios' that would unfold quickly 'if we do not address these issues without further delay'. Shareholders could form an association to agitate for action, make a complaint to ASIC, instigate legal action or talk directly to the media. 'Any of these would be potentially catastrophic. Indeed one or more may already be inevitable.'

The private doubts and internal ructions were never revealed to shareholders. Instead, they were told that a new test would be conducted on the pill to satisfy the Department of Consumer and Employment Protection, even though according to Finnin Shell had tested the pill in 2004 'and found a 4.09 per cent' fuel saving. 'Some of you have asked why we haven't released this and other tests on the fuel pill,' Finnin wrote to shareholders on 16 February. 'Unfortunately many test results are protected by strict confidentiality agreements . . . the confidentiality agreements are designed to stop test results being misused in inappropriate promotions. Unfortunately it also limits our ability to defend ourselves.'

The dud pill wasn't the only problem. In mid-February, Finnin found out that an audit on Firepower's finances, which he had been led to believe was being conducted by KPMG, had stalled. KPMG had stopped work months earlier because it was owed more than $100 000 for previous work. This also came as unwelcome news to Huston, the lawyer who had been brought in to bring Firepower to a listing in London.

'A listing cannot be achieved without audited financial statements which is the most important task for the company to complete as soon as possible,' Huston wrote to Finnin on 7 March. 'Next following completion of that task is the preparation and completion of a business plan.'

Finnin was facing a massive storm. The pill was a fraud, there were no financials and there was no business plan. To make matters worse, Huston's legal advice was that the shareholders were entitled to look at the books.

Firepower attempted to counter the inclement weather by commissioning Wilkinson Media to organise an elaborate series of shareholder meetings in Perth, Sydney, Melbourne, Brisbane, Adelaide, Hobart and Darwin. The public relations firm scoured the country to find an academic who was prepared to say the pill had potential fuel-saving qualities. After several qualified scientists turned them down, including experts from the University of Queensland, they settled on Dr Stephen Hall from the School of Mechanical and Manufacturing Engineering at the University of New South Wales. Hall, who charged $1600, plus $200 an hour for speaking to the media, was not an expert on fuel-saving devices. In fact, he had only ever conducted one fuel-saving experiment. But Wilkinson Media didn't ask him to find out if the pill worked; it merely asked him to review the results of previous tests that had been presented by Firepower. Hall found fault with them, but none of his concerns were made public.

What was presented to shareholders was a relatively unscientific one-off test in which Hall measured the calorific value of a container fuel that had the pill added to it. In other words, he measured how much energy was released from the fuel once it was burned. Hall found that the pill might have added 1 per cent of calorific value to the fuel, which, in scientific terms, meant very little if anything. Rather than say this though, Firepower issued a press release with a generic quote from Hall: 'Increased power allows a car to use less fuel for a given trip, therefore improving fuel economy.'

For the shareholder meetings, which began on 3 March, a tactical decision was made that only Finnin would speak, with Johnston being restricted to visual recordings played at predetermined intervals. The meetings also featured live crosses to Gregory Klumov in Russia, who assured shareholders the multimillion-dollar contracts were in place.

Finnin began each of the carefully choreographed meetings with an apology for the 'utterly inadequate' communication to shareholders. 'Firepower is a company built on the vision of one man, Tim Johnston, and his amazing ability to generate business,' he continued. 'It is also built on your money. You have invested in Tim's dream, and for that I congratulate you.'

The shareholder meetings succeeded in dampening, if not extinguishing, shareholder concern, but further trouble was just around the corner. On 2 April 2007, the *Sydney Morning Herald* carried a story saying that the Australian Securities and Investments Commission was investigating Firepower.

Wilkinson urged Firepower not to overreact. 'There is not a lot in this SMH story other than the announcement of the inquiry which we are already aware of,' he counselled Johnston via email. 'Contact Russell Crowe and Peter Holmes à Court and brief them on our strategy.'

A few days later, Orbital delivered its verdict.

18 THE
MONEY PIT

It was Ross Graham, the mining magnate, who kept Firepower alive. But having handed over $10 million by the end of February 2007, to allow Johnston to sort out the non-existent carbon credit side of the business, Graham was suddenly confronted by the reality that Johnston owed money everywhere.

The news came in a series of phone calls. 'I started receiving calls from creditors of the Defendant [Firepower] complaining that contractual obligations that Johnston had entered into had not been honoured,' Graham later told the Federal Court in July 2008. 'In particular, I received telephone calls threatening to commence proceedings or to wind up the Defendant and the Firepower business.'

That caller was Tim Miles from Tasman Motorsports, the V8 racing car team that Firepower sponsored and whose other director was Moss's friend James Henderson from Dynamic Sports and Entertainment Group, which at that point was still supposed to be managing Firepower's many sponsorships but was also owed money. The court documents reveal that Miles informed Graham that the Tasman team was owed $1.3 million, and that he 'was an insolvency expert . . . and would have no difficulty in causing trouble for Firepower'.

Tasman had never breathed a word publicly about the fact that it wasn't being paid. In fact, there had been a deathly silence from most of the Firepower-sponsored sports teams and personalities in response to the stories that continued to be published by the *Herald*.

One exception was Peter Holmes à Court, who publicly defended Firepower, stating in the *Sydney Morning Herald* on 8 August 2007 it had met all its obligations to the Rabbitohs and that 'they have been good to work with'. He said the ASIC inquiry into Firepower was a 'non issue' for the club because 'they have met all of their obligations in a seven-figure sponsorship'. Holmes à Court's line was consistent with his earlier press release of 9 November 2006 welcoming Firepower on board as a sponsor: 'Two of the biggest issues in the world today are harmful fuel emissions and rising fuel prices. Firepower has developed the technology to tackle all these issues head on. As we speak, Firepower's fuel technology is helping leading industries around the globe to enhance automotive performance, improve fuel technology, lower maintenance costs and increase equipment life—culminating in a reduction in environmental impact. Russell and I have been particularly keen to take the club forward in a socially responsible fashion and Firepower certainly fulfills [*sic*] that criteria. Firepower is an Australian success story, operating in 50 countries globally and currently expanding rapidly to new markets. Firepower is an emerging brand that is already a global leader in its category. Like Souths, Firepower is prepared to roll its sleeves up and invest in the future—we welcome their support.'

The other defender of Firepower was the Western Force.

On 20 January 2007 in the *Sydney Morning Herald*, Peter O'Meara, the club's chief executive, said the *Herald*'s questioning and scrutiny of Firepower was jeopardising the good work the company did for sport in Australia. 'This is putting at risk some relationships that exist in Australian sport and if you continue to pursue the angle, how is it in the interests of Australian sport or the promotion of Australian sport?' The consistent line from the Western Force club spokesman was: 'They pay their bills, and we are comfortable with our sponsorship.'

But the Federal Court documents show that Shane Richardson, Johnston's old rugby teammate from his schooldays in Brisbane and the then chief executive officer of the Rabbitohs, was one of the creditors on the phone to Graham. So too were 'some of the rugby players from the Western Force' and Johnston's own public relations man, Peter Wilkinson, whose firm had billed Firepower for hundreds of thousands of dollars. Internal firepower emails show how some of the sportsmen who were initially happy to climb on board the Firepower fairytale later scrambled to rewrite their private deals after questions were raised about Firepower's alleged fuel technology.

For instance, Force coach John Mitchell was getting a payment valued at $100 000 a year from Firepower. The three-year agreement, which began in October 2006 but was ended early at Mitchell's insistence, allowed him 'to be paid in full or convert part of the fee to a combination of [Firepower] shares and/or personal holiday travel'. He had initially decided to take $60 000 in cash and $40 000 worth of Firepower shares, according to one document. But only days after the *Herald*'s first critical story his agent, John Fordham, asked that the contract be changed. He now wanted the whole amount in cash. 'John Mitchell will review his position concerning shares when the company determines its listing position,' Fordham wrote. Western Force player Scott Staniforth, who was getting

$50 000 a year in payments from Firepower, also later requested his payment in shares be varied. The documents indicate that, until the *Herald* began writing about Firepower, neither the Australian Rugby Union nor the Western Force was even aware of all of the agreements in which its employees were entangled. In the days after the *Herald*'s first story, Fordham wrote to then Force CEO Peter O'Meara informing him that Firepower had deals with Ryan Cross and Cameron Shepherd.

'I had been meaning to provide you with this background before the start of the Super 14 season,' he said, 'but because of the recent publicity concerning Firepower, I thought it appropriate to bring this forward. These arrangements are based on each player's future career development and will involve them in making occasional appearances for Firepower that will not in any way involve above-line advertising or the usage of the intellectual properties of the Western Force or the Australian Wallabies. I felt comfortable making these private arrangements in view of Firepower being a major sponsor and supporter of the Western Force.' All of the sportsmen eventually appeared to have trouble getting paid, a fact repeatedly denied publicly at the time.

An email from Johnston to Graham, dated 14 March 2007, shows that Firepower was having trouble even meeting its payroll. 'Unfortunately we did not finish our chat last week about finances and investment mate,' Johnston wrote. 'As we discussed . . . it is difficult to forecast to the exact week when the actual large payments from Europe will begin. We do know that once they start the entire company globally is profitable and can fund the expansion itself. (Then watch the share price go through the roof).

'However short term we need your help mate. Our immediate needs are for about $700 000 please . . . Rosco I thought I would put this in writing for you to consider today as we need your help due for payroll this Friday . . . Thanks again for your genuine support and friendship Rosco. See Ya, Timmy.'

In late March and early April 2007, Graham began to make his own inquiries about the financial position of Firepower, canvassing opinions from staff—including Finnin, who expressed his concern that all the investors were about to lose their money.

'I recall discussing the large number of overdue creditors with Johnston in or around March 2007,' Graham later told the Federal Court. 'Johnston assured me he was still pursuing a listing on the AIM board in London but that he needed more money to continue to keep the Firepower business running. He also said to me words to the effect that: "The contracts in Russia and other areas haven't come through as we expected but they are still coming, everything is still sweet, it's all go. It just hasn't happened yet."

'About that time I made a decision that because of my previous investment and because 1200 other investors had put money into the Firepower business, in order to get the Firepower business to a float so that all of the investors got a return on their funds, I would make available another sum to a maximum of ten million dollars to the Defendant.'

Graham's continued support had followed his signing of the joint venture with Johnston to exclusively distribute Firepower products in Australia, New Zealand and the Pacific Islands. This involved the formation of yet another company, called Firepower Australia Pacific. It was the announcement of the formation of this company that had prompted the phone calls from creditors.

Johnston had sold Graham on the idea of an exclusive deal to distribute Firepower products, but had failed to mention the other agreements that were already in place. Then it emerged that Johnston had also sold the marketing rights for the fuel pill to Stephen Moss, the 23-year-old entrepreneurial son of Bill Moss. This prompted Graham to fly to Sydney, meeting Stephen Moss at the Westin Hotel.

'Ross Graham appears on the scene,' recalls Bill Moss. 'Ross has his accountant and they try to heavy Steve. They say, "You don't have the rights, we have just bought it." Stephen says, "No, I have the rights, I have a contract." Turns out they both have contracts. So, it has been sold twice.'

Stephen Moss's plan had been to sell the fuel pill across the country, using radio and newspaper promotions that would have involved giving away free samples through the *Daily Telegraph*. But before he could begin, Firepower issued a blanket recall on the product.

The reason for the recall was to allow Firepower to blindside the inquiry into the pill by the Western Australian Department of Consumer and Employment Protection by arguing that the recall meant consumers were no longer at risk and therefore the department was acting outside its jurisdiction and wasting taxpayer money by continuing to take an interest. Why the desperate change in strategy? Firepower had just received a copy of the Orbital test on the liquid product, the report it had hoped would deflect any doubts over the veracity of its fuel-saving claims. It knew the department was due a copy, as per the legal agreement, though this didn't happen for another month. There was good reason for the delay: Orbital had found the liquid didn't work.

Firepower was running on empty.

At the prospect of impending doom, life can sometimes acquire a wilder flavour, a strange sense of perspective.

Finnin hoped that if he could just buy some more time, he might be able to pull off a miracle and turn the company around. It would, after all, take just one of Johnston's big contracts to come good. He bought that time at the shareholder meetings by promising to produce a full set of figures to investors by 30 September 2007. He figured, correctly, that the shareholders were as desperate as he was and would allow them six months of breathing space.

But reality soon rained down on him like a hot meteor shower. Until now he had largely been excluded from Firepower's finances. Now internal figures showed the operation was burning between $1.2 million and $1.5 million a month. He couldn't be sure where even the next dollar was going to come from; the company was effectively at a standstill. Superannuation contributions weren't being paid, creditors were investigating legal options, and many trading accounts were either withdrawn or on hold, including those of the chemical blenders and the freight companies.

In this atmosphere, on 16 April Finnin was called to a meeting at the Westin Hotel in Sydney with Johnston and Graham and their legal representatives. Both parties agreed it wasn't working out. 'We agreed on a termination payment,' Finnin reveals, 'and a deed for this was drawn up.' The severance package came to about $3 million, but was never paid. Other events would provide Johnston with an excuse not to bother. In May, members of the Victoria Police knocked on Finnin's door with a search warrant and took away his computers. He was being accused of child-sex offences, a matter that would eventually reach the courts and be made public.

For now, Finnin kept the matter private and continued in his role as the loyal chief executive, marvelling at Johnston's boundless optimism. Just weeks after the meeting at the Westin Hotel, Johnston wrote to Finnin from Britain where he and his wife were spending increasing amounts of time in five-star hotels and executive apartments in upmarket Mayfair: 'Great meetings in London, will update you asap. Please do not appoint an auditor until we discuss. The reason is that certain NomAds and brokers in London prefer and have certain relationships.'

But Finnin had already approached Ernst & Young and PricewaterhouseCoopers to provide quotes on a cost and pro-posed time frame for the global audit. He passed on Johnston's news to them, but not very convincingly. 'There are plans to raise a further $20 million to enable us to meet our IPO requirements,' he wrote to Ernst & Young on 18 May. 'I am assured by the chairman that this is being done now. On his return from London yesterday, I have been told this has been accomplished.'

But no money had been raised, and both of the big auditing firms eventually declined to do the audit because of Firepower's risk profile. Finnin had been unable to supply key information to the auditors because he himself had been unable to obtain it from Firepower.

Any inkling Finnin may have had about being on the outer was confirmed in an email from Johnston to senior Firepower staff on 31 May 2007 in which, without prior warning and after weeks of being what Finnin described to me as 'in virtual hiding' from senior management, he announced the creation of another new joint venture called Firepower International. 'Firepower International has extensive connections throughout the world and will work with us to develop the business around the world, including China, Europe, USA, Mexico, Middle East and other regions,' wrote Johnston. 'Firepower International will operate across many regions specifically targeting large international clients. This can range from large steel works in China to the government of Mexico to ships in Greece as well as the pill sales.'

In effect, Finnin says, Johnston had just created a shadow Firepower. And had done so without any consultation.

'I saw the issue as another attempt by Johnston to simply

abdicate his responsibilities as chairman and once again engage in flights of fancy,' Finnin says. 'It was another sign of a man seriously deluded as to his own capability and ability to manage a business quickly descending into high farce. He simply wasn't capable and the email was more about him, his state of mind, than it was ever about anything else.'

Firepower International was Stephen Moss and his business partner, Corey Cooney. 'Mr Bill Moss has also agreed to join the board and offer his support,' Johnston enthused in the 31 May email. 'In the next few weeks Steven [sic] and Bill will be travelling to a number of countries and will have discussions with our management in these regions to inform them of our relationship and the potential clients of their territory . . . Please join me in welcoming Stephen, Bill, and Corey to the Firepower team.'

According to Bill Moss, Firepower International came about after his son confronted Johnston over the original contract for the rights to the pills. 'Stephen comes back and tells me, "I have got this deal, not only has he given me the rights to Australia, he has given me the rights to the world,"' Bill Moss recalls. 'My advice to him was: don't you go anywhere near this.' He says his son didn't listen.

Though Johnston continued to talk up the possibility of getting the company listed in London by September 2007, the financial crisis was deepening.

'Gents, please note we have a requirement for $2.9 million this week and a cash at bank balance of $88k, a significant shortfall,' wrote Gary Conwell, the company's chief financial officer to Finnin and other senior managers, on 11 June. 'We have a very large Tsunami of creditors that have run out of patience and we are being gazetted by D&B [Dun & Bradstreet, providers of credit information] for non payment of creditors which will cause further final demands and potential legal action to be taken. I am concerned that this will ultimately cascade into a downward spiral that we will not be able to control.'

The person who came to the rescue time and time again was Ross Graham, the mining magnate. Court documents show that on 14 and 15 May 2007 he authorised money transfers of $1.4 million. The significance of the dates was that the fifteenth of every month was when everyone associated with Firepower got paid. This included the staff, Johnston's contractors around the world, the Sydney Kings basketball team, the rugby players Johnston sponsored at the Western Force and what was left of his other sponsorships.

In June, Graham transferred another $1.6 million, prompting a grateful note on 20 June from Finnin. 'I wanted to thank you for ensuring the Waite Group [a recruitment company that was a major creditor] got paid and indeed that the salaries of the local Australian staff also got paid,' he wrote. 'I am extremely grateful for your continued patience and forbearance under what must be trying circumstances for you. Your support and continued good faith is both admirable and most welcome at a crucial time for the business. I know you must be "tearing your hair out", what's left of it. Welcome to my world.'

On 11 July, four days before the next pay cycle for the staff and sportspeople, Graham authorised the transfer of another $1.5 million; on 20 July another $300 000; on 24 July, another $240 000; and on 27 July another $400 000. The cycle continued into August and September, with the transfer of another $2.25 million, until the total of his loans reached $8 455 000 'for the purpose of enabling the Defendant to make payment of debts due to various creditors'. He would eventually be owed $25 million.

According to Federal Court documents, Johnston was still overseas during this period, supposedly raising money for the proposed listing—the time frame for which had now blown out to November 2007.

'I recall speaking to Johnston,' Graham told the court. '[He] told me words to the effect that: "I have four lots of $5 million from four joint-venture partners around the world. There is that much money over here I don't know which money to take first. Some people are talking about taking $20 million, there are money trees everywhere. The first $10 million that I raise is coming back to you Ross".' Internal Firepower emails show that Johnston remained untroubled by the problems at home. For the Rugby World Cup in France in September and October 2007 he booked accommodation in thirteenth-century castles—one was a nineteen-bed mansion with a swimming pool built into an ancient trout basin—for himself and a party of more than ten. He flew by private jet to the group games in Montpellier and Bordeaux, and the quarter-final games in Marseilles. The emails show he booked Chateau de Montelegre, promoted as 'a medieval jewel beckoning from the thirteenth century' that cost £11 375 for the dates of 22 September to 9 October. Johnston's secretary then organised other accommodation closer to Paris from 9 October to 23 October for the semi-finals and asked Johnston to choose between the Domaine de Montreveil, costing £14 886, or the less luxurious Chateau de Foulz at £8549.

Johnston had been hailed as a messiah when he first appeared on the basketball scene, but now people weren't so sure.

A few weeks after he bought the Sydney Kings, Johnston had walked into the humble Alexandria Basketball Stadium and proudly watched his team train. After the session, the players gathered at his feet and he enthralled them with stories about the fuel technology contracts he had all over the world. He told them how his company was about to list on the stock exchange in London and they were all about to enter a new era of endless promise that would see them play tournaments abroad. 'We all walked away thinking, "Wow, this is big time",' one player later told the *Sydney Morning Herald* on 31 May 2008. 'This is a major corporation that wants to be involved with us. He sold it unbelievably well.'

Kings coach Brian Goorjian says Johnston talked about how he [Goorjian] was going to be in charge of identifying talent from around the world to bring to the Kings. 'African players,' he says, 'I was going to be a world agent.'

Johnston offered a prize for the coveted player-of-the-season award: a pair of business-class seats on a plane to Bali for a free stay in his holiday mansion, complete with a driver, a chef and a maid.

Johnston took full control of the Kings in February 2007 and purchased a set of leather armchairs for the sidelines so he could view his team in comfort. But as time went on, the players saw less of their owner. He was always doing a big deal somewhere. One day it was in China, the next in Russia. 'We all thought, "This just gets better and better",' one player told the *Sydney Morning Herald* in the May 2008 article.

Administratively, however, the Kings was in chaos. What had started as a $1.3 million debt when Johnston walked in the door began to get worse. 'For the life of me I can't understand why he did no due diligence before buying the team,' one former member of the Kings staff says. 'There was all this talk about an international competition, a sort of champion-of-champions tournament. But there were invoices left in drawers for $80 000 that were unpaid and he never enforced a system to get on top of it.'

Insiders say the franchise was insolvent from June 2007, almost three months out from the new basketball season, and possibly earlier than that. A liquidator would later find it had been insolvent from the moment Johnston walked in.

But Johnston allowed the Kings to continue to trade, and the National Basketball League continued to maintain the club was meeting its financial commitments. To admit that the competition's biggest club and biggest television drawcard had problems would have been to risk the entire 2007/08 season.

From the time of the ownership switch, the players began receiving their monthly payments late. At first it was just a few days, then a week. Rarely would the sum arrive on time. Yet amidst the boundless optimism, it seemed hardly worth worrying about.

Things only started to go noticeably awry when Johnston proposed a grandiose basketball trip to China in July. He told the players he could use them to leverage deals in China and Indonesia, a percentage of which would go straight to the Kings' operational budget. The proposal had the players excited, but they naturally wanted to be paid for their time. Johnston promised them $1000 each for the week they would be away. An estimated 50 million television viewers watched the Kings play in China, with one of their opponents, Chinese superstar Yao Ming, a major drawcard. But it would be another six months before the players saw their money, and then it was only half what they'd been promised.

When the season started, the problems continued. The wages were late but nobody could ever reach Johnston; credit cards were being used to pay off credit cards. Rumours began to circulate that contractors weren't being paid—the cheer-leaders, the Sydney Entertainment Centre, the guy who announced the games, media companies, advertising agencies, the rent on the apartment for the American import players. By January 2008 the Kings were in full-blown crisis with its front office in chaos and creditors lining up outside the door. Players, their bank accounts empty, would go to their captain, Jason Smith, on the fifteenth of every month—the date they were meant to be paid—and ask if he had heard anything.

Smith felt awful. He tried to extract information from the owners but felt he was being spun one lie after another. There was always an excuse. Money was always about to be transferred from Europe or somewhere else. He and the players were offered 100 000 free shares in Firepower as a form of apology. But, by now wary of Johnston and his wife Sandra, who was getting increasingly involved in the day-to-day running of the club, the captain decided not to tell his fellow players about the offer, figuring the shares were worthless anyway.

Brian Goorjian describes how in the days leading up to the fifteenth of the month everyone associated with the team started to get anxious. 'No one could ever get a hold of Tim, or he was in Russia or on his way back from London,' he says. 'Then the fifteenth of the month would come around and there was no money there . . . and I'm getting calls. The rent on the stadium where we train hadn't been paid, the caller at the games hadn't been paid, the phones had been turned off, Foxtel had been turned off . . . there were people putting stuff on their own credit cards . . . I was a nervous wreck all the time. I had no understanding of what Firepower was, nor did the players. It wasn't something we could see or touch.'

Johnston also offered Goorjian Firepower shares—250 000 of them—by way of compensation. But the coach just shook his head. 'My code was broken when I lost my code with the players. In twenty-two years, I have never let the guys down in that form . . . I felt like a horse's ass a lot of the time. So I went back to the team and said "this is all shit".'

Two weeks into January, with the team topping the National Basketball League ladder, and despite all the off-court dramas, boasting one of the best win-loss records in its history, Goorjian gathered the players at the Alexandria stadium training ground. They decided that to beat Firepower they would have to win the championship.

'We resolved that after you win the thing, your value goes a lot higher as a player and we'd see the season out,' one unnamed Kings player later told the *Sydney Morning Herald*. 'We decided nothing can penetrate us, our playing group, no matter what happens. We played on.'

The beginning of the end of the relationship between Firepower and the Rabbitohs came in late August 2007 when the allegations against Finnin were made public in the Melbourne Magistrates Court. It was revealed that police had searched Finnin's Sandringham home on 15 May and taken away a computer. Finnin had appeared in court to try to retrieve the computer and it was then that the nature of the allegations against him came out. Though he denied the accusations— and Firepower issued a statement saying he had a right to a presumption of innocence and had yet to be charged—Finnin was dumped as chief executive that day. The allegations and his dumping made front-page news and would appear to have been the last straw in the strained relationship between the Rabbitohs and its sponsor.

Under the three-year agreement drawn up for the Rabbitohs, the club was to receive 50 per cent of all gross profits made from any business brought to Firepower. This secret sales commission was on top of the company's widely publicised $1 million a year sponsorship deal.

The initial plan had been to brand and market the Firepower pills using images of the Rabbitohs players. 'Peter Holmes à Court has asked if he and Russell can get a supply of pills to test/promote,' reads one email sent by Christopher Green, an employee of a firm hired by Firepower, to Tim Johnston on 6 October 2006, shortly before Crowe revealed the Firepower sponsorship to millions of viewers on the Jay Leno television show in the United States. 'They are both very enthusiastic about the potential of the pill and want to try it for themselves. Can we get a box sent to Souths? Peter has already begun his sales role, he's in Fiji on holidays and sent me a note saying he'd had dinner with a ship owner who buys two million gallons of diesel a year, and he wants a trial ASAP. Peter says he knows many of the largest ship owners in the world and he'll be tapping them all for Firepower.'

But, like the pills themselves, the planned contract with the Rabbitohs was legally flawed. It was drawn up using a company name—Firepower Pty Ltd—that bore no relationship to Firepower. The name was borrowed from a small family business in Queensland that installs security screens—and married with a false Australian Company Number. Quite amazingly, nobody checked these details.

Green, who later went to work with Holmes à Court at a company called The Passionate Group, says no Firepower product was ever sold. 'The 50 per cent gross profits was a standard clause in all their sponsorship contracts—or so they told us—and we never received a cent from this initiative as we didn't try to make any sales,' he says. 'The reference to Peter speaking to shipping companies in Fiji was not entirely accurate. Peter was in Fiji on holidays at the time the email was sent and I was engaging in some banter with a new sponsor. We did request some pills to try, but we were unable to draw any conclusions from the tests on the pills and formed no opinion about the product ever.'

In October 2007, the Rabbitohs took the unprecedented step of dumping Firepower as a sponsor, something that had never happened before in the NRL competition. Several existing and prospective new sponsors were unhappy with the continued association between the club and the negative headlines generated by Firepower. 'We've taken an opportunity to move on,' Holmes à Court told ABC television's *Lateline* business program on 24 October. 'How the company conducts themselves among their investors is really not my business. I just should be appreciative that these guys took a risk with us, they helped provide the platform that now makes us the number one most marketable team in rugby league.'

The Western Force was not so courageous. By May 2007, the *Sydney Morning Herald* had begun exposing the web of secret payments involving the players at the club and the links between those players, some Western Force staff and Firepower. The newspaper also reported that some of the players and the club weren't being paid sponsorship monies owed them by Firepower—stories the Western Force and Firepower vehemently denied.

There was speculation that some of the players, including Matt Giteau, were reconsidering their careers, and this too was reported. But when other newspapers came across the same information and tried to publish it, the stories were denied. Internal Firepower email correspondence from late May shows that when the *Australian* asked questions about whether the sponsorships were being honoured, the newspaper was misled.

It would later emerge in the Federal Court that the stories were, in fact, true. Ross Graham revealed he'd had another meeting with Johnston in November 2007 where he was asked for more money to pay the rugby players and the Western Force. Graham handed over another $1.3 million in December. It included $605 000 for Matt Giteau, $170 000 for Drew Mitchell, $110 000 for Scott Staniforth, $70 000 for the player agent John Fordham (an invoice on behalf of a client), and $200 000 for the Western Force.

A happy last Christmas from the self-proclaimed Santa Claus.

EPILOGUE

A variety of theories have been advanced to explain how a fraud the size of Firepower came about.

Some of those most intimately involved with the company have been accused by each other at one time or another of plotting to bring it down. Each, it was said, wanted to drive Firepower into liquidation in order to purchase the remnants of the business cheaply. The premise for this theory was that the fuel-saving technology worked but Tim Johnston—or someone else, depending on who was telling the tale—deliberately suppressed results that showed marvellous fuel savings, intending to defraud Firepower investors out of the rights to the technology.

At one point, Johnston persuaded Bill Moss that Les Stein was behind a plot to discredit Firepower, and produced an email claiming that Stein was the source of the *Sydney Morning Herald* stories. Johnston told John Finnin that Moss was in fact the source of the negative stories. Yet he told mining magnate Ross Graham that Moss was circling Firepower like a corporate shark—a story that enabled Johnston to swindle almost

$25 million from Graham. Meanwhile, Warren Anderson claimed it was Graham who was trying to take over the company.

It was all complete nonsense. But throughout 2007 the conjecture continued. The wilder theories were fed by Firepower's various and disparate political and military connections, such as the intimate dinners Johnston enjoyed at the residence of then Australian Prime Minister John Howard; his hiring of the US lobbyist James Wholey; his connection to a Chinese arms dealer; his relationship with the former Romanian diplomat George Teleman; from Johnston's claimed links, however tenuous or unsubstantiated, to agencies like the CIA and the KGB.

One former Firepower contractor, who declined to be identified, swore privately that tests done by the Russian military had staggering implications for armed services worldwide and that the White House had stepped in to ensure they never saw the light of day. The Firepower liquids had the ability to allow entire armies to cover vast distances with greater efficiency, at the same time virtually eliminating the need for the servicing of vital engine components. Whoever had access to this technology would have a critical advantage during any potential conflict, and the Americans certainly didn't want it in the hands of their old Cold War foe.

A former Firepower employee, who also declined to be named, suggested that Guenter Nolte, who headed up Firepower's European operations and was close to Frank Timis, the Romanian-Australian businessman, had obtained fantastic results from a leading European testing agency. But, the story goes, he was withholding the results until he was paid money owed to him by Johnston.

Though there was no evidence to back up any of the supposition, and stories about Johnston had been appearing in the *Sydney Morning Herald* for more than twelve months, some people—most of all the shareholders—were simply unwilling to believe that Firepower was a fraud—most likely the biggest, and certainly the most spectacular, in Australian history. These shareholders had never received anything that even resembled a proper disclosure of the risk involved. Fewer of them had any real knowledge about the fuel-saving technology industry. They simply relied on the word of others—most often that of trusted financial advisors. Johnston played on the fact that most people were so keen to jump on the chance to make money that they wouldn't stop to check the facts.

Deirdre Clark worked for Quentin Ward from 2005 to 2007 as one of his front-office staff in Perth and was there during the period he offered Firepower shares to his clients in his role as financial advisor. She recalls that people were falling over themselves to get the shares. During a two-week period in early 2006, just before Firepower was again supposed to list, she witnessed firsthand the frenzied buying.

'I'd get phone calls saying, "Oh I want to put money in, keep it [the share offer] open, tell Quentin to keep it open",' she would tell the *Four Corners* program in July 2008. 'So it was exciting times, I suppose, and we all got carried away with the hype of it.'

Clark piled in herself, purchasing hundreds of thousands of dollars worth of the useless stock at ever increasing prices. She told *Four Corners* that when Firepower didn't list, 'they always had excuses, they always had reasons and they were good reasons. I'm trying to think of one now . . . just off the top of my head I can't think of a reason'.

Many high-profile sporting figures were caught up in the same staggering tale of deceit. They too rushed headlong over a cliff, as internal Firepower documents attest. Some of the personal agreements with individual sportsmen were highly questionable. For instance, one Wallaby player (it is unclear from the documents who) entered a $50000-a-year sponsorship deal with the same fake Firepower entity—Firepower Pty Ltd—as the Rabbitohs had done. The 'heads of agreement' allowed for 5 per cent commission on the value of all business the player brought to Firepower, on top of the $50000 annual payment.

It was the same modus operandi Johnston had used with Austrade, when he got the taxpayer-funded agency to enter into a service agreement with a company called Firepower Group Pty Ltd, which didn't exist. Johnston's story has almost fairytale qualities. It was as if he was deliberately leaving a trail of breadcrumbs as he set off on his destructive journey. It was almost as if he wished someone to follow him, and catch him.

By March 2008, as the Sydney Kings marched into the play-off finals, the club's financial problems began filling the back pages of the national dailies. And the story behind the story—Firepower—gained traction in every major media outlet in the country. It helped that Goorjian and the Kings players weren't afraid to say they weren't being paid either their salaries or their superannuation, despite threats by Johnston to take legal action against them for speaking out.

The plight of the basketball players brought home to the public for the first time the danger that Firepower posed to the various sporting codes they loved—that all that once-easy money may ultimately exact a terrible price. In this atmosphere of uncertainty, the Kings made it all the way to the five-match National Basketball League finals against the Melbourne Tigers. Having staged what is generally regarded as the greatest comeback in NBL history in the fourth game to give themselves a chance at the title, they lost the fifth and deciding game. In the public's eyes, they were champions anyway.

During the period of the finals, captain Jason Smith had been calling the Kings' front office, unwilling to give up on the issue of the players' pay. By this point, the Kings had only one full-time administrative staff member left—an associate of Johnston's. The other employees had resigned. Smith's calls were ignored, as were his emails. And whenever he called Sandra Johnston, he'd hear her say: 'Hello? Hello? Hello? Can't hear you. Hello?' before she hung up.

In May, Smith took the issue to the Industrial Relations Commission, forcing the hand of a seemingly reluctant NBL. The NBL, which had bent its rules about owners having to live in the home city of their team to grant Johnston his ownership licence, was clearly afraid about what might happen to the league without its most popular franchise. Now, the NBL threatened to cancel Johnston's licence unless he paid up.

Johnston continued to dally and fib until finally, on 12 June 2008, a liquidator was appointed to the franchise. After twenty years, the Kings were dead.

The Western Force players and other creditors, previously reluctant to talk, suddenly came out with their own tales of financial woe. It emerged that Firepower owed money everywhere—to players, to teams, to suppliers. But by now, Johnston was nowhere to be seen. He had abandoned his $5 million palatial mansion on the Gold Coast, where he had lived since selling his Perth abode, and flown out of Australia only days before the Kings went under. He took up residence in a rented upmarket apartment in London's Park Lane, with occasional first-class flights to his lavish Bali holiday retreat. Johnston refused to answer questions from the Kings' court-appointed liquidator and was soon threatened with arrest. But it was a hollow threat given he was abroad and quite clearly had no intention of returning home.

The only Firepower-related person to appear at this time was Warren Anderson. On 18 June 2008 in the *Australian*, Anderson came to Johnston's defence, claiming the fuel technology had been unfairly demonised. He admitted the pill was 'not so bloody good' but claimed that Firepower's other products could deliver huge windfalls to shareholders and that Johnston had been, in the words of the newspaper, stitched up by the Kings and by the Western Force. 'Tim was good enough to step in and help out the Kings and the Western Force when they were in need and now because he can't continue they're turning on him,' he said. 'Forget the millions he's given them, they're kicking him in the guts.'

Anderson said Johnston was a 'decent bloke' whom he considered a friend, and that he was in London trying to raise additional funds from overseas investors with the view to listing Firepower. 'Tim's made some terrible mistakes, I'm not saying he's the best runner of business,' Anderson continued. 'But he's not a crook, he's not a share ramper, he's not trying to steal from the company, he's just trying to get this thing across the line.'

No one else showed any sympathy for Johnston. The international media latched onto the colourful tale and were soon referring to him as 'the most wanted man in Australia'. Back home, on 19 June the *Daily Telegraph* printed a mock 'Wanted' poster featuring Johnston's portrait: 'For regicide after the callous death of the Kings and turning players', coaches' and staff's lives into hell. Also wanted by liquidators, Western Force, South Sydney Rabbitohs, Matt Giteau . . .'

Despite all this, it would be another month—and more than twelve months after they began their investigation—before the Australian Securities and Investments Commission moved against Firepower. On 21 July 2008, ASIC filed an action in the Federal Court against companies associated with Johnston and with property developer Warren Anderson, barrister Les Stein and former WA Police Minister Gordon Hill. It also took action against Quentin Ward, the financial advisor and former bankrupt who was believed to have sold more than $40 million of the shares in Perth. ASIC alleged that the individuals and companies named were involved in selling shares in Firepower to members of the public in breach of the *Corporations Act*. It alleged that proper disclosure was not made to those who bought the shares and that this did not allow the investors to make a proper assessment of the risks involved.

The move by the regulator, though generally welcomed, drew stinging criticism from *Crikey* commentator Michael Pascoe, who continued to follow the story. The move, he said, had come too late. 'Let's take a quick reality check here,' Pascoe wrote on 22 July. 'Firepower was very, very publicly proclaiming that it could turn lead into gold, water into wine, grow hair on a billiard ball and cure the common cold. And tomorrow it was going to deliver peace in the Middle East and raise Diana Windsor from the grave.

'OK, Johnston and his cronies didn't make those exact claims, but their magic fuel additive promises were every bit as ridiculous. That ASIC was either incapable of smelling the rat itself or simply not interested in doing anything about it is nearly as criminal as the actual scam. Johnston's success—the theft of $100 million or so—means that our securities and investment watchdog is no smarter than the gullible people who chose to believe in miracles when promised massive investment returns and the sporting bodies prepared to act dumb when bribed with sponsorship millions.'

Once people finally accepted Firepower was all a con, the desire for an explanation grew almost unbearable. Public meetings were held. Concerned and angry shareholders rallied. The early work on a number of planned class actions was begun—legal cases that would target not Johnston but those who had allowed the shares to be sold.

The first private company to move against Firepower was its own lawyers, Johnson Winter & Slattery. The firm was owed nearly $70 000 and, after dumping Firepower as a client, it moved to have the company put into liquidation. Ross Graham, the mining magnate who had invested and lent Johnston $25 million, eventually joined this action in the Federal Court and it was he who, after a brief legal fight, succeeded in putting Firepower's Australian operations into liquidation in early July. After a further legal fight, the British Virgin Islands' arm was put into liquidation in late September.

The court-appointed liquidator, Bryan Hughes, from the Perth firm Pitcher Partners, soon went public with his belief that Johnston had stashed up to $38 millions in overseas bank accounts and was planning to use the money to build a replica company called Green Power Corporation, using the same corporate logo and the same fake products. Hughes revealed that Johnston had teamed up with Frank Timis, the Romanian-Australian businessman who had once claimed to have found oil off the coast of Greece.

'I have no doubt they are establishing a new business called Green Power,' Hughes told the *Sydney Morning Herald* on 2 September. 'I'm not sure what jurisdiction they've registered in, but I know they've been operating out of London and they've been making efforts to acquire and obtain the stock of Firepower to kick the business off with—it's just version three as far as I can see.'

Days later, on 6 September, Warren Anderson—who was alleged to have made $26 million from selling his Firepower shares—lashed out in the *West Australian* at the Firepower shareholders, accusing most of the 1200 people who had lost their investments of being victims of their own greed.

'They were stabbing themselves in the f...ing streets to get these shares. They were murdering each other. In 2006, they couldn't get them quick enough. They were going to

Quentin Ward and Tim Johnston, and I get phone calls asking me if I want to sell some shares. From Quentin Ward and Tim Johnston. I said, "Sure, I'll sell some shares. Why wouldn't I?",' he said. 'I never went out and promoted the company. Ross Graham was Mr Johnston's partner at the time and he was promoting the product. I don't even know those shareholders. They talk about being sympathetic towards them because they are unsophisticated shareholders. Bulls . . . most of them had accountants and bloody lawyers and Christ knows what. They are just sh...y because in their greed they grabbed these shares hoping to treble and quadruple and quintuple their money.'

Hughes, the liquidator, issued a terse statement that day to the media in response. 'I was extremely surprised at Mr Anderson's attack on shareholders,' he said. 'Firstly, it seems peculiar to have to point this out to Mr Anderson, however it is a fact that people invest in companies with an expectation that they will make money. This is the purpose of investing and to imply that there is something wrong, or that the shareholders were "greedy" because they had an expectation they were going to make money is absurd.'

Hughes's statement went on for two pages. 'If he is saying the company had nothing and the shareholders' beliefs were unfounded, then the question arises at what point did he become aware of this, and what did he do to inform the shareholders or the authorities? . . . It [Firepower] has no assets, it has no business, it has no intellectual property, it has no distribution network for its product, it has no reason for anyone to invest money in it.'

Finally, Tim Johnston stepped forward, albeit from the safety of London. Despite months avoiding both Hughes and the court-appointed liquidator of the Sydney Kings, and refusing to file a comprehensive defence to the court action undertaken by ASIC, Johnston declared his innocence in an interview with the

Australian's Europe correspondent Peter Wilson on Thursday 25 September 2008.

'You will see: we will eventually be vindicated and our investors will be well rewarded,' Johnston said, claiming that Firepower's shareholders 'will be delighted very soon, when they find out what is really happening'. He added: 'I have read this stuff about me fleeing to all sorts of places, but I have been based right here in London for almost two years.'

Insisting that Firepower's products did indeed reduce fuel consumption and carbon emissions, Johnston said the company's problem was that it had taken too long to market its products in countries such as Russia, and had run out of money. In relation to his sports-marketing strategy, he said: 'We thought it would build up the brand and get us access to top-level business contacts. It was a good decision based on our predicted revenues but they fell short.'

He claimed the oil industry was behind the criticism of his firm. 'We have got products to reduce oil use and help the environment, so why are we being made out to be fricking arseholes? You have to wonder who is behind that and who doesn't want this to work. There are no missing millions—I have been doing my utmost to protect the shareholders. I have not become a wealthy man out of Firepower.'

He even defended the fuel pills. 'We have plenty of tests to prove they work but we have copped these vicious attacks saying the products can't possibly work so anyone in the business must be a conman. It has had a terrible effect on my name and my family, and hurt a lot of good people who have worked hard for the company. But eventually the truth will come out.'

During the interview, Johnston sat for a photographer for the image that would appear with the story on the front page. His once dyed and slicked-back hair was now grey and limp. His pale eyes stared at the camera, small and fixed and unremorseful. He was an unrepentant defender of his actions, so calm he seemed almost plausible. Someone who had never told a lie; or at least none that mattered.

Some, seeing the photo and reading the interview, said Johnston was deluded and self-absorbed. Those who had invested their life savings in his venture clung to his claims with a dead man's grip. Those who knew him best just laughed out loud.

Tim Johnston was no longer just a name. Through his actions in fooling everyone from the prime minister down, he had become a kind of bushranger figure onto which a multitude of opinions could be projected, and in relation to which the boundaries of justice and human frailty could be debated, on and on.

At the very least, his case highlighted apparent flaws in the regulatory system. Shareholders complained loudly that if ASIC had been more proactive instead of reactive, if it had listened to the complaints made to it about Firepower from mid-2006, then much of the damage could have been lessened. Some media commentators raised similar questions. 'So why did it take . . . the SMH to bring the Firepower empire down?' wrote *Crikey* founder Stephen Mayne, an activist for the rights of shareholders, on 22 July 2008.

It wasn't as if the characters involved in Firepower were unknown to the authorities. For instance, Quentin Ward was linked to a previous fraud in the mid-1990s that ASIC had investigated. Ward had sold shares to his clients in a bogus Cook Island insurance company called Century Insurance Limited that cost investors more than $2 million—a large sum at the time. He had been prosecuted by ASIC for his role in the con, was bankrupted and had been banned by ASIC from 1995 until 1998 from dealing in securities or from giving investment advice. But at the end of the ban, Ward reapplied for his financial planners licence and ASIC returned it.

Michael van Rens, another key player, had also been

previously investigated by ASIC. In addition, in 2003 and 2004—at the same time he was selling shares in Firepower—he was the subject of action by the Australian Prudential Regulation Authority, which disqualified him from acting as a trustee, investment manager or custodian of a superannuation entity. Both actions related to the fact that van Rens was a trustee of Perth's Strategic Capital Superannuation Fund, whose funds were seized by APRA after investigators were only able to locate about $13 million under management, despite advice that the fund had about $24 million. Some of the shares purchased by the superannuation fund were in Firepower.

Most shareholders concluded that Austrade had allowed itself to be compromised. The taxpayer-funded entity had provided Johnston with credibility; it had afforded him an entrée into the highest echelons of society, to the prime minister, the Governor-General, the president of Pakistan, to business leaders and diplomats all over the world; and Austrade hadn't even taken the time to realise that its commercial arrangement was with a business that didn't exist—that even the name on the contract had been faked.

Some shareholders concluded—without any proof—that it was clearly too embarrassing for the authorities to ever allow Johnston onto a stand to tell his side of the story. They pointed to the fact that the action taken by ASIC was civil action in the courts. ASIC alleged Johnston had sold the shares without giving proper disclosure and if found guilty those who suffered a loss would be entitled to compensation from him. But Johnston was never charged with fraud—a criminal offence—and this meant ASIC was unable to apply for his extradition back to Australia to face the charges. So if Johnston wanted to, and had the means and sufficient funds to do so, he simply had to stay out of the country to avoid facing shareholders.

He could in fact just start all over again, somewhere else.

SOURCES

This account is based upon interviews with the main participants in the Firepower affair; upon the many thousands of pages of internal company emails that were kindly provided to me by former Firepower staff and by those who purchased shares in the company; upon newsletters and communications to shareholders; upon Federal Court documents; and upon the precious few other records that shed light on the life of Tim Johnston, including the 1991 Gyles Royal Commission into the building industry. Some of this information came to me on the understanding that its various sources would not be identified publicly. I am very grateful to everyone who talked to me but I would like to single out John Finnin, the former chief executive of Firepower, for being so frank and for being so generous with his time. I am equally grateful to Ken Gracey, Dave Tate and Frank Collier, Johnston's former employees. Others who spoke freely or who answered specific questions via email include:

Ray Whitham, Barry Barmby, Ian Forrest, Jim Grebe, Carol Grebe, Edwin Perry, Graeme Drummond, Don Spiteri,

Ian Robertson, Dr Damon Honnery, Dr Michael J. Brear, Dr Jeremy Foster, Dr Roy Douglas, Steve Yu, Len Mijat, Elaine Hautau, Trevor Nairn, Zorica McCarthy, Bill Moss AM, Brian Goorjian, Jason Smith, The Hon Julie Bishop MP, Peter Holmes à Court, Christopher Green, Air Chief Marshal Angus Houston, Rear Admiral Davyd Thomas, Commodore Kevin Taylor, Air Marshal Errol McCormack, Graeme Clegg and Warren Anderson.

CHAPTER 1

Pages 2–3: Background on Split-Cycle Technology was drawn from articles in the *Australian Financial Review* on 13 July 1997, page 56, 'High-tech saga cycles on' by Paul Syvret; the *Newcastle Herald* on 4 December 2000, page 8, 'End of a sorry saga' by Jeff Corbett; and *Business Review Weekly* on 23 May 2002, page 24, 'Whatever happened to . . .' by Tim Treadgold.

Pages 3–4: Background on Red River company was drawn from articles in the *Australian Financial Review* on 10 May 1994, page 24, 'Red River reckons it can run motor cars on water' by Nick Tabakoff; *Australian Financial Review* on 12 May 1994, page 38, 'Red River's meteoric rise comes to an end' by Nick Tabakoff; *The Age* on 14 May 1994, page 27, 'Car blaze sends Red River into a spin' by Tony Kaye; *Australian Financial Review* on 16 May 1994, page 24, 'Black friday blaze fuels Red River run' by Nick Tabakoff; *The Age* on 18 May 1994, page 27, 'Red River suspends shares trade' by Tony Kaye; *Australian Financial Review* on 17 June 1994, page 39, 'Flurry with a singe on top' by Nick Tabakoff; and *Australian Financial Review* on 9 August 1994, page 28, 'Whitewater ride for Red River' by Nick Tabakoff.

Pages 5–7: Background on Save the World Air Inc taken from 'A fuel and his money' by Ben Hills, *Sydney Morning Herald*, 28 April 2001, page 31.

United States Securities and Exchange Commission, press release number 43057, 20 July 2000.

United States Securities and Exchange Commission, litigation release number 19469, 17 November 2005.

United States Securities and Exchange Commission, litigation release number 17603, 9 July 2002.

Stock Patrol, 'Stock or schlock?', 19 July 2000, www.stockpatrol.com/article/key/saveworld.

Pages 8–9: Background on Peter Brock drawn from an article in the *Australian* on 9 September 2006, page 51, 'Boy driven to become legend' by Robert Wilson; the *Bulletin* on 12 September 2006, 'Brock and Holden bust up' by Bill Tuckey; and from Bev Brock *Peter Brock: Living with a Legend*, Pan Macmillan, Sydney, 2004, pp 159–78.

Page 9: Brock's comments about the Energy Polariser were reported after his death in Melbourne's *Herald Sun* on 16 September 2006, page 26, in an article titled 'Peter Brock tribute' by Paul Gover.

Page 13: Power Plan International testimonials drawn from an article in the Automobile Association of New Zealand *Directions* magazine, September 1992, pp 26–30.

CHAPTER 2

Pages 19–22: Actions recorded by the Royal Commission into Productivity in the Building Industry in New South Wales— Roger Vincent Gyles, Royal Commissioner. Information taken from an electronic transcript of the hearings in 1991 and from Part 2 of the report of the hearings (p 9, pp 16–17 and pp 161–3).

An account of the events at Knebel Kitchens was also drawn from the *Sydney Morning Herald*, 3 June 1991, page 8, 'Executive heavied to quit, inquiry told' by Malcolm Brown.

Background on Tim Bristow was, in part, drawn from the book by Kevin Perkins, *Bristow: Last of the Hard Men*, Gary Allen, Sydney, 2003.

Background on Lenny McPherson was drawn from the *Sydney Morning Herald*, 19 November 1994, page 31, 'A cut above a common criminal' by Malcolm Brown.

Background on Jack 'Mad Dog' Cooper was drawn from an article in the *Sun Herald* on 18 August 1991, page 42, 'Threats on city building sites' by Keith Gosman and from an article in the *Sun Herald* on 17 April 1994, page 16, 'Murder in the carpark' by Evan Whitton.

Pages 23–25: The references to a US Coast Guard commander called Harold G. Reed that PSP, and later Tim Johnston, claimed to have endorsed certain products appears to be a reference to a seminar on 8 November 1978 in the United States conducted by the 12th Coast Guard District engineering branch, though there is no actual Harold G. Reed mentioned in the report of the proceedings. Some of Johnston's distributors were supplied with a copy of the proceedings of the seminar as alleged proof of the connection with the US Coast Guard.

The references to W.E. Becker are drawn from numerous brochures advertising Tim Johnston's variously named products and were supplied by former business partners of Tim Johnston. They do not wish to be identified. A reference to W.E. Becker endorsing the Fuel Magic pill being sold in Western Australia in 2000 was accessed from the website www.my.com.au/fuelmagic/results.htm on 21/9/2000. It was supplied by one of these sources.

Similarly, under the headline 'Tests returned from international laboratories', Tim Johnston often misrepresented the nature of those tests. They were not done to determine that his products worked. For instance, there are continuous references to J.W. Mitchell, a New Zealand government analyst. It is drawn from a letter dated 17 March 1992 written by Mr Mitchell to an unknown recipient. It reads in full: 'Fuel Conditioner: Received 4/3/92 a plastic bottle labelled "Super Conditioner" containing a yellow oily liquid. Further identification "TL 10SC12" was advised. Analysis was required to determine whether this was a petroleum-derived product. The infra-red spectrum of the product showed that it was primarily hydrocarbon in composition. The sample was ashed and was found to contain very low residue (0.004 per cent). The hydrocarbon nature of the product makes it extremely likely that it is petroleum-derived. The result for ash indicates that the product is free of additives containing inorganic substances.'

Pages 25–28: Tim Johnston's actions are recorded in an article in the Automobile Association of New Zealand *Directions* magazine, September 1992, pp 26–30.

CHAPTER 3
Pages 32–37: Victor Melnikov's account of money laundering activity in Nauru was reported in *The Age*, 30 October 1999, page 1, by David Hilzenrath.

The Financial Action Task Force's concern about money laundering is contained in its 1998/99 annual report.

The US State Department's concern about money laundering is contained in a report drawn up in 1998 but not released publicly until February 1999.

The activities of Prok Bank, Prok Trade House and Prok Enterprises are drawn from the following newspaper articles— the *New Zealand Herald*, 18 February 2000, 'Inquiry into mystery internet bank' by Chris Daniels; the *New Zealand Herald*, 17 October 1998, 'Russian traders to Prok get new backers' by Joe Helm; the *National Business Review*, 16 October 1998, 'Prok back from the dead' by Deborah Hill; the *National Business Review* 24 January 1997, 'Fraud office calls a halt to prok bank investigation' by Frances O'Sullivan; the *National Business Review*, 27 September 1996 'Capital currents—Prok schlock' by Frances O'Sullivan; the *National Business Review*, 20 September 1996, 'SFO investigates Prok laundering claim' by Frances O'Sullivan; the *National Business Review*, 13 September 1996, 'Meurant tried to net fishing deal in office' by Belinda Milnes; the *National Business Review*, 24 May 1996, 'From Russia— without much love' by Belinda Milnes; *The Evening Post*, 1 February 1996, 'Meurant strikes off for political wilderness' by Sarah Boyd; *The Asian Wall Street Journal*, 29 August 1995, page 19, 'New Zealand politician dismissed'.

Professor Gennadiy B. Rozenblit is described in a number of undated brochures as having tested the Supertech Fuel Conditioner sold by Tim Johnston through his TLC companies and having achieved a 9 per cent fuel saving. Professor Rozenblit was also alleged to have found that the product extended the working life of injectors by over 1200 per cent, reduced toxic emissions by up to 50 per cent and reduced maintenance on valves, exhaust manifolds and piston rings. This alleged endorsement was later extended to other products sold by Tim Johnston.

SOURCES

The typical description for Professor Rozenblit is contained in a brochure advertising the wares of Tim Johnston's former Singapore-based offshoot Global Lubricants & Conditioners Pte Ltd. He was said to be the director of Technical Sciences and Mechanics at Kharkov State Academy of Railway Transport in the Ukraine.

Pages 36–37: Tim Johnston's undated CV was obtained from Ray Whitham. It was drawn from documents promoting TL Chemplex Automotive Group Ltd and was originally printed in a distributor information brochure entitled 'Introducing the Chemplex Auto-enhancer'. It reads in full: 'Timothy F. Johnston. Mr Johnston is an internationally recognized businessman with many years experience in the Oil and Transport industries. Mr Johnston is a member of the prestigious Chartered Institute of Transport of London with Honors degrees in Transport Management, Business Management and Marketing. Having lived and worked in various parts of the world, Mr Johnston has a natural feel for international trade and negotiations. Many multimedia articles have been written as well as radio and Television interviews about the international success of businesses headed by Mr Johnston. Previously employed as Group General Manager for the giant TNT Transport company in Australia, Mr Johnston has for the past 8 years been Managing Director of the marketing divisions of T.L.C. Limited and U.S. Lubricants International. His current position is Chairman of the Board of U.S. Lubricants and T.L.C. Limited.'

Pages 38–39: TLC promotional brochures obtained from Ray Whitham and from former business partners of Tim Johnston in New Zealand who do not wish to be identified. Tim Johnston is also captured on video giving his presentations. Copies of these videos and source notes for Johnston's white board demonstrations were supplied to the author on the basis that the sources not be identified. The quotes are taken from 'The Pollution Solution' TLC (NZ) Ltd Licencees Information Manual, dated August 1998, but there are many versions of this brochure and the words are remarkably similar.

CHAPTER 4

Page 41: Background on Jim Grebe obtained from personal interviews and from www.chemplexauto.com.

Pages 41–43: Background on the chemical Ferrocene was drawn from the scientific journal Pure & Applied Chemistry, vol. 60, No 4, pp 445–51, 1988 'The productive scientific career of Charles J. Pedersen supplemented by an account of the discovery of crown ethers'; from the *Journal of Aerosol Science*, vol. 29, Supplement 1, pp S617–S618, 1998 'The effect of ferrocene addition on particle formation and burnout in combustion processes' by M. Kasper, K. Sattler, K. Siegmann and U. Matter; from a letter written by Jean-Pierre Cheynet of the International Organisation for Standardisation (ISO), which sets the global standards for fuel, to members on 11 October 2006 warning about the adverse effects of Ferrocene-laced fuel; from an extract of Inhalation Toxicology, vol. 12, Supplement 1 to issue 6, 15 June 2000, pp 63–82 'Investigation of chronic toxic and carcinogenic effects of gasoline engine exhausts deriving from fuel without and with ferrocene additive' by L. Peters, H. Ernst, W. Koch, W. Bartsch, B. Bellmann, O. Creutzenberg, H.G. Hoymann, C. Dasenbrock and U. Heinrich; from an abstract of an SAE International technical paper number 2006-01-3448 'Influence of ferrocene on engine and vehicle performance' by Atsushi Kameoka of the Japan Automobile Research Institute; and from the manual used to set fuel specifications around the world, the Worldwide Fuel Charter. The information obtained was from page 22 of the September 2006 edition of the charter; and from technical information provided by the Chevron oil company on gasoline refining and testing and on antiknock compounds on its website www.chevron.com.

Page 44: The reference to Jim Grebe being an 'exclusive Chemplex distributor, serving Southern California', is in an undated brochure used by Tim Johnston to advertise the Chemplex Valve & Injection Purge product—a copy of which was supplied by Carol Grebe.

Pages 45–49: Background on Graeme Clegg obtained in an interview with the author. It was also partly drawn from http://newimageasia.com/article1.php (accessed 7/2/2008) and from www.graemeclegg.com (accessed 31/8/2008). Clegg spoke freely about himself and was generous with his time. Further information was obtained from former employees of Total Image and of New Image International. They did so on the basis that they would not be identified. When Firepower went into liquidation in July 2008 New Image International was named in the Federal Court as a creditor.

Background on Leadership Dynamics obtained from Wikipedia that cites a 1976 book by Nathaniel Lande called *Mindstyles, Lifestyles: A Comprehensive Overview of Today's Life-changing Philosophies*, Price Stern Sloan, Los Angeles, 1976, pp 138, 143 and 144, and from various other Internet sources that regularly quote from the 1972 book by Gene Church and Conrad D. Carnes, *The Pit: A Group Encounter Defiled*, Outerbridge and Lazard, New York, 1972.

Page 49: A reference to Dr Roy Douglas allegedly testing the New Image International fuel pill was obtained from the internet as recently as 24 October 2008 from New Image International Malaysia at: www.newimageasia.com.my/power pillfe3_productinfo.html.

This site states that the 'PowerPill is made by New Image International under US Lubricants International'—the same company spruiked by Tim Johnston.

Pages 50–53: TLC USA's alleged interest in setting up a manufacturing base in Malaysia was reported in the *Business Times* (also known as *Business Today*) newspaper, a division of WorldSources Inc, on 13 February 1998, 'US additives producer eyes base in Malaysia'. It was obtained through Factiva.

The reference to the Automobile Association of Malaysia is drawn from a letter dated 10 February 1998 written to Ian Robertson—Tim Johnston's then business partner in Asia— by the AA's general manager Khir Anuar Mohamad. It reads in full: 'Product test result: I refer to our earlier discussion pertaining to the above matter. I have no objection to let you have a copy of the test result for your research and development purposes. A copy of which is enclosed for your attention. But however, the test result should not be used for any promotion or publication activities unless approval is given. Could we have your understanding on this matter?' The two-page report from the AA reads, in part, 'the saving on fuel cost is minimal' but claims the product reduces air pollution. The test was conducted on the open road and no laboratory work was done.

A report on the launch of the PowerMax products in Malaysia was reported in the *Sun* newspaper in its 'Wheels' section on 8 May 1998 'PowerMax comes to Pahang'; in the *Sunday Star* 'Wheels' section 1 March 1998, 'Tonic to give your car a boost', that quotes an endorsement from 'W.E. Becker, general services manager for General Motors Corporation' who was said to have tested the product; and in several other unidentifiable Chinese, English and Malaysian-language newspapers in February, March and April 1998. Another English-language headline, dated 1 March 1998 in the motoring section on an unidentified Sunday newspaper, was 'Medicine for your car'. Tim Johnston features in many of the photographs that accompany the articles.

The wonders of the PowerMax products were also reported by the *New Straits Times* on 23 January 1998, page 3 of the shopping section, 'Wonder pill for your vehicle'. The article talked about the 'revolutionary new product that has been widely used in the United States of America and Europe but has just been marketed in Malaysia'. It described the manufacturer—Tested Lubricants and Conditioners—as an American company and that the products were backed up by tests conducted by 'various organizations and companies including General Motors, Ford Motor Company, Caterpillar and the Singapore Standards Institute'.

A video was made of the Singapore launch on 9 October 1998, a copy of which was obtained by the author. Photographs of the event also later appeared in a 'technical manual' for later versions of Tim Johnston's products.

The *Good Morning Singapore* television segment was used by Tim Johnston in later video promotions, and copies of these were also obtained by the author.

Pages 53–54: The 21 September 1998 test by the Productivity Standards Board of Singapore is a two-page document addressed to The Lubricants & Conditioners Pte Ltd, 1 Sophia Road #07-06, Peace Centre, Singapore. It was one of two tests carried out by the PSB. The second was conducted on 5 October 1998 using a Hyundai Excel car. This second trial was aimed at measuring any reduction in emissions from using the PowerMax products. The outcomes of the two tests are unclear. They involved driving the cars from Singapore to Malaysia and then back again. They did not appear to involve any laboratory work.

The quotes are extracted from a letter written on 31 July 2000 by Jim Grebe to Mr James Kimberly, Great Western Petroleum, North Fremantle, Western Australia. Mr Kimberly was a customer of Tim Johnston at the time.

CHAPTER 5

Page 56: Information on the engine-cleaning machine partly drawn from an undated brochure entitled 'The New Revolutionary Power Purge System—Ask for the Tune-up of the 21st Century.' Brochure supplied by Ray Whitham.

Page 57: The Tim Johnston quote 'Let's crank this up and make some serious money and have some fun doing it' is drawn from a letter from Tim Johnston to Ray Whitham and Steven Clegg dated 26/11/1998 on TLC Chemplex Automotive Group Inc letterhead.

Page 60: Undated TL Chemplex Automotive Group Ltd brochure supplied by Ray Whitham.

Pages 61–62: Quotes taken from a letter Ray Whitham wrote to his lawyer, Edward Cox, in April 2002 that outlined his dealings with Tim Johnston.

CHAPTER 6

Page 69: The quotes relating to the results of the University of Western Australia test on the Fuel Magic pill are taken from a press release issued by the WA Ministry of Fair Trading issued on 21 December 2000, 'Magic fuel pill discredited in tests'. It is available at: www.docep.wa.gov.au/Corporate/Media/statements/2000/December/Magic_Fuel_Pill_Di.html.

Page 70: The quotes from Magistrate Jeremy Packington were obtained from a press release issued by the renamed WA Ministry of Fair Trading, now called the Department of Consumer and Employment Protection, on 31 October 2003, 'Fuel Magic pills—Magic moment in Court'. It is available at: www.docep.wa.gov.au/Corporate/Media/statements/2003/October/Fuel_Magic_pills.html.

The article entitled 'Eight Best Ways to Still Make a Fortune from Scratch in Australia Today' by Mal Emery was accessed from the internet but has since been removed. Mal's views can be accessed at: www.malemery.com.

Mr Emery's manual 'How To Turn An Ordinary Business Into An Extraordinary Business—The 9 Indisputable Laws Of Speed Wealth' is available for sale at: www.plustenmarketing.com/malemery/extrabus.html.

Page 71: The extracts are taken from SAE International/The Engineering Society For Advanced Mobility Land Sea Air and Space—technical paper 900154, 'Effects of Ferrocene as a Gasoline Additive on Exhaust Emissions and Fuel Consumption of Catalyst Equipped Vehicles' by K.P. Schug, H.J. Guttmann, A.W. Preuss and K. Schodlich. Paper prepared for the International Congress and Exposition, Detroit, Michigan 26 Feb–2 March 1990.

The alleged tests done by Angel N. Gonzales were in November 1999 but he did not sign off on them until 8 February 2000.

He is alleged to have achieved a 42 per cent improvement in economy on a Nissan 720 pickup truck and a 36 per cent improvement in economy on a Nissan Sentra B14 car by adding a product called the 'Fuel Wonder Drug'. A certificate signed by Mr Gonzales states that the Fuel Wonder Drug was in fact the Power Pill FE3. In Australia, the product was re-branded as the Fuel Magic Pill.

Pages 78–79: The claims for the fuel pills packaged by Steve Yu in China were obtained from the packaging on the pill and from interviews with former business partners of Tim Johnston who declined to be identified but who were intimately involved with what happened.

Pages 79–80: An account of what happened at Gold Leaf Enterprises was supplied by Dave Tate and confirmed by other former employees of Tim Johnston, including Ken Gracey.

CHAPTER 7
Page 81: Facts about Russian Railways originally appeared in literature supplied by Tim Johnston's former business partners and was confirmed at: www.eng.rzd.ru/wps/portal/rzdeng?STRUCTURE_ID=4.

References to Russian Railways are scattered throughout many Firepower documents. An impending contract with Russian Railways features extensively in a Firepower company profile dated 1 September 2004 page 7 and pp 24–25. It in part reads: 'Professor Evgeny Kossov, a department head with the Russian Railways Research Institute has advised that the FP4000 Fuel Conditioner will be part of the fuel specification for a "new fuel" being developed for the Russian Railways. One of Professor Kossov's responsibilities is to write the fuel specifications for the

Russian Railways which must be met for all fuel deliveries to that organisation. Professor Kossov has advised that the current consumption of diesel fuel by the approximately 20 000 locomotives under his control is 14 billion litres per annum. . . . this would equate to net revenue (after deducting the cost of the product to FH [Firepower] of in excess of USD $50m per annum.'

A document accessed from Firepower's business partner in Greece, BioChemical Hellas (www.biochemical.gr), states that the Russian Railways trial took place using one locomotive over a six-month period between July 2000 and January 2001, and resulted in a 5.1 per cent fuel saving. There is a picture of an unidentified man standing in front of a train but no detail about how the trial was conducted.

Page 82: The claim that the Russian Railways would recommend Firepower to other railways across Eastern Europe is made on page 7 of the Firepower company profile dated 1 September 2004.

The allegation that Tim Johnston was paying Professor Kossov was confirmed by a former business partner of Tim Johnston and implied in documents sighted by the author.

The author was given several matching accounts of Tim Johnston's trip to India in May 2001. One was from former Firepower employee Frank Collier, who accompanied Tim Johnston. A second account was captured on local television and later used in a promotional video obtained by the author. A third account was accessed from the internet. It was an article by the journalist Vasanthi Hariprakash on 1 June 2001, 'PowerMax: the magic brown pill to boost your vehicle engine power'. The quotes that begin 'it is to your vehicle what Viagra is to mankind' are taken from this article, based on promotional material, and from the television story that aired in India. The article was accessed from the internet at: www.india markets.com/imo/industry/pollutioncontrol/pollutionfea30.asp on 29 January 2007.

A fourth account was taken from an article in *The New India Express*, Bangalore 1 June 2001, 'Now, Viagra pill for automobiles'.

Page 83: An account of Tim Johnston's meeting with Mugunthe's business rivals was supplied by Johnston's former employee Frank Collier.

Page 84: An account of the trial in Pontianak was drawn from diary notes of the trip supplied by former Tim Johnston employee Frank Collier. The claim that Tim Johnston's product achieved a fuel saving of 6.27 per cent was made in a Firepower company profile dated 1 September 2004, page 20, and in several later documents issued to shareholders, Firepower employees and contractors. The claim that the Indonesian power monopoly was using the products was first made in the same company profile on page 8 and then later repeated in the other documents.

The claim that the Firepower products achieved a 16 per cent saving on a Thai military truck and bus is made in the same company profile on page 20. An account of the note drawing Austrade's attention to the trial was given by a former business partner of Tim Johnston, who declined to be identified.

Pages 86–87: Quotes are drawn from *The Sunday Times*, 22 May 2005, 'The Gusher'. Part of the story of Regal Petroleum is also drawn from this article.

Page 90: The details of the deal with Peter Matthews, the inventor of the newer Firepower liquids, and an account of his dealings with Firepower are drawn from documents lodged in the Supreme Court of Western Australia, reference number CIV 2391 of 2005. 'TPS Group Pty Ltd v Matthews & Versalife Pty Ltd'.

CHAPTER 8

Page 95: An account of the arrest of a couple in Great Britain over the alleged bribes that were allegedly paid to secure the frigate contract was obtained from a report in the Romanian newspaper *Jurnalul National*, 22 January 2007, by Paul Cristian Radu and Valentin Zaschievici.

The quote is taken from the *Four Corners* program 'Liar, Liar, Pants on Fire', broadcast on 21 July 2008.

Page 95: The letter from Jacqueline Davison later appeared in a newsletter to Firepower shareholders in June 2004 (*Firepower News*, vol. 1, Issue 1).

Page 97: Gregory Klumov's background and the quotes used are drawn from the *Sydney Morning Herald*, 20 October 2003, page 31, 'Russian born, Australian made' by Deborah Snow.

The appointment of the Irbis Group as distributors of the Firepower products was announced to in a newsletter to Firepower shareholders in June 2004 (*Firepower News*, vol. 1, Issue 1). It read: 'This is as a direct result of the impressive trial of Firepower products conducted by the Russian Railways in the first half of 2001'.

Pages 100–101: Information drawn from a newsletter to Firepower shareholders in June 2004 (*Firepower News*, vol. 1, Issue 1).

Pages 101–103: The Firepower company profile is dated 1 September 2004.

CHAPTER 9

Page 106: The quotes from Tim Johnston are taken from the Firepower company profile dated 1 September 2004, pages 12 and 18.

Page 106: An account of the proceedings of the product development meetings is drawn from documents lodged in the Supreme Court of Western Australia, reference number CIV 2391 of 2005. 'TPS Group Pty Ltd v Matthews & Versalife Pty Ltd'.

Page 107: The quotes are taken from a two-page company announcement to shareholders by Tim Johnston on 6 October 2004.

Page 112: Quotes were obtained from *Firepower News*, vol. 2, Issue 1, June 2005.

Pages 112–113: The quotes are taken from publicly available Austrade documents advertising Australia Week In Moscow 10–15 May 2005. They include a document titled 'Briefing Package' handed out to exhibitors; a press release accessed from the Austrade Website on 13 December 2006 'Opportunities For Exporters to Capture The Russian Market' and dated 9 February 2005; and a 122-page document in both Russian and English produced for the trade fair.

Details of the show *A Day in the life of a Successful Australian Business* were included in a newsletter to Firepower shareholders in June 2005.

Page 115: The quote from Tim Johnston about the reception to Firepower in London's banking and broking community was obtained from a newsletter to shareholders in June 2005, page 8.

CHAPTER 10

Page 118: The invitation to Tim Johnston to the official reception at Parliament House, Canberra was reproduced in a newsletter to shareholders in June 2005, page 7.

Page 119: Quotes taken from two *Pak Tribune* online reports, the first dated 4 September 2005, 'Australian company intends to invest $35 million in Pakistan' (accessed on 15/12/2006 from www.paktribune.com/news/print/php?id=117940), and the second dated 6 September 2005, 'Wide scope for Australian investor in energy development activities: Jadoon' (accessed on 15/12/2006 from www.paktribune.com/news/print.php?id=118273).

The *Dawn* newspaper clipping is dated 7 September 2005, 'Australia to set up petroleum plant', and was originally forwarded to Tim Johnston by Austrade.

Page 120: The photograph of the Prime Minister John Howard appeared in *Firepower News* vol. 1, Issue 2, page 1, dated March 2006, 'Prime Minister witnesses Firepower agreement with Pakistan Government'.

Page 124: The quotes from the *Australian* are taken from an article on 23 June 2008, page 29, 'Mr Fix-It's hot property:

kingpin slam-dunks Firepower shares to pocket $20m' by Anthony Klan.

Page 128: The list of companies Firepower was said to be developing a relationship with is listed in a newsletter to shareholders, *Firepower News* vol. 2, Issue 1, June 2005, page 6.

CHAPTER 11

Page 131: An account of a meeting between the Australian ambassador Robert Tyson and the Russian Senate is contained in a newsletter to Firepower shareholders in March 2006, *Firepower News*, vol. 1, Issue 2, page 2.

Page 132: The quote from Tim Johnston is taken from the same newsletter to Firepower shareholders in March 2006, *Firepower News*, vol. 1, Issue 2, page 2.

Page 135: The quote is taken from an English translation of a report on the trial on an Icarus brand bus in Astana that is dated 28 September 2005.

The quotes from the report on the Firepower trial at MMK is taken from an undated English translation.

The account of the trial on four dump trucks in the mining town of Zhezkazgan was obtained from an Engish translation of a report dated 23 December 2005.

Page 140: A transcript of the judgment of *Loutchansky v The Times Newspapers Ltd & Ors* was accessed on 2/1/2007 from: www.bailii.org/ew/cases/EWCA/Civ/2001/1805.html.
The judgment provides some background information on Mr Luchansky (also spelled Loutchansky).

An English-language translation of an interview with Mr Luchansky after he won the court case by the journalist Sandris Tocs was accessed from www.baltkurs.com/english/archive/fall_2001/profile.htm on 6 June 2007.

CHAPTER 12

Page 142: The quote is taken from an email by Les Stein to Eileen Carr, dated 21 September 2005, that was also forwarded to other senior Firepower contractors and employees, including Firepower chairman Tim Johnston.

The memo from Carr to Johnston about her proposed structure for Firepower was attached to an email on 26 October 2005.

Page 143: The quote from ASIC is taken from documents lodged in the Federal Court on 21 July 2008.

Page 144: Quotes are taken from emails sent by Errol McCormack to Tim Johnston on 28 March 2006 and on 4 April 2006.

Page 147: The quotes are drawn from an undated Firepower company profile that updates the original company profile dated September 2004. This document was known as the 'Firepower Update Document' and the author was given three different versions by shareholders ranging from 20 pages to 94 pages in length.

Page 148: The original reference to a test at the Singapore Institute of Standards and Industrial Research was a letter dated 9 December 1994 and is addressed to one of Tim Johnston's former associates Mr Calvin V King at Techni-Lube Singapore Pte Ltd.

Pages 148–149: The quotes are taken from undated documents advertising Firepower products during 2006 and from the documents known as the 'Firepower Update Document', which the author was given three different versions of by shareholders ranging from 20 pages to 94 pages in length. The shareholders were given the documents by their investment advisors during 2006. The quotes from the Firepower website were retrieved on 19 July 2007. The website has since been closed.

Page 151: All references to Firepower were removed from the Austrade website in early 2007 after the *Sydney Morning Herald* began writing about the company.

Page 151: The quotes are taken from an article in the *Sydney Morning Herald*, 16 June 2006, page 21, 'Russian oil gunning for Firepower's founder' by Benjamin Seeder; from the business section of the *West Australian*, 17 June 2006, 'Meeting fire with Firepower' by Benjamin Seeder; and from the *Bulletin*, 28 June 2006, vol. 124, No 27, 'Peter the Great' by Nick Tabakoff.

Page 153: The email from Tim d'Emden to his clients was sent on 28 June 2006 and it outlined the events that took place on the trip to Moscow. The summary begins: 'Arrived Moscow with Premier Peter Beattie who was representing the Australian Government and under police escort driven to our hotel opposite Red Square/Kremlin (wow) . . . our involvement was to meet and greet and discuss through an interpreter and act as investors from Australia in the company.'

The quote about the size of Firepower's alleged contracts was taken from the business section of the *West Australian*, 17 June 2006, 'Meeting fire with Firepower' by Benjamin Seeder.

SOURCES

CHAPTER 13

Page 157: The quote from Peter Holmes à Court is taken from the *Sydney Morning Herald*, 20 January 2007, page 37, 'Into the dragon's lair' by Jacquelin Magnay.

Pages 158–159: The quote from the *Daily Telegraph* is taken from the article 'The power of none' by Paul Kent. It appeared on 7 June 2008 on page 88.

Page 161–162: The quotes from Tim Johnston are taken from the *Sunday Times* (Perth), 18 March 2007, 'Fire in the belly' by Nick Taylor.

Page 164: The reference to Caltex and Ampol being a Firepower customer first appeared in a newsletter to shareholders in March 2006, *Firepower News*, vol. 1, Issue 2, page 12. It quoted 'business manager' Lance Burns.

CHAPTER 14

Pages 167–168: Quotes are from an email from John Finnin to Les Stein and Tim Johnston on 3 August 2006.

Page 168: Quotes are from an email from John Finnin to Kim Stokeld on 15 August 2006.

Page 174: The reference to Firepower in the *Adelaide Advertiser* was in an article on 5 September 2006, page 22, 'Local celebrities fuel company float' by Rebekah Devlin, Candice Keller and Naomi Jellicoe.

Page 174: Firepower's plans to sponsor rugby teams in Russia are outlined in a 55-page document titled, 'Russian Rugby The New Frontier', dated December 2006.

CHAPTER 15

Page 181: The quote from Russell Hinder is taken from the *Four Corners* program 'Liar, liar, pants on fire', broadcast on 21 July 2008 on ABC television.

Page 184: The quotes from Tim Johnston are taken from the *Sunday Times* (Perth), 18 March 2007, 'Fire in the belly' by Nick Taylor.

The quote from the *Daily Telegraph* is taken from the article 'The power of none' by Paul Kent. It appeared on 7 June 2008 on page 88.

Pages 188–189: The quote from Robert Northcoate is taken from the *Four Corners* program 'Liar, Liar, Pants on Fire', broadcast on 21 July 2008 on ABC television.

CHAPTER 16

Page 197: The reference to Canada Bay Council is drawn from a notice of motion put forward by councillor Neil Kenzler for the City of Canada Bay Council meeting agenda of 21 November 2006. It proposed using Firepower products in five garbage trucks. 'The proposed trial by Cleanaway, Firepower and Techenomics in January 2007 is seeking to reduce the exhaust emissions and volume of fuel used by Cleanaway in its waste contract with the City of Canada Bay,' the notice of motion read.

The reference to meetings with ministerial staff to discuss using Firepower products in Sydney's ferries is based on emails from Peter Richard and Chris Adsett from Techenomics to Tim Johnston in September and October 2006 about the meetings, and on a copy of the presentation made at the time.

Page 202: A recording of the meeting at the Perth Convention Centre on 14 December 2006 was kindly provided by a shareholder on the condition of anonymity.

CHAPTER 17

Page 205: The first critical story about Firepower was carried by the *Sydney Morning Herald* on 8 January 2007, page 1, 'Deals and more deals: the rise of man with a magic mystery pill' by the present author.

Pages 208–209: The quotes from Tim Johnston are taken from a two-page statement to shareholders issued on 10 January 2007, 'Response to *Sydney Morning Herald* articles 8th and 10th January 2007'.

Page 211: The *Sydney Morning Herald* story was carried on 5 February 2007, page 4, 'Firepower's pill under scrutiny' by the present author.

Page 219: The *Sydney Morning Herald* story was carried on 2 April 2007, page 3, 'Watchdog's sniff at fuel firm may end up biting sports stars' by the present author.

CHAPTER 18

Page 220: The quote from Peter Holmes à Court is taken from an article in the *Sydney Morning Herald*, 8 August 2007, page 32, 'Firepower fallout a non-issue, say Souths' by Andrew Webster, Rupert Guinness and Jessica Halloran.

Page 221: The quote from Peter O'Meara is taken from the *Sydney Morning Herald*, 20 January 2007, page 37, 'Into the dragon's lair' by Jacquelin Magnay.

Page 221: The quote from the Western Force spokesman is taken from an article in the *Sydney Morning Herald*, 8 August 2007, page 32, 'Firepower fallout a non-issue, say Souths' by Andrew Webster, Rupert Guinness and Jessica Halloran.

Page 230: The quote from the Sydney Kings player and the account of the demise of the Sydney Kings is taken from an article in the *Sydney Morning Herald*, 31 May 2008, page 69, 'From Kings to paupers' by Jessica Halloran.